The complete guide to Starting and Running a bookshop

MALCOLM GIBSON

The
Booksellers Association
of the United Kingdom & Ireland Ltd

The Booksellers Association of the United Kingdom & Ireland Ltd

First Edition published in 1988 by Malcolm Stewart Books

Second Edition Published in 1999 by
The Booksellers Association of the United Kingdom & Ireland Ltd

Reprinted 2002

Printed by Biddles, Guildford.

ISBN 0907972144

Contents

Part one
The world of bookselling

Part two
The business of bookselling

Appendices

Acknowledgements - to the first edition

I have tried to write this book drawing on my experience and understanding of the book trade. That experience has been greatly enriched by the contributions of many colleagues within the trade over the years and I am enormously grateful for the numerous friendships that I have been privileged to share. To list personally all who have helped shape my view of the book trade and who have contributed, wittingly or otherwise, to this book would be impossible. I hope they can see their contribution and accept my thanks for their help and their insight. I would, however, like to acknowledge a few individuals who have been particularly important and generous to me.

The person who individually has most helped to shape my perspective on bookselling is my chairman, Ainslie Thin. His limitless support, encouragement and advice has been invaluable. Without that support I would have been unable to undertake my many book trade activities outside booksellers James Thin Ltd. I would also wish to thank Tim Godfray, the Chief Executive of the Booksellers Association, who I am pleased to consider an old friend – as well as a true fount of wisdom.

As far as this book is concerned I must pay due respect to the author of the first edition, Malcolm Breckman. His broad outline appeared even more masterful as I struggled to impose some structure on my writings about what has become a very different book trade in the ten years since his book appeared. I must also pay an enormous debt of gratitude to my editor, Jennifer Creswick, who has patiently transformed my turgid text into something much more readable.

Finally, I would thank my family who have selflessly and generously tolerated my disappearance into our study for many more hours than I had ever dreamed likely, and who provided support, coffee and occasionally something stronger if writing was proceeding with some difficulty.

M. R. G.

Edinburgh, 1998

Update for the second edition

I have received significant help and encouragement from a number of members of the trade, for which I am grateful. In particular I would like to thank Meryl Halls at the BA for both her patience and also her willingness to find answers to my various questions. Special thanks are also due to David Hicks at BTBS for helping me to keep a sharpened approach to life!

Malcolm Gibson

Malcolm Gibson Marketing

Edinburgh 2003

1

Part one
The world of bookselling

1. The business of bookselling

Spending one's time surrounded by books – and making money at the same time – is the opportunity that almost everyone who loves books dreams of.

Reality is rather different. If the dream is to provide genuine satisfaction, and be allowed to continue, some hard-headed business direction must intervene.

That said, bookselling does offer a wonderful opportunity to participate in the cultural well-being of society. Most people who survive as booksellers learn to recognise that, although not every book they sell is necessarily edifying, there is at least something worthwhile in most of the titles they deal in. Bookselling offers the chance to help people towards a greater understanding of themselves, their circumstances and the world around them, bringing with it the sense of social responsibility that is important to many of us. There is also a social satisfaction which comes from being involved with so many like-minded people associated with the world of books – not only the readers who are our customers, but authors, publishers, librarians, teachers and even fellow-traders.

This is probably one of the major reasons why bookselling is seen as different from much of the retail world. The traditional byword was that "books are different". They are, but that does not mean we should ignore the experience that the rest of the retail world may have to offer.

The opening chapters of this book aim to give readers who are thinking seriously about opening a bookshop an insight into how the various elements of the book trade interact and operate. The hope is that they will recognise an industry which is open and welcoming to all, even though a new business may be a source of competition.

The retail environment

In any high street, city centre shopping centre, or out-of-town retail complex you will be confronted with an array of different types of shop. At first sight they may seem to have little connection with each other. A bit of analysis, however, reveals certain patterns.

There are those shops which sell particular types of products, whereas others (such as department stores) sell a wide variety of goods. There are some aiming at particular types of people, and others which seem to impose no limit on their potential clientele. There are shops which are clearly a part of large groups with many outlets, and still more which are clearly very local, "small" businesses. On a British high street, the analysis might produce the kind of list given in Figure 1.1.

Shops selling particular products	K Shoes Richer Music Tie Rack Waterstone's
Shops selling a wide variety of goods	Woolworths Debenhams
Focused target audience	Poundstretcher Liberty
Broad target audience	BhS Marks & Spencer Boots
Part of a large group	Next Halfords Tesco
Independent stores	Local stores

Figure 1.1 The retail environment: types of shop in the UK

This, very superficially, illustrates the wide variation within the retail scene. The desegregation of retailing can be analysed in terms of product range, target market, and ownership. It is also important to recognise the differing shopping arenas that are developing. Not only are there the traditional town centre shopping sites such as the high streets and other street shopping areas, there are also in-town shopping centres, peripheral shopping centres (which often have more space for bigger shops and parking) and the very large regional shopping centres that are often located on old industrial sites well away from any urban development. On top of these physical shopping areas there are also the traditional mail order operations, book clubs, and the newer Internet retailers.

Profitability

Bookselling is not usually a hugely profitable business. Once we admit that, it does nevertheless offer many people a very reasonable standard of living, providing they develop and exercise their bookselling skills and business acumen.

Getting an idea of the profitability of individual booksellers is not easy. Some of the bigger companies have their profitability examined in the financial pages of the national press or in *The Bookseller*, the book trade weekly, on an annual basis. Others will have filed their accounts at Companies House, but go unreported. Many are small companies and as such, work to far less stringent reporting requirements. The general view is that, to ensure continued business growth, a company needs to return a net profit figure of around 5% of turnover. If the return is much lower than this, then there are likely to be continuing difficulties with its long-term funding and development.

This optimum level of return suggests that for a small bookshop with an annual turnover of around £400,000 to develop, it might realistically need to yield a net profit, after all expenses have been deducted, of some £20,000 per annum.

Within the trade there are undoubtedly companies which do achieve this level of return (indeed, a number manage to do still better, particularly where the premises are freehold rather then leased). There are also, however, many other companies which fail to perform to this level.

Where a bookshop does fail to generate enough gross margin to cover its expenses, the financial result is obviously a loss. It may be a catastrophic loss resulting in effective closure through bankruptcy, or it may be a more manageable loss which can be reversed through the next year's trading, provided the bank is understanding – and willing to continue supporting the business.

Some people new to bookselling see this low level of financial return as business failure, and they try to move to another business. For others, potential financial success is only a part of the reason they are involved in the book trade. Some fortunate folk may be financially independent to the degree where the income from their bookshop is irrelevant, or they may be prepared to accept a small return in the light of the enjoyment and independence the business gives them.

Nevertheless, it would be extremely rash to set out with anything but the intention of making a bookshop work financially. You must plan with the basic aim of survival, and the hope of significant improvement later. As well as detailed planning, any previous experience of the book trade will be valuable at this stage.

What is involved?

Running a bookshop calls for many of the same qualities involved in making any other retail business work. You will need personal energy, enthusiasm, vision and a determination to succeed.

You will also need the help and support of those immediately around you since you will inevitably work long hours, particularly at the start-up of the business and at such busy times of the year as Christmas. If this is likely to put unsustainable stress on your personal life, it is probably better to recognise this now rather than too late.

Bookshops, like every other sort of shop, can generate money, but they need start-up capital and investment if they are to work and you will need some realistic personal capital at your disposal. Assuming you can put a good business plan together then you will probably be able to get financial support from your bank, but you will still need access to some start-up funding.

Skills

To keep your bookshop moving in the right direction, you will need to have – or to develop – a range of financial, business and management skills.

Considerable people skills are another prerequisite. You will be dealing on a regular basis with your staff, with your suppliers and, most important of all, with your customers. All of them will need rather different things from you, things that you must be able to provide on demand.

On top of all these skills you must develop a further range specific to the book trade. You will need to understand the various supply chains that operate; the terms that are used; the range of product; and how best to market it. Figure 1.2 gives you an overview.

Business skills	Spotting profitable opportunities Negotiating good terms with suppliers
Management skills	Controlling and directing the business Planning and implementation
Financial skills	Running business accounts Controlling costs
People skills	Finding the right staff Training and motivating staff
IT skills	Identifying suitable systems Maximising system efficiency Reducing system costs
Marketing skills	Spotting opportunities to exploit Marketing your bookshop
Book trade skills	Understanding the supply chain Memorising details of authors, titles etc.

Figure 1.2 Some of the skills needed to run a bookshop

Filling the gaps

You would not be reading this book if you did not have many of these complex skills already. Inevitably, some will be weaker than others and some non-existent. Do not worry unduly; considerable help is available, provided you have the dedication to take advantage of it.

You may prefer to take the long view and go through a full-time business studies course. However, most business, management and financial skills can be learnt by taking courses at local educational establishments and many run evening classes or short, intensive courses aimed at getting people started in business.

Book trade knowledge and skills are a bit harder to come by, but by no means impossible. You can learn by working with an established bookseller, particularly one who is committed to the training and development of staff (If you do follow this route it will inspire you, one hopes, to do likewise for your staff once you are established as a bookseller in your own right).

You may also find other booksellers within your general locality who are prepared to share some of their skills. BA Branch meetings provide some opportunity for meeting such potential saviours.

Is bookselling for you?

It should be said that you are more likely to make a success of bookselling if you can combine some sound business acumen with an abiding enthusiasm for books. There have been successful booksellers who had little enthusiasm for books, but they were rare creatures. There have been many more cases of people who loved books but lacked business acumen. Sadly, most of the businesses they set up struggled, and many eventually failed. The complex mix of skills which makes for successful bookselling will respond to training and dedicated effort, but do not lose sight of the books.

Bookselling is unlikely to yield a very high level of material reward, but tends to more than compensate for this by providing a stimulating level of job satisfaction. It is a difficult, subjective measure, but in a world that is becoming increasingly polarised between those looking for vast financial returns and those wanting to take a more holistic and satisfying approach to life, then bookselling has a lot to offer as a career.

If you feel that you have the necessary interests and skills and are likely to be content with a more modest living, then you are probably well suited to bookselling. Read on.

2. The world of the book

For centuries the book existed only as handwritten manuscript but, with the invention of printing, it became more widespread and the written word became the major mechanism through which information was passed between people, and from culture to culture. Until quite recently it remained just about the only medium through which information was transferred from person to person in anything approaching a mass audience.

More recent developments in technology broadened the mechanisms for information transfer. Film, radio, and then television provided early competition for the book. It was predicted that these "new media" would eliminate the written word from our lives, but the book proved far more resilient than many thought.

Today it is subjected to more competitive forces than ever before. Television now offers a vast range of channels – satellite, cable and, digital/interactive; radio stations proliferate; we may chose between video, audio books, electronic books, multimedia CD-ROMs, online information services and now the Internet – and still people buy books.

So does this mean that existing (and potential) booksellers can be assured of a continuing market in the light of all this competition? After all, it is well over five centuries since Gutenberg first printed his Bible. It seems unlikely.

Booksellers must consider carefully the entirety of the world in which they are operating or may be about to enter. In marketing terms it is known as the macro-environment. If they do not they may find that, strategically, they are outflanked. The book today, as seen by most booksellers, should involve as many of the possible media variants as it can. In the early 1980s books on tape were a rarity, whereas most bookshops now have quite a thriving market in audio or talking books. Many booksellers have also taken up multimedia, but the size and composition of the potential market for it is not yet properly established.

Many general and academic bookshops have set up their own web sites on the Internet and whilst some merely advertise their services, many are actively selling books over the Internet. A number of booksellers, such as Amazon.com deal exclusively over the Internet, thus avoiding the need for retail premises. The academic market for textbooks and the professional market for handbooks are felt particularly likely to be subject to serious electronic inroads by electronic publishing initiatives. It is entirely possible that booksellers will manage to ensure their place in such a supply chain. So booksellers now need to take as broad a view of "the book" as possible. The concept will certainly include maps, atlases, and talking books. It may well include video, multimedia and other new technology developments. Part of a bookseller's success lies in the way the market is perceived. Yesterday's booksellers were quite distinctly sellers of printed books. Today's should see their role as purveyors of information in its broadest sense.

That said, one must remember that there are more than 1,000,000 titles in print (and that around 115,000 new titles, including new editions etc., were published during 2000). Very few booksellers would keep anything approaching the whole range of this vast, diverse output, but many will keep a broad representation.

The book is far from moribund; it is simply subject to more competition than ever before.

Trends in bookselling

It is much simpler to look at historical trends than to try to predict the future. In bookselling, however, even the historical trends have become difficult to interpret. In 1995, the collapse of the Net Book Agreement, which for almost a century had ensured that most book prices were fixed by their publishers, caused a fundamental shift in the competitive nature of the trade. In ways like this some developments have been abruptly dislocated and others have gained undue prominence.

Any aspiring bookseller needs to know the sort of influences they are likely to be faced with and needs to get some feeling for where today's bookselling has come from. An immediate example is shopfitting. Twenty years ago, shelving in bookshops served merely to show books – there was little emphasis on design. Now, the retail environment leads customers to expect high standards of display and the days of amateur shopfitting are probably gone for ever. As a result the entry costs to bookselling have risen significantly.

So the retail book trade has followed many of the trends to be seen within the general area of retail development in the UK. If it has failed to keep up – and this is certainly a just accusation – then it is because the sector's relatively low profitability has hindered investment and development.

In terms of its trading activity the British book trade has seen a prolonged and major shift away from the small independent bookseller towards the multiple chain bookseller. The process started very gradually, when the first branch of Waterstone's opened outside London in 1983, but it accelerated with great force over the next ten years as Waterstone's and Dillons between them opened branches in most population centres of any size.

Other chains such as Books etc., Hammicks, Ottakar's and Volume One also opened considerable numbers of shops. Huge areas of new bookselling space were fitted out, but significantly the increase in the overall value of books bought by the public was not of the same order. The process was all about market share rather than wholesale expansion of the marketplace for books.

A large factor in the growth of the new shops was the introduction of far more marketing activity and major shopfitting investment into bookselling. This was strongly supported by the state of the property market during the late 1980s, when retailers could often get very favourable letting terms, in the form of financial inducements, in new shopping developments.

The new shops looked good, particularly when compared with the often under-capitalised existing bookshops. They were generally bigger and carried a much more significant stock range. What is more, the new shops held author events, took out advertising in local newspapers and put on excellent window displays. The dowdy and traditional image of bookselling was being picked up, shaken, and hung out anew.

In many instances all this new space and activity did not produce thousands of new readers who had previously been denied access to bookshops. Rather, it led to a shift in market share away from the smaller independent bookshops towards the larger, and generally more comprehensively stocked, multiple-shop chains. This meant that a number of the smaller, and not so small, bookshops closed when faced with new competition.

The period between 1995 and 2002 saw the failure of a substantial number of traditional booksellers. Mostly these were purchased by other, stronger, groups but the diversity of the retail bookselling environment was dramatically changed through this process of concentration. In some cases the original trading names survived and in others they disappeared forever. Amongst the bookselling groups that saw their ownership change in this period were Austicks, Heffers, John Smith, and James Thin.

A number of small, but highly thought of, booksellers also failed but were not taken over by bigger companies. Perhaps the most notable of these was the closure of the women's book specialist, Silver Moon , in Charing Cross Road where increasing rentals rendered the future impossible.

Bookseller strategies

Several distinct strategies could be perceived in the opening plans of the chains. Some, such as Books etc. appeared to opt for a geographical cohesion, on the basis that saturation, particularly in a heavily populated area, would lead to more effective marketing, and also insulate the group against heavy competitive pressure.

Others, such as Waterstone's and Dillons, tended to opt for larger population centres where there was a tertiary education establishment, i.e. a college or university. This gave them a large enough catchment area to keep book sales high and supported sales of their academic books. The shops tended to be large, holding extensive stock ranges. The movement broadly mirrored the development of the superstores in the United States.

Most of the other chains adopted a strategy which seemed to avoid the largest population centres where competition from Waterstone's and Dillons was almost a foregone conclusion. They quite often opened in shopping centres and other prime pitches, but within the more secondary towns.

This process continued more or less steadily through to 1995. When the Net Book Agreement collapsed there was an initial lull in bookshop openings, but they soon began again. It was noticeable, however, that most of the principal new shops belonged to the mid-sized chains, such as Books etc. Ottakar's, and Hammicks.

There were two main strategies at work here. On the one hand there was the development of a much smaller, more flexible trading format by some groups, such as Ottakar's. This would enable them to open in smaller towns, but also to be rather more flexible in their property requirements. The second strategy was to adopt the more capital intensive philosophy of the "category-killers". This is an aggressive model imported from the United States and based on the principle that if a store can be big enough to hold almost every possible type of book, then it will attract customers from far and wide.

In 1997 Waterstone's opened the largest bookshop in the UK in fifty years. It is located in Glasgow and trades from about 28,000 square feet across five floors. Refurbishment costs alone were estimated to be in the region of £3,000,000. Subsequently, however, there have been even bigger bookshops opening in the UK.

The same year also saw what will probably prove to have been one of the most significant of the post-NBA changes. The London-based bookseller, Books etc., was bought by US bookseller Borders, the world's second-largest bookseller. Borders have now opened super-stores not just in central London, but also in a number of major population areas such as Manchester, Glasgow and Edinburgh.

Another change in the UK bookselling environment was the formation of a new company, the HMV Media Group, which led to Waterstone's and Dillons combining to trade as a single company within its book division. The result has been the development of a very large, up-market bookseller – a move attributed to a response, at least partially, to the entry of Borders into the UK market.

WH Smith also saw a number of changes whereby they purchased the John Menzies retail operation and after a period of management repositioning greatly strengthened their book offering throughout the group in both their mainstream and their travel shops. The result has been a powerful and popular range of books generally offered at very competitive prices. This is perceived to be ensuring their competitive position against both local booksellers and importantly the major supermarkets, who have become much more interested in books since the collapse of the Net Book Agreement.

It is not just the general market where there have been changes; the academic market has also seen dramatic movement. In 1998 the Leeds-based bookseller, Austicks, was purchased by Blackwell. They also purchased, in 1999, the Cambridge-based bookseller, Heffers, and in 2002 bought the academic bookshops of the failed James Thin group. Another apparently strong Glasgow-based academic bookseller, John Smith, was bought by Coutts Information Service.

This period also saw the gradual development of a number of specialist Internet based booksellers who were able to operate effectively in this new environment. The highest profile new entrant was undoubtedly the US-based Internet leader, Amazon, who offered vast book ranges at heavily discounted prices. Another company that was able to successfully use the technology was Swotbooks.com which aimed to supply textbooks to students using on-line ordering and payment. Consolidation continues: in 2003 Ottakar's bought the general bookshops from Hammicks.

ISBNs

Alongside retail revolution, the second major trend within the book trade has concerned technology. The process dates back to the development in the 1960s of the robust system of product numbering known as the International Standard Book Number (ISBN), one of the most beneficial developments in the recent history of the book. The ISBN uniquely and permanently identifies each title, regardless of where in the world it is published, and it has acted as a gateway to computerising the book trade.

The ISBN makes it possible to differentiate between similar authors and titles in a way that is ideally suited to computerised techniques. With the single number, tracing and identifying books, ordering them, and controlling stock can be comfortably achieved using computer systems.

A close ally of the ISBN is the barcode that is found on the back of almost every book. This is a machine-readable code which allows a computer system to identify precisely which book is being sold.

Understanding just how ISBNs work is essential for understanding how a great deal of today's book trade technology works. An explanation of the working mechanisms for them is given in Appendix 2, together with an example of a barcode and related ISBN.

With the ISBN set up, an International Standard Serial Number (ISSN) system was also developed, principally for journals and newspapers although it will sometimes appear in tandem with an ISBN in multi-volume serial publications. It consists of an eight-digit number, divided by a hyphen into two four-digit groupings.

The growing role of technology

The enormous leaps in the computer's availability and capability, and the falling costs of hardware have allowed far more use to be made of computerised processes than could have been imagined, even fifteen years ago. The development of fast means of communications has been even more critical. In 1997 modems tended to operate on conventional telephone lines at a speed of about 28 Kbps. The industry standard swiftly accelerated to 56 Kbps but this was still a major constraint on the electronic medium becoming fully utilised The real change came with the introduction of broadband connection where vastly faster speeds of information transfer were possible.

The impact of these developments is highly significant since from its early uses in electronic ordering (facilitated by the ISBN), computerisation has now moved into almost every area of a bookshop's activity.

Almost every bookshop, like any business, will use word processing and spreadsheets today. The book-keeping, invoicing and accountancy functions of the bookshop will almost certainly be computerised, using a variety of off-the-peg software packages. The stock control operation will also be computerised, usually by means of specialised software packages in this case. Marketing will be supported by database and/or graphics packages. Communications will be conducted either by electronic data interchange, fax, or e-mail.

One area of major (and very positive) change is that bibliography is now almost universally accessed using CD-ROM at the lower end, and on-line for the more serious high level users.

The technology is here to stay, whether we like it or not. For those who feel comfortable with it, technology produces few difficulties except the frustrating occasional tendency of failing to do what was wanted of it. For those who are unhappy with technology many processes can still be done manually, though whether there is time to do them this way is another question.

The world of publicity

One of the enormous advantages that the world of books enjoys over many other industries is the volume of free, and generally favourable, publicity that books receive in the media. New cars, by contrast, are reviewed almost exclusively in the specialist press, and the overall coverage is a fraction of that given to books.

Almost every newspaper and magazine devotes editorial space to new books. Some give far more than others, but the overall effect is to let the general public know about many of the books new in the shops and to generate a sense of excitement and need. Reviews do sell books.

For committed readers, there are also several non-trade journals which concern themselves almost exclusively with books. The best known of these are the weekly *Times Literary Supplement* and the *London Review of Books*, published fortnightly.

As well as providing review coverage, the media tend also to be awed by the celebrity status that attaches to many leading writers. Some have become superstars in their own right, and many of our most popular authors are accorded almost the sort of media attention normally reserved for Hollywood stars. Interviews with them are often given leading feature positions; their divorces make the headlines.

All this means that books are continuously finding themselves in the limelight. Sometimes it is because of something an author has, or has not, done; at other times it is because a new book deals with a controversial subject or adopts an unorthodox view. As booksellers we should be ready to make the most of this sort of coverage: it is a rare gift which many other retailers would dearly love.

Bookish events

Publicity for books is also generated through a diverse range of specialised book-based events. Book prizes form a major category here, and can vary from the highly publicised Booker Prize for Fiction with its televised centrepiece, the awards dinner, all the way through to a small prize awarded for the best book review by a pupil at your local school.

The principal book prizes all receive carefully cultivated publicity. From the general bookseller's point of view perhaps the most notable are the Man Booker Prize in October, the Whitbread Prize in January and the Orange Prize for Fiction, all of which frequently create controversy. There is a whole raft of other prizes for both fiction and non-fiction. All of them draw attention to books and, in the process, stimulate readers to become involved by buying and reading the books concerned.

Book festivals are another useful mechanism for creating widespread awareness of books through media involvement. The Edinburgh International Book Festival, started in 1983, has gone from strength to strength and is among the most famous. Others include the Cheltenham Festival of Literature and the Hay Festival, which has attracted sponsorship from the *Sunday Times*. The star-studded casts of authors visiting festivals to give readings usually create an instant success with the press, radio and television companies, both local and national, and thousands of readers revel in the opportunity to see, hear and perhaps meet their favourite writers.

An important entry in the calendar of book events is World Book Day. This is an international event held around about Easter each year in celebration of the book. In the UK it has become very significant, thanks mainly to the activities of a high-profile marketing team put together through co-operative action by the Booksellers Association and the Publishers Association. The day is almost always judged a resounding success.

Media activity like this is good for business because it creates an aura of excitement and enthusiasm around books. As booksellers we can help to feed that process through co-operation and attractive in-store display. After all, the more enthusiasm there is for what we sell, the more people are likely to want to be part of it, and will buy books as a result. In short, it is a nice symbiosis between commerce and art.

3. The book trade

Anyone thinking about entering an industry that is new to them needs to be aware of what type of world they may be joining. If you are to open a bookshop you need a sense of the way the book trade operates, for you are more likely to get on if you generally "go with the flow".

The structure of the trade

The book trade is a mature industry that has developed over hundreds of years. During that time its constituent parts have taken on quite specialised and distinct functions along the seemingly endless chain linking authors to the reading public. This functional segregation has evolved because the core business skills required at any one stage are frequently unique – if a company spans more than one function the wider range of skills involved is often incompatible with a good financial return.

So it is the authors who write; the literary agents who place their work with publishers; and the publishers who bring the work to the stage where it is ready for production and, later, for sale. Meanwhile, printers and binders have transformed what was the manuscript into its final form for delivery to distributors, who move the smaller orders to retailers. They sell the authors' works in ones and twos to the general public, or occasionally in larger numbers to such institutions as libraries.

At several levels there is also an organisation involved in representing the affairs of its members – authors, publishers or booksellers, for example – within the wider book trade. Further information on some of these bodies will be given later in this chapter and in the appendices.

Any general summary like this is bound to be shown wrong occasionally. Some authors have developed their own successful publishing operation; some publishers run a very effective distribution operation. The overlap between a publishing house and a bookselling business has been far less successful over time. This is probably due to a wide difference in objectives, for to say that both are involved in selling as many books as possible to the reading public is, unfortunately, to over-simplify the case.

Bookselling in the retail economy

It is estimated that the total UK retail turnover in books is in the region of £1,800 million. On this basis, bookselling accounts for somewhere around 1 per cent of the UK retail economy.

One of the enduring difficulties the book trade faces is that despite the very high number of titles published every year, around 117,000 in 2000, total consumer expenditure on books remains low. This situation is aggravated by the continuing decline in institutional sales as local government cutbacks bite into book-buying budgets.

Booksellers

In early 1998, it was estimated that there were some 60,000 retail outlets which stocked books in the UK. Of these, approximately 3,300 were members of the Booksellers Association of the United Kingdom and Ireland (BA). Not all booksellers join the BA but the great divide is between the shops whose primary business is bookselling and those for which bookselling is a secondary activity. There are many other outlets where ranges of books are regularly sold – such places as supermarkets, garden centres, department stores and service stations.

There are several distinct groupings within this range of shops selling books. In the first group, i.e. the booksellers, there is a traditional division between the independent businesses and those which are one part of a multiple group. The distinction must be made carefully, since a number of the multiple groups are independently (rather than corporately) owned.

A useful way to see the impact of these different groupings of booksellers is to look at the estimated share of the market that "belongs" to them. The analysis shown in Figure 3.1 also reveals the breadth of the different markets for books.

Source of purchase	% Market share
Bookshops	29.4%
Book/stationery shops	19.3%
Supermarkets	7.4%
Bargain Bookshops	6.4%
Other shops	13%
Book clubs	10.2%
Other direct sales	9.7%
Other	4.6%

Figure 3.1 Market share, by volume, between booksellers (source: Books & the Consumer, 2001)

In terms of trends over the period 1998 to 2001 growth in share of volume sales was experienced by chain booksellers, bargain bookshops, supermarkets and other direct sales. All the other types of outlet showed a decline in their share of volume sales over the period. It is instructive also to look at the market share amongst booksellers when measured by the value of sales rather than simple volume. This gives an indication of the mix of sales betweeen higher-priced hardback books and lower-priced paperbacks (the level of price discounting will also exert some effect, although it is harder to evaluate). Figure 3.2 below illustrates this market share division.

Source of purchase	% Market share
Bookshops	36.7%
Book/stationery shops	20.7%
Supermarkets	5.1%
Bargain Bookshops	3.2%
Other shops	10%
Book clubs	9.5%
Other direct sales	11%
Other	3.7%

Figure 3.2 Market share by value of sales (source: Books & the Consumer, 2001)

Again in terms of growth in share of value sales over the period 1998 to 2001 the winners were the chain bookshops, bargain bookshops, supermarkets and other direct sales.

The other main difference between booksellers is in the arena for their main business. There is a fairly obvious difference between academic and general bookshops, but there are also religious bookshops, shops dealing chiefly in children's books, and others which specialise in library or school supply. Some of these booksellers have formed special-interest groups within the Booksellers Asssociation's membership. Figure 3.3 shows the numbers involved.

Type of bookseller	Number in BA membership
Children's	145
Academic, professional and specialist	181
Christian	329
Export	22
Library suppliers	42
School suppliers	136
Internet	49

Figure 3.3 BA membership by group (source: BA Directory of Members 2002)

Comparing 2002 with 1997, a gap of five years, the change in some areas has been marked. The 1997 total for academic, professional and specialist booksellers fell from 207 by 12.5%, and library booksellers fell from 67 by 37%. There was a slight increase in the number of export booksellers and school suppliers, but the Internet booksellers group is an entirely new addition over the 1997 summary. The current edition of the *Directory of Booksellers Association Members* provides further information on the level of interest in certain subjects, and in the geographical distribution of booksellers throughout the UK.

Publishers

The variety of booksellers is matched by a huge range of publishers, from the "single-handed" cottage industry end of the market all the way through to vast multinational organisations. Indeed, the internationalisation of publishing and "conglomeration" within the industry has been a cause of concern to observers in recent years. Many rue the passing of what they thought of as its "character".

Publishing, like bookselling, also has areas where specialisation becomes important. Often a publishing house will have a strong reputation for a specific type of book. The reputation is generally based on the sound editorial judgement of those involved in the publishing process allied with a very professional awareness of the needs of the market and the gaps to be filled.

In some of the bigger companies there is a parallel where such expertise tends to lie in imprints. In the UK, Random House, for example, is a part of a multinational media group. It has a number of famous general imprints like Transworld, Jonathan Cape and Arrow, but it also has a range of specialist imprints, such as Pimlico and Vintage.

At the opposite end of the publishing industry, where there are surprisingly few restrictions on entry, many new businesses start each year. Not all succeed, but a good number do, even though they may publish only one title a year.

The management consultancy KPMG, which has done a lot of work on the book trade supply chain, report that 17,000 of the publishers on the Whitaker database may be considered as active, having published at least one book between 1994 and 1996. Such a multiplicity of potential suppliers causes booksellers huge difficulty, since each publisher usually has its own terms of trade. A useful summary of this report can be found on the BA website.

Distributors

Many publishers have found that the skills needed to publish books are very different from those needed to organise the distribution of their books to retailers. The operation calls for specific and methodical logistical skills which are not necessarily a main part of publishing. So the trade now includes specialised distribution companies which receive bulk deliveries of books direct from the printer and warehouse them until they go out to retailers.

The distributor will usually handle the books' physical distribution and invoicing and may also take on the representation of the publisher's list, using its own force of sales representatives. It will also be responsible for regular reporting to the publisher on the sales progress on the books. In exchange it is paid a negotiated fee dependent on the number of functions it performs. Occasionally a publisher may supply a big order for a single title directly from the printer to a customer at an extra discount. The saving in cost to the publisher with the books not going through the distributor, and thus incurring fees often covers this extra discount.

Devolving this area of the operation to a distributor allows publishers time to develop better publishing skills and to avoid building the often significant, for example warehouse, shelving, stock management systems, staffing etc., overheads associated with distribution. The use of distributors also gives booksellers the chance to route orders for a variety of publishers to one supplier, receive a single delivery and statement in return, and thereby save costs.

Wholesalers

Wholesalers function as specialist booksellers who sell their books on to other bookshops. They use all the stock selection skills that any successful bookseller does, but with a different market in view.

Their principal role is to provide a much faster delivery service than most publishers can manage. They can achieve this by focusing on keeping the better-selling titles from a publisher's range always in stock, ignoring the slower-moving titles and saving themselves from cluttering up their warehouses. They make their money from the higher discounts they receive from publishers in return for bulk-buying.

Many of the major wholesalers now make computerised systems available to their customers, at a cost, and provide on-going support for those systems. They are usually customised to the wholesaler's own systems and so make ordering much simpler and faster. The wholesalers also usually have a catalogue of the titles they have available arranged by category – thus allowing booksellers to see at a glance what is available on Feng Shui, for instance, regardless of who publishes them. Help and support in the form of Buyers Notes for new titles is also a useful benefit for the customers of wholesalers since it allows them to see at a glance what are likely to be the best titles across a range of publishers' books.

Perhaps the biggest benefit of dealing with a wholesaler is the ability to pull so many disparate publishers into one account. This allows significant savings in time and cost since there is only one delivery to be unpacked and reconciled; one invoice to be managed; and then one monthly statement to be settled when due. Since every action costs, removing the volume of statements from a booksellers operation can be a lifesaver. The caveat, of course, is the risk involved in putting too many eggs in one basket. Each bookseller has to make their own mind up on that!

Book clubs

The book club concept is that of mail order bookselling with incentives and rewards for purchasing. Incentives are generally offered in the form of heavily discounted introductory books in return for some form of commitment to future purchases. Colourful advertising appears in most of the Sunday newspaper magazines.

A slight variation on the book club is the sort of operation which sells to children by putting on book fairs at schools. Here the children usually pay the full price for their books, but the school receives a financial reward for the volume of sales made at the fair.

Specialist bookshops, even small independents, may be able to build up a list of customers interested in, say, nautical books, with a view to offering a similar sort of operation. However, they would be well advised to look carefully at the economics and logistics of such activity before plunging in.

Trade information

Still with the idea of getting a feel of the trade before trying to enter it, it is useful to look at back issues of the trade journals (particularly the weeklies). It will give you an insight into current issues, as well as practical information on the routine business.

The trade journal of record is *The Bookseller,* published on Fridays. It was established in 1858 and, despite its title, covers all functions within the trade – one current shoutline is "Where the book trade meets each week". The news coverage is good and it carries well-informed articles on everything from new authors to latest developments in technology. Its letters pages provide a lively forum. There is also the weekly listing of new publications from the Whitaker database and bookshop bestsellers lists derived from BookTrack. The journal is also available on-line at www.thebookseller.com. A basic service is available to everyone, but a subscription, providing a user name and a password, is needed to access certain areas of the web site.

The second weekly trade paper, *Publishing News*, dates from 1979. It also covers the whole trade spectrum, but is perhaps more lightweight in approach than *The Bookseller*. The impression is rather tabloid which, given the very personal nature of the industry, has its uses.

Books in the Media is part of the Whitaker Group. As the title suggests, it concentrates on giving booksellers and others useful information on books related to, or getting a mention on, radio and television, with only brief general trade news items. It also features bestseller lists, most-reviewed books, prize information and is likely to interest general booksellers keen to tie in their promotional efforts. *Books in the Media* can be viewed easily on *The Bookseller* website.

A relative newcomer to the world of book trade journals is *Logos*. It is a quarterly, with rather more of the aura of scholarly publishing to it, and carries in-depth articles on the issues which unite, divide, excite and concern all those deeply involved in the world of books whether they be booksellers, publishers, librarians or scholars.

Contact details for these and the other organisations described below are given in Appendix 3.

Trade associations and other bodies

The Booksellers Association and the Publishers Association are the two principal book trade organisations.

The Booksellers Association

The Booksellers Association of the United Kingdom and Ireland Ltd. (BA), set up in 1895, represents its members' interests in many spheres: legal issues, international affairs (it belongs to both the European and the International Booksellers Federation), contacts with government departments, professional contact and training all come within its mandate. Its activities are described more fully in Appendix 1.

The Publishers Association

The Publishers Association (PA), established in 1896, looks after the interests of its publisher members in a broadly similar way, nationally and internationally. Within the UK, it has worked with the BA on the campaign against VAT on books and its legal concerns include the protection of copyright in the new digital environment. Like the BA, it has special-interest divisions representing educational and academic publishers.

There are numerous other important bodies involved generally with the book trade and new booksellers may well find it useful to know something about their activities. The organisations are often able to provide helpful advice and assistance to anyone working in the industry.

Book Trust

Book Trust is a book trade-supported charity which aims to broaden awareness and interest in books and reading throughout the UK. Its main office is at Book House in Wandsworth, south-west London. A similar organisation, Scottish Book Trust, is based at the Scottish Book Centre in Edinburgh.

Publishing Training Centre at Book House

Also based in Wandsworth, the Centre is the principal focus for publisher training within the UK and, increasingly, internationally. The organisation was formerly known as Book House Training Centre (BHTC) and is the trading division of the Unwin Charitable Foundation.

The Centre is devoted to raising professional standards in publishing. Its training courses, ranging across most functions from basic copy-editing to the latest production processes, marketing and exporting, are available to all involved in the industry. Regular course brochures are issued and can be obtained on request, or alternatively their course programme can be found on their website at www.train4publishing.co.uk.

Book Industry Communication

BIC is a joint company set up by the BA and the PA together with the Library Association and the British Library. Its first aim is the establishment of trade-wide electronic standards within the UK book trade and it also works to ensure that international compatibility is maintained through the standards that become established.

Its work becomes ever more essential in a time of increasing electronic and computerised communication. As well as working towards the development of robust communications standards, it can advise booksellers and publishers on the standards most suited to their needs.

London Book Fair

The London Book Fair (LBF), set up in the 1970s as a fair for small and specialist publishers to show their product to booksellers, has become a major annual exhibition and forum for the British book trade. It is held in the middle of March and in recent years has taken place in Olympia, west London. Many

UK, and a growing number of international, publishers take exhibition stands and use the event as an opportunity to meet their existing customers, win new ones and generally let the trade know about their forthcoming titles and the direction their company is taking.

For booksellers the LBF provides the opportunity both to talk to individual publishers (especially those whose representatives do not call) and to make new business contacts. The opening day (a Sunday) is usually designated "Booksellers Day", with a special emphasis put on retailers' interests in that day's parallel programme of events. Frequently publishers will be offering special discount terms for orders placed at the LBF.

Further information on this essential book trade event can be found on the LBF website at www.lbf-virtual.com. You can also pre-register for the LBF on the web site.

BTBS The book trade charity

BTBS is the trade's own welfare charity. It is often the most appropriate channel through which assistance and support can be given to those members of the trade who find themselves in difficult circumstances. **BTBS** expresses, in a range of practical ways, the responsibility that the community of the book trade - both individuals and companies - has towards its less fortunate colleagues. The prime objective of the charity is to provide assistance for people in need throughout the UK who have worked in functions relating to the publishing and selling of books for a period of at least twelve months, and their immediate dependent relatives.

The approach of **BTBS** can perhaps best be summarised in this quotation from their web site (www.booktradecharity.demon.co.uk)

"We are a charitable organisation which expresses the collective concern of the book trade for the personal welfare of past and present colleagues throughout the UK.

We provide support services tailored to the needs of book trade people and their dependents, and which are not readily available from other sources. These include advice, accommodation and financial help.

We aim to provide these services within our own means, through efficiently managed resources supplemented by active fundraising. We will also form alliances with other organisations where this will be in the best interests of our beneficiaries."

The address and helpline phone number for **BTBS** can be found in the relevant appendix.

4. The customer

A bookshop without customers is a sad and lifeless thing. No customers mean no income – and certain death – so the lion's share of your effort must go on attracting as many customers as possible to your bookshop.

Take care, however, not to spread your marketing effort so widely and thinly that it fails to attract anyone. To be all things to all people is almost impossible – although it is also the daily challenge most booksellers face.

Book-buyer profiles

Before you start to think seriously about opening a bookshop you should look carefully at the sort of people who might buy books from you. If you can begin to characterise them in some way, then you may be able to work out how many potential real customers, as opposed to people, there will be in the area where you hope to open.

If you are opening a Science Fiction bookshop, then you know that your target market is relatively limited, but that the customers you do reach are liable to buy significant quantities of books from you. If it is an academic bookshop that you are planning, then your customer profile will be quite different. It will consist mainly of students buying books for their courses and may gradually extend as the academic staff perhaps start buying their books from you as well.

A general bookseller has a harder task, since establishing a profile of the average book-buyer is far from easy. He (but, say the researchers, more likely she) is probably broadly middle class and earning an average or higher salary. This does not help enormously so we have to look deeper into some of the reasons for buying books.

What the customer wants

There is little to suggest that customers setting out to buy books have considerations vastly different from anyone else deciding where to go shopping. Consumer research shows that shoppers want:

Ease of parking	Most shopping trips involve a car
Convenient location	Ease of access is important
Value for money	An increasingly critical motivation factor
Good range	Saves the need to look elsewhere

The same factors are likely to weigh with bookshop customers, with an extra emphasis on a good range of product. For many book-buyers this is an overriding, critical factor. The buyer either wants to find an enormous, eclectic range of titles, or else a broad range within a specialised area.

An important fifth factor for bookshop customers is the provision of good service.

Ancillary service is an important ingredient of the bookshop's offer to customers. A smaller bookshop cannot possibly carry the stock range of a 25,000 square foot bookstore. What it can do, however, is compensate with a higher level of personal and dedicated customer service.

Customer loyalty

In an ideal world every potential book-buyer in your catchment area would come to you to buy their books, spurning all other purchase opportunities. In the real world, however, you will have competitors trying to entice your customers away – with enhanced service offers or through promotional pricing, for instance. On top of this many customers will buy books where they happen to see them, or where it is easiest for them to park.

The idea of customer loyalty is far from new: supermarkets have run increasingly sophisticated schemes to encourage it for years now, starting with the Co-op dividend and working up to smart cards. After the Net Book Agreement ended schemes designed to increase the chance of customers returning to a particular bookshop for future purchases were on many booksellers' minds, too.

Nevertheless, it seems unlikely that any one bookseller, except perhaps the major national multiple stores, will be able to offer such lucrative incentive schemes. Few can provide such wide accessibility of stores and availability of titles to guarantee that customers never buy books elsewhere.

In spite of this, the question seems never to go away and, in terms of a local bookshop, one avenue to explore may be reader cards which confer some suitable benefit after a certain value of purchases has been made. Alternatively, loyal customers may be offered some form of running discount. The options are limited only by your imagination, and your need to show a profit in the end.

The ideal customer

The ideal customer is surely the person who comes into the shop regularly to browse and goes on to buy at least one book on each and every visit. It is the regularity which is important since opportune customers will always be just that – unpredictable in their visits and their purchases.

With regular customers the bookseller gets to know their reading tastes and it becomes easier to assess what they might like to buy. These books can then be brought (gently) to their attention. Done well, this approach helps form a bond between customer and bookshop without any sense of being thought "pushy". The bond usually results in considerable customer loyalty.

Regular purchases add up over the year. Add to this the likelihood that satisfied customers will tell their friends about your bookshop, and one regular and happy customer can lead to twenty or thirty others, each with a similar potential. Try calculating the value of this over a five-year timescale and it will give you a good indication of the importance of satisfied customers to your business.

Customer service

To be successful, customer service must be both consistent and personal.

The consistency is best developed through training your staff to make sure that standards of service always meet your expectation. The personal element comes from having employed the right staff in the first place. Some people have a very balanced personality which enables them to feel comfortable with customers on a one-to-one basis and they can make even the most difficult situations seem easy and pleasant. Such individuals are worth their weight in gold: recruit them to your staff if at all possible.

Even where your staff do not rise to such a high standard you can still help them to provide a good service by showing them how you want customer relations to be approached. You can give them "lines" to use in certain situations if necessary. With time, they will find their own solutions, and grow as a result..

Customers are looking for all kinds of help and advice when they seek service from a bookshop. Some simply want to know whether you have a book in stock or not. If you do not, but it's in print, this is an opportunity to create a sale through effective service.

Customer service is critically important in reassuring customers in their purchases, an area high on any bookshop's agenda. Many customers know what they want, which is fine. Others will be less certain, particularly when buying a book as a gift, and even more so for a child. Helpful reassurance is often needed to finalise a sale, but beware of blindly recommending everything in the shop.

Other customers may be looking for detailed bibliographical help; the mailing of books to friends; advice on comparable authors; details of any customer accounts you may operate – the list can seem endless. The critical thing to remember is that for the customer the enquiry is important, no matter how trivial it may seem to you.

The Internet customer

Whilst it is not necessarily easy to understand the customers who visit your shop in person, it is relatively easy to see them. You do not have this luxury when you are dealing with customers who are either ordering from you over the Internet or who have a query that you are trying to answer. The mere fact that they are actually in contact with you suggests that they have successfully overcome a wide range of issues such as finding your web site, having trust, and being willing to spend the time.

There are many marketing issues that, whilst not necessarily unique, are particularly pertinent to the Internet customer. Some of these issues are discussed in Chapter 15 on marketing. It is important to understand, however, the developing profile of the sort of people who may wish to deal with you electronically.

In the early days of the Internet there were relatively few users who had the skills, time, or ability to pay the high costs of being on-line. This situation has rapidly changed with the growing acceptance and understanding of the Internet and also the dramatically faster access possibilities coupled with substantially reduced on-line costs. It is no longer the geek who is likely to wish to deal with you electronically; it is as likely to be absolutely any of your existing customers, or very geographically remote people who either have an interest in your specialisation or else have some other reason why they might wish to deal with you – perhaps they now live in Canada but were born in your town.

Clearly easy of parking and the convenience of your location are of no relevance to the Internet Customer. They will, however, still be interested in value for money and the availability of a good range. Additionally they are likely to be much more interested in the speed with which your web site responds to their requests for information, the effectiveness of your search engines, and also the efficiency with which you are able to back up your supply to their orders.

5. Business planning

Early on you should recognise that the core of your potential business is planning. Anyone who is likely to invest in the business will want to see a business plan. This includes you, for you have most at risk.

The business plan is the starting point of your project. It is well worth taking the time to look at some of the many books available on the formulation of business plans (there is a selection listed in the bibliography below) before you start on your own.

Any successful business plan (for almost any business) will cover certain common areas in some detail, under the following headings.

Business objectives

On a personal basis you may have many objectives for your bookshop, but the overriding aim is survival. Your potential backers will be predominantly interested in two objectives supporting this goal.

The objectives can be expressed generally as:

1. To generate sufficient profits to allow the owner(s) to draw an acceptable income (sometimes referred to as a "satisfactory rate of return on capital invested") and to provide sufficient funds to reinvest in the business and ensure its continued growth;
2. To have sufficient finance and long-term cash inflow to enable the business to meet its debts and therefore continue trading.

These will not be the sole objectives of the business. You will undoubtedly have others targeting different sections of your business plan, but everything must support the two critical objectives if the business is to prosper.

The remainder of your business plan will broadly set out how you intend to achieve the two objectives. There are many ways of presenting the information, but all business plans will cover a number of key areas.

Sales and potential market

No matter what your business, you must have customers if you are to continue trading. Consequently your business plan must demonstrate that you have researched your market and are satisfied that there are enough customers out there looking for your type of bookshop to make it a success.

You would normally be expected to have looked at such factors as location, competition, sales targets, stock range, customer services and marketing policies. All these should be included in this area of the plan.

Costs

A critical part of your plan must set out the likely costs that the business will face. The first year will carry start-up as well as running costs.

You should differentiate between costs relating to expenditure on items which are used up in a given period of trading, such as the costs of stock sold, wages paid, heating etc., and expenditure used to purchase assets. Note that some costs (such as stock costs) depend entirely on the level and volume of sales, while others (such as electricity) are fixed regardless of sales volume. The fixed costs are usually called "overheads".

Your formulation of objectives within this section of the business plan will be very closely linked to your sales targets and investment intentions.

Profits

This part of the planning will provide some of the essential answers as to whether your sales and cost objectives are realistic. You will need to test that your sales will bring in sufficient revenue to cover all the costs of the business and still provide you with the acceptable income forecast in your main objectives. Once you have made your first estimates of costs and revenue you will probably have to make at least some minor changes to the original sales and costs objectives.

Investment and finance

The very nature of a business requires you to invest in it. This part of your business plan will set objectives as to how that investment will be put to use, and what further measures will be necessary to finance the business.

The amount of money that you will need to invest in the projected bookshop will be determined primarily by the scale of its business; the stock levels you will need to carry to keep the bookshop running; and whether you plan to buy freehold or leasehold premises.

If your bookshop aims to supply institutions and businesses to any significant degree you may also have to take the level of credit sales into account, since payment will not be made immediately in cash. This will have important implications for your cash flow and your exposure to potential bad debt.

Seasonal trading peaks over the year are another consideration. Every bookshop has busy and quiet periods which tend to coincide with recognisable calendar events. General bookshops in tourist areas usually have good summer and Christmas periods. Academic bookshops see a huge rise in turnover at the beginning of terms and semesters, particularly in October.

At such times your bookshop would be cash-generating, but for much of the rest of the year it will be cash-hungry. You will have to predict the likely cash flow for the business so that you can see when you will need additional financial support.

Once you have estimated how much money is needed for investment, and when it is needed, you should consider the right type of finance to apply for.

Business and administrative controls

By the time you have finished the business plan you will have set a number of objectives relating to the main areas as outlined above. With these set, you proceed to create systems to put your plans into action. You will also need to meet a number of legal requirements so that you are able to fulfil such things as your tax obligations.

Generally you should detail your proposed systems and policies for:

- maintaining the security of cash and merchandise;
- recording all the transactions of the business;
- monitoring sales;
- ordering stock from suppliers;
- recruitment, training and management of staff;
- operating a payroll;
- handling customer complaints;
- ensuring compliance with legislation affecting the business.

Most of these business controls are discussed in the course of this book, but further details can be found in business administration or management textbooks.

The process

Drawing up a valid business plan is not something to be undertaken lightly. It is time-consuming, but it is a very real backbone to your business and will pay you back for the effort.

The checklist below highlights the main steps to follow in generating a successful business plan. As in any planning exercise, the right order of approach makes it easier. Following the process in this logical sequence will help you reach an accurate assessment of your potential business.

1. Identify the potential constraints on your business.
2. Decide on your overall business aims.
3. Examine the bookselling environment.
4. Identify your strengths and weaknesses.
5. Identify threats and opportunities.
6. Formulate your business objectives.
7. Gather detailed information on your probable location and market.
8. Identify and assess strategies that will allow you to reach your objectives.
9. Produce a detailed plan of action with forecasts for sales, costs and profits.
10. Establish investment and financial needs.
11. Implement the plan.
12. Measure progress and review the plan.

You may find it useful to look at a business plan development software package. They are available commercially, or you may be able to get a free software package from your bank. Such packages tend to take users through a pre-defined process and then build the information you have provided into an acceptable and easily understandable format.

When things do go to plan?

Armed with your business plan, you should be able to decide with reasonable confidence whether your bookshop will pay. You will also have the necessary documentation to take to your bank in search of help in getting your business off the ground.

Clearly this is just the start of the process, but it is a critical milestone. Once past it, you can move on to the more practical issues involved in running a bookshop, which are discussed in the second part of this book.

And when things don't work out

A word of caution - with even the best organised businesses things do not always go as expected. One might think that the bigger businesses with their much greater resources are better buffered against mishap, but often when things go wrong for them they go wrong on a much bigger scale and even their resources are inadequate to see them through. If you are smaller, with fewer resources, then you are just that bit more vulnerable to things not quite going as you hoped.

Any business plan has an element of risk in it – an ambitious target, an expectation of development etc. Sometimes these turn out to be possibilities that become too unrealistic and fail to materialise. As a result a variance will come into the plan. It may be relatively minor, but it may not! If a large sales increase has been projected and costs based upon this ambitious budget are incurred, but the sales increase does not happen, then financial difficulties are likely to occur.

It may be that the bank, on seeing the results, is unwilling to extend their borrowing facilities to you. It may be that come payment date for your suppliers you simply do not have funds available.

It is critically important that you do not continue to trade when you know you have inadequate resources to cover any debts you may incur. If you do, then you have broken the law by trading unlawfully, and you may incur serious penalties. It is important that your control mechanisms allow you to monitor your financial position carefully so that you are aware when your cash flow may be tight. Another indicator of difficulties may be where suppliers put you on stop. This means that they are unwilling to supply more goods to you until they get paid for stock that has already been supplied. If you are on top of the situation you can take steps to ease the pressure by either cutting back your spending, or else arranging additional cover from the bank in advance.

People do not like shocks. If you know that there is trouble ahead you should discuss the matter carefully with your accountants first. They may be able to show you some possible courses of action, and they may also suggest that you talk to your bank. The bank is likely, but not guaranteed, to be more understanding if they are aware of the situation and of your plans to set things right.

It may be possible to sell your business if it is failing, but this is always going to be much harder than selling a successful business. There is the possibility, however, that another business may have the experience and resources to overcome the problems you are having. Do not expect best price however!

If things have reached the point where there are no exit routes then there are usually two courses of action open to you. You can seek the Court's protection through an Administration Order, or else the company goes into liquidation, either at your request, or more usually at the request of one of your creditors. This may be the bank, or the Inland Revenue (if there is tax owing) or even one of your suppliers. When any of these actions happen you lose control of your business and it is taken over by appointed managers. Their task will be to maximise the value of any assets so that as many of your outstanding debts as possible can be paid off.

If you believe this sort of action may be heading your way it is critical that you have good advice from your lawyers and your accountants. Your actions in the build up to the end will be examined carefully and you may become legally liable for actions which subsequently become seen as unlawful.

2

Part two
The business of bookselling

6. Location, location, location

It was guru Tom Peters who allegedly first joked that the three secrets of retailing were "location, location and location". Little has changed really, which is why when opening a new bookshop you should be so careful to end up in the right location for your business.

Picture this scene (which you may know well already). Your bookshop is in a reasonable part of town, conveniently close to a major shopping area – which means a lot of passers-by each day. In ten years, you have built up a good trade. Then a new shopping centre opens right at the other end of the town. Suddenly, you are stranded in the wrong place. Although the shopping area survives, all the passing custom has now migrated. Business falls dramatically. A number of neighbouring shops close. Unfortunately, there are still fifteen years left on your lease. What do you do next?

Alternatively, a major competitor may open a new bookshop in your town and has all the advantages of choosing a location to suit today's shopping pattern, rather than the pattern you used to find a site ten years before. The competitor also benefits from a bright, newly fitted shop with a wide range of fresh stock, plus a glittery opening.

These things happen to us all. The choice of location is one of the main areas of risk in bookselling.

Demographics

One of the first things to look at when choosing a potential new location is the demographics of the town. The idea is to get an early indication of the sort of "fit" a possible bookshop might have with the town's population.

The following list will give you some initial criteria to work from.

- What is the population of the town?
- What is the population of the immediate catchment area?
- What sort of people live and work there?
- What proportion of people are owner-occupiers?
- How affluent are they?
- How well educated are they?
- What is the unemployment rate?

Visit the public library and look at some local council publications for statistics and the local papers to build up the picture. The statistical reviews of the UK which TSO produces are helpful and the demographic reports for the area from specialist companies like Experian (www.experian.com, or CACI (www.caci.co.uk) are invaluable. However, you will normally need to supply a very specific brief on what sort of information you are looking for and if you have not used such services before you may find it a difficult and time-consuming process.

You should also be careful in interpreting the statistics since unless you know your way around them, you might end up drawing the wrong conclusions.

When you come to assess the possible long-term future for the town, some further indicators which you might consider are listed below.

- What is the main source of employment in the area?
- Are the long-term prospects for continuing employment good?
- Are there any tertiary education establishments in the area?
- Is the area experiencing economic growth or recession?
- Do people commute into the area or do they go elsewhere during the day?

Where the success or failure of a general bookshop is concerned the principal – but by no means sole – consideration seems to be the proportion of "middle-class" residents in the area. If that proportion of the town's population is well covered in the 25 to 45-year-old age range, the ABC1 socio-economic range, and predominantly in employment, then the chances of success go up a good deal.

Primary and secondary location

For almost every bookseller it is the world passing the front door which provides most of the trade right through the year. A specialist bookshop can end up being sought out by those who know it exists. It may then become what is known as a "destination store". Similarly, a business specialising in export may only need an office, but for most booksellers it is passing trade which regularly rings the till.

This makes the volume and quality of the passing custom critical to the bookshop, whether established or prospective. If there are too few people passing the shop the number coming in and then buying something may be too low to sustain the business. Equally, if most of the passers-by are not in the least bit interested, for whatever reason, in buying books then the business is in trouble. If you have ever played the game of Monopoly you will know that property costs are higher in Mayfair than in the Old Kent Road. For booksellers, real life is the same: a question of the volume and value of the passing custom.

Goad plans, a tool used by estate agents, are invaluable here. These are large-scale maps of the shopping areas of almost every town marking the outline shape of each shop, with details of the current occupier. Get hold of one and you can picture the shopping areas from your office and see quite clearly what is prime and what is secondary within the town.

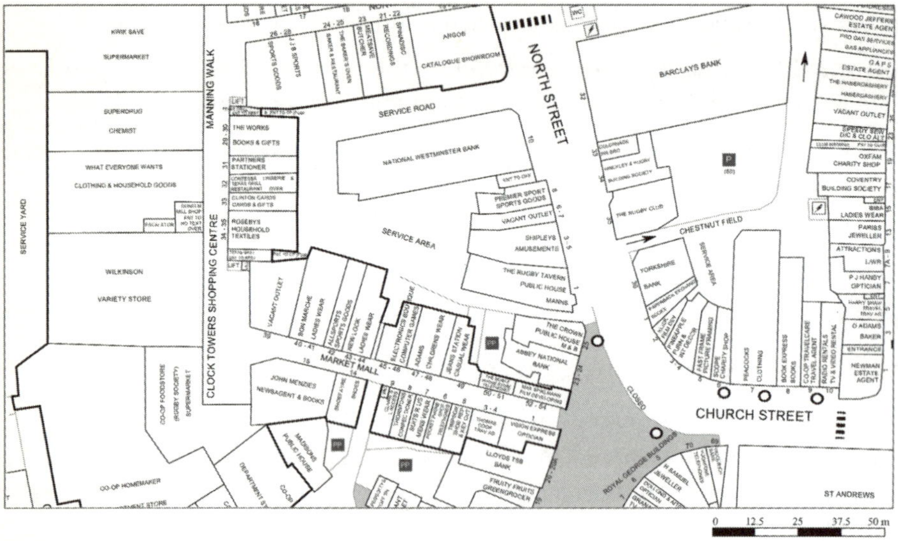

Figure 6.1 An illustrative Goad plan

Extract reproduced from Rugby Town Plan, 2003 edition of Goad plan

That ideal corner location with busy, affluent streets on either side will be attractive to every retailer. The landlord simply needs to stick out for the highest offer – and a bookseller is unlikely to be profitable enough to afford the rent that this kind of property will command.

Balancing primary and secondary

The dilemma that most booksellers face is that they cannot afford the costs of being where they know the volume and quality of customers are near-perfect. These “prime” pitches, as they are called, command enormous rent and rates which are simply out of reach.

The choice then lies between finding a property close enough to the main shopping area to be busy, but far enough away to carry an affordable rent. This sort of pitch is known as “near-prime”; further away from the best part of town, the pitch becomes “secondary”. You need to be very aware of what the impact might be if a new bookshop opens in a better position than you. Many, many traditional bookshops have failed simply because somebody chose to gamble on paying a higher rental and opening in a better location. Ultimately it may not work for them with the higher costs, but it will almost certainly kill your business in the process.

It is also worth taking a very careful look at how busy any potential location is at varying times of the day. Never try to save money by cutting out professional advice, either. Consult estates specialists before entering into any negotiations.

Figure 6.2 below summarises the various factors differentiating primary and secondary locations. You will need to weigh up how much each factor may affect your business.

	Pros	Cons
PRIMARY LOCATION	● High visibility and footfall. ● More affluent client base. ● Surroundings conducive to customers spending more time and money. ● May be possible to eliminate competition in secondary location.	● Generally high rent and rates cost. ● Covering overheads may prove impossible.
SECONDARY LOCATION	● Generally lower rent and rates cost. ● Potentially better chance of business coping with overheads. ● If specialist, may become a destination store.	● Lower footfall. ● Less affluent client base. ● Surroundings less agreeable. ● More vulnerable to competition in primary location.

Figure 6.2 Primary and secondary location

Unit Size

The next critical factor in the search for a location is the size of unit you are looking for. Many retail units may be either too small or too large for the bookshop you are planning.

It is also important to recognise that you are not alone; other retailers will also be seeking new units. As soon as a particular size or format of retail unit becomes popular, it will get scarcer and, in strict accordance with the law of supply and demand, the asking price will go up. The demand for retail space fluctuates all the time. When there is a glut of it and little demand, you can secure a very good deal. If demand is outstripping supply competition – and prices – will increase. This can be damaging to bookshops, which are often unable to compete with the levels of rental that fashion shops may be willing to pay.

If you follow the new shop planning process covered in later chapters of this book you will get some indication of the size of unit you need for your business. Your budget will also suggest what level of rent you can afford. With these two factors in mind you can then start exploring the possibilities. Again, Goad plans are quite helpful since they will show, in outline, what areas of the town may offer units of the size you are looking for.

Unit Shape

In terms of rent, you will probably be better off with a narrow shop, so long as it is not ridiculously so. This is because such a unit has what is called a helpful "zoning". This means that the layout of the shop unit provides a smaller area in the more expensive zones.

Figure 6.3 below illustrates the difference. Shop A is a wide but shallow unit giving a very good shop window overlooking the main street. It therefore has a lot of space at the very front of the shop, which is the most expensive area. As a result, rent and rates will be high.

Shop B has the narrow front, but goes back a long way. Its floor area is the same as shop A's, but because there is less space in the expensive front part of the shop the rent and rates will be proportionately lower.

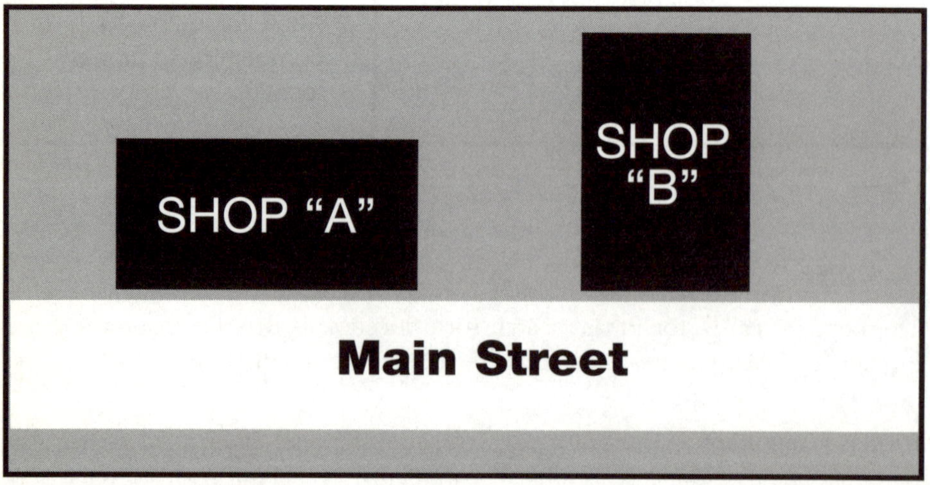

Figure 6.3 Unit shapes

The unit's shape is important in several other ways, too. A straightforward box is good for allowing maximum visibility through the shop and also tends to make shopfitting a bit easier, but you may think it a bit "clinical" and potentially boring. A unit on two floors may well mean almost twice as many staff to keep your shop secure. It may also mean having two till points and, if you are using computers to any great degree, building a network within the shop. Such things may not cause you any problems, but you should consider them before you commit yourself.

A unit with lots of bits and pieces jutting off a central area can often be converted into a very attractive bookshop. The greater length of the run of wall space, where you can put extra wall shelving, is an advantage. Against this, the shop-fitting will be more expensive and the nooks and crannies may give you some serious shoplifting problems after you open.

Any long section of plate glass window (often found on corner sites) can make for difficult shopfitting. If you are to maximise the wall space devoted to shelving you will have to find some way of blanking out the glass and putting shelving along the inside. Some of the solutions to this are not very enticing from the street.

Shopping centres

The shopping centre concept, first developed in the US, has found very general favour in the UK and is a growing feature of the retail property scene. It may have a lot to do with the ease of shopping under cover in an uncertain climate or it may depend more on the now standard provision of easy parking. To many shoppers, these are distinct advantages over traditional open-air high streets.

Many towns not only have main and secondary shopping streets now, they also have two or more shopping centres, often with competition from out-of-town retail locations as well. A number of the larger out-of-town sites are known as "regional centres" reflecting the strategic nature of their location providing access to wide geographical areas. Some examples of such developments are Bluewater in Kent, Meadowhall in Sheffield, Cribbs Causeway in Bristol. They have a huge catchment area and develop their attraction by providing an all-in-one shopping experience for the family. Almost by definition they have thousands of free car parking spaces for customers, although future legislation aimed at controlling car usage may impose charges for such parking.

All of this makes your choice of bookshop location particularly difficult, and you need some detailed knowledge of local shopping patterns.

To booksellers, one advantage of having a unit within a shopping centre is that the centre is usually managed. This means that there are some controls over the shopping environment and that certain minimum retail standards are maintained. On the other hand this control may be an unwelcome source of additional cost!

It may also be a chance to get an "exclusivity clause" included in your lease, stipulating that yours is the only bookshop in the centre. This can be a real bonus since it means that you can develop with less risk of immediate competition.

Competition

In a free market philosophy competition is a wonderful thing: it drives competitors to providing the best possible service for customers at the lowest possible price. If one company cannot survive the competition and goes to the wall, so be it. The customer ends up with the best value for money. That's the philosophy.

In practice, the complete absence of competition is probably a bad thing, encouraging sloppy thinking and methods. With nowhere else for customers to buy their books, inefficiency becomes acceptable.

At the other end of the scale, extreme competition is also bad. If a competitor is always undercutting your prices or forcing you to put huge resources into providing what for you is an unreal level of service, then your future is probably risky. Your customers will find they get a better deal from the competitor. Additional difficulties may well be imposed by the conditions of your lease since unless you can find somebody to take on the lease you may be forced, either legally or economically, to continue trading despite the business making a loss if the lease requires it.

When the competition is simply a plethora of nearby bookshops, you may well be as good as they are, but customers are presented with so much choice that they will shop wherever it suits, often with little loyalty. In this case the slices of the cake can simply become too small for you to survive. You may well also find it harder to keep your staff if the other bookshops are offering better pay or conditions. You may feel what you are offering is reasonable and that your staff are loyal, but they all have their own costs to bear. It may be worth considering other, creative, ways of keeping your staff with you, since to lose them may make life extraordinarily difficult for you. Reasonable competition is another thing altogether. It will force you to keep on your toes and look for service improvements wherever possible. Without extreme pressure, you can make a go of things by being comparatively aggressive about your marketing.

Competition, either existing or potential, is a crucial factor in opening a new bookshop and it will be considered again later in this chapter.

Rent and rates

If you own the freehold of your premises rent will not really be an issue for you. You will still need to assess a notional rent for accounting procedures, but you will be freed from continuously working out whether you can pay it.

For other booksellers, rents are a critical part of the business mix. You must pay a landlord rent to be able to trade out of premises and, the better the premises, the higher the rent. There are some cases where the cultural impact of a bookshop produces some form of rental concession – a bookseller may, for instance, only have to pay 70% of the market rental that a butcher or fashion shop would pay – but they are comparatively rare.

In general terms a bookseller wishing to trade from reasonably visible and busy premises would expect to pay a rental amounting to around 10% of total turnover. So, if the rent is going to be £40,000 per annum, the bookseller needs to be reasonably confident of making sales of at least £400,000 before signing the lease.

Some booksellers will be able to trade successfully from premises where the rent is well below this level; others may wish they were in a situation where they were only paying 10% on rent. Generally, however, provided you still have a reasonable location, the lower your rent, the more profitable your bookshop is liable to be.

The other main form of property cost which every trader has to bear is rates, the local government tax based on an assessment of the value of the property. The level of your trading or the profitability of the business are not taken into consideration.

Locating a new bookshop

Most retailers will want to trade in an area with a major centre of population that is suited to their projected business. An academic bookseller normally wants a shop not only in a town offering tertiary education, but also in a location near the college or university. Sometimes specialist booksellers feel they will be sought out for their specialisation, almost regardless of location, while an Internet bookshop obviously faces a quite different situation.

A general bookseller will usually want a shop in a town with a fair-sized population. The trouble is that every other bookseller tends to want to be there too, so you are unlikely to find an ideal location without another bookshop or without one starting up after you have got going.

It is increasingly important to build a view of how easy it will be for customers to get to you. Is there nearby parking? Are the local bus or train services good and reliable? It is essential to get a feel for what future developments for an area may be and visiting the Local Authority's Planning Department will be invaluable. If customers are likely to find it difficult to park nearby, due to parking restrictions, or awkward one-way systems, then you should be very wary about the potential for the location.

The other trouble is that the demand for sites in main shopping areas, from all sorts of other retailers, is high, and this means that the rents will tend to be higher, pro rata, than in the less favoured shopping streets. So at first sight it looks as if your choice is between moderate rents with little competition but not much business, and a high level of business, but with guaranteed competition and rents that may lose you some sleep.

Assuming that you have no pre-defined town where you wish to open your bookshop, you need to devise a list of towns with what you feel is potential. After that, you start looking for specific sites within these target towns.

It is important to be organised about this since taking off in your car and touring the UK to look for sites is unlikely to produce much more than road rage.

Assessing a location's sales potential

If everyone bought books equally the likely spend on books in any town would relate directly to the size of the population – the bigger the town, the more spent on books. Unfortunately it is not so simple as this.

Traditionally demographic analysis looked at the standard socio-economic groupings – A, B, C1, C2, D and E. Modern demographic analysis considers these groupings too broad for today's marketing methods. The analysis now tends to look at population in terms of lifestyle groupings on the grounds that people with similar lifestyles tend to have similar needs and wants. Typically, some thirty different groupings have been identified.

For most towns in the UK a demographic provider can identify for you the relative proportions of each of the lifestyle groupings in the catchment area. If you know what groupings interest you most it is then relatively easy to see which towns have the largest number of potential customers in the groupings. You then have your target list of towns to seek sites in.

Few booksellers have access to research detailed enough to enable them to assess the relative importance of each of the different lifestyle groupings, so they can only really look at broad socio-economic groupings. These suggest that book-buying tends to become more active as people move to the higher levels of the conventional socio-economic classification. So a town with a high proportion of ABC1 households tends to offer a greater book-buying potential than a town with a large C2DE population.

Remember, however, that the size of town is as important as the relative proportion of each socio-economic group. A large town with a very low proportion of AB households may well have a higher book buying potential than a small town with a high proportion of ABs.

Catchment areas

The size of the catchment area is important in any assessment of potential. As a general rule the larger the town, the greater the gravitational pull on the surrounding area, since the shopping facilities are likely to be that much better.

Many of the fully functional geodemographic systems provide very accurate assessments of the size of each town's catchment area. You can, however, assess the relative strengths of nearby towns using a formula which takes into account the factors of population size and distance. The approximate limits to the catchment area of one shopping place in miles relative to another can be calculated by using it as follows:

$$\text{Limit to the catchment area of centre A} = \frac{\text{Distance A to B}}{1 + \sqrt{(\text{Population of B}) \div (\text{Population of A})}}$$

A worked example of the formula is shown in Figure 6.4 below. The formula takes no real account of such complicating factors as public transport or the size and quality of a town's shopping area, but it does give some preliminary idea of the town's potential.

If the distance between towns A and B is 7 miles, and the population of town A is 41,000 and of town B is 68,000, the break-even point where neither town predominates will be:

$$= \frac{7}{1 + \sqrt{(68{,}000 \div 41{,}000)}}$$

$$= \frac{7}{1 + \sqrt{1.658}}$$

$$= \frac{7}{2.287}$$

$$= 3.06$$

So the population living more than 3.06 miles from town A is more likely to shop in town B than in A. In this way you build up a picture of how town A and its surrounding towns affect the shopping potential of town B.

Figure 6.4 Calculating catchment size

The objective of this phase in the search is to come up with a list of towns with the potential of enough book buyers to make a bookshop a viable prospect. You are unlikely to be the first person who has thought of opening a bookshop there, of course, so the next stage of the search process is equally critical.

Assessing the competition

For a new bookshop the competitive situation brings an element of choice – you can choose to open in another town if you feel the chances in your first choice are too limited. Such an option is rarely available to an existing bookshop.

Any bookshop that wants to survive must see competition as coming from all directions. Its sources can be broadly categorised, since each demands slightly different techniques of assessment. Some possible competitive variables are:

- small independent bookshops;
- non-specialist chains with a strong book emphasis – WH Smith, etc.;
- supermarkets and other chains such as Woolworths where books form an increasingly significant sector of turnover;
- specialist bookselling chains – Ottakar's, Waterstone's etc.;
- Internet bookshops;
- other leisure areas competing for potential customers' discretionary spending.

We shall come across the final form of competition when looking at marketing in Chapter 15 and since it influences every bookshop in the land it is simply identified here, without further discussion, while we focus instead on the immediate bookselling competition.

The first stage is desk research. The Booksellers Association's annual *Directory of Members* lists every member business in the country arranged geographically by town. Simply checking the target town will give you a listing of the "recognised" bookshops, i.e. those who see bookselling as a sufficiently important part of their business to become members of the BA.

Other bookshops may have opened up since the current directory was produced, however, and you need to know about them sooner rather than later. So your next task is a walk around town. The walk will also help you to identify the other local sources of books. Second-hand bookshops are obvious, but you also need to know whether the local supermarkets sell books. You should end up with a list of all the book outlets in your chosen town, with their locations (ideally to be marked on a town map so that you can see their relation to any site you may identify) – plus an opinion on how effective they are at bookselling.

To assess how effective the competition is at bookselling there are all kinds of possible indicators to work from. Some people find it useful to construct a scoring system to apply weightings to each factor. Ideally you should try to look at the town twice, on a busy Saturday and at a quieter time, too – say a Tuesday afternoon. If you only look in the week before Christmas you may be misled; come the dreary February afternoons a new realism will strike you.

Try answering the following questions to get a fair idea of the competitive potential a shop would offer, should you open nearby.

- What size of floor area is devoted to books?
- What is the state of the premises? Newly painted or a bit ragged?
- How wide a range of stock is carried?
- How well is the stock displayed? Lots of face-out, or a bit disorganised?
- What services are provided for customers?
- Is the stock looking fresh, or has it become a bit tired?
- Is price used as a promotional tool and if so, how vigorously?
- Are the promotions well displayed and well sited?
- Are the promotions current and appropriate?
- How busy is the street or centre where the shop is located?
- How busy is the shop itself?
- How many staff are around?
- How interactive with the customers are they?
- Is their advice, when questioned, helpful?
- How effective is the stock control? Are there lots of old titles around?

It is also important to weigh up carefully all the different sources of competition, and how their offer to your potential customers might affect your business.

A branch of WH Smith or a relatively strong book section in a supermarket could mean a lot of bestsellers for sale at far lower prices than you could afford to match. Depending on the proximity of these shops to your possible location and the kind of customers you are targeting, this could mean that your shop was severely affected by price competition.

Equally, a branch of one of the leading specialist bookshop chains nearby may mean that you would be unable to compete on range of stock, but there may still be openings if you feel you can provide a significantly better service to prospective customers. Do not underestimate the competitive pressure these shops generate, however.

When Tim Waterstone was still running his eponymous chain he observed: "The point about general bookselling is that somebody who is prepared to take a much bigger site and have a much bigger stock is going to win at the end of the day. People want to see a vast amount of books in front of them. That's what general bookselling is about." He has seen a lot of changes since then, but general bookselling has not.

The objective of this phase of the search is to narrow down your list of target towns in such a way as to give you some certainty of the success of the bookshop you might open in any of them if a suitable property comes up.

Size matters

At some point you will need to determine both the optimum size of your shop and the likely turnover that it may achieve. The conventional measure that you would need for these calculations is the level of sales that are likely to be generated from every square foot of your shop, known as the sales per square foot. This measure can either be used to cover the sales divided by the total sales floor area, or the sales divided by the total shop area including back office space. Clearly it is important to identify what criteria are being used when you are using these figures for comparative purposes.

Recent research suggests that during 1998 the main chain booksellers were generating sales of between £300 and £500 per square foot. This is a broad generalisation and spans such a wide range because sales per square foot is a measure not only of marketing ability and efficiency of stock operations, but also of location. A bookshop in a busy central London location must generate a far greater density of sales than a rural bookshop. The footfall is very much higher, but equally such sales levels are necessary to help support the very high rental costs that will be incurred at such a location.

You must therefore try to pick an anticipated level of sales per square foot for your proposed shop. The guides given will have to be modified to suit the specific location, but they should give you a broad indication of both the size of shop you would need to generate a projected turnover and the turnover you are likely to generate from a given space.

As an example of this we might use a town where you estimate that a sales density of £250 per square foot is realistic. If your business plan suggests that you need to generate an annual turnover of £750,000 then you can now work out that you need to look for premises of around 3,000 square foot. If, on the other hand, you are looking at premises comprising 2,000 square foot, you can estimate that a possible turnover will be in the region of £500,000 per annum.

Buying a going concern

The advantage of taking over an established bookshop is that everything is already in place and you are not forced into early decisions about shopfitting, stock range, bibliographical tools and so on. Neither do you have to initiate business contacts with suppliers, staff and customers. To a certain extent you can let the business ride while you take some time deciding how far, if at all, the inherited ways of running the business might be developed, modified or changed altogether.

A going concern offers you a degree of certainty. The bookshop is likely to be as busy in your first week as it was in the previous owner's last. Your accountants should have carefully examined the financial and business records of the business, and this should give you a fairly good idea of what to expect in the coming year by way of turnover, gross profit and ultimately net profit.

Clearly all this must be paid for. The price you are likely to pay for the business will be higher than the value of its physical assets. The additional payment, i.e. the difference between what you pay for the business and the total value of its physical assets, is called goodwill and is, in effect, a payment for the expectation that the bookshop's record of profitability will be maintained. There is no guarantee of this, however, and you should be very careful to avoid buying the proverbial "pig in a poke".

It is important to try to understand the real reasons for the sale and also the likely future developments within the shop's catchment area. If the sale is because a large new bookshop is opening around the corner, or that the town centre is being decimated by a newly opened nearby shopping complex, then you have to find this out for yourself, since it may well make a critical impact upon your future trading and profitability.

Vendors generally tend to take a rather optimistic view of the value of their shops, fixtures, fittings and other assets. Get professional advice on the validity of the estimates and aim to negotiate down to what you believe them truly to be worth.

Taking over the stock

Purchase of stock is one area where you need to be particularly careful. If the sale of stock is to be included in a deal, you will probably see the price advertised with "plus SAV", which stands for "stock at value". The stock will almost certainly be worth less to you than it cost the present owner (who will probably be aiming to recoup the cost), so you must assess its real value to you.

You should make sure that you take over only the recently bought stock that is still actively selling. The present owner can get rid of the old stock as they wish. If the stock control system does not distinguish between the old and the new it may be better simply not to take the stock unless you are confident of being able to assess its quality yourself. This leaves you to buy completely fresh stock, but that may be a better option than being saddled with unsaleable items. If you feel you need to do this, however, why not start the whole business from scratch, since there are bound to be other things you will not like either?

You may well be offered the stock at what seems a generous, written-down value, in other words a sum calculated as an arbitrary percentage off the stock's total value at retail prices. This might seem quite a good offer since it will certainly be cheaper than you could buy it. You must remember, however, that the only value (written down or otherwise) of an unsaleable book is zero. If the stock contains more than a tiny proportion of such books you must be extremely careful – or negotiate the stock value down to a level where you believe you really can make some money from it.

Landlords and agents

It is popularly thought that there is a very special part of hell reserved for landlords but at some point in your search for a property you will have to deal with landlords or agents.

Ever so occasionally a landlord or agent may feel that having a bookshop around is a benefit in the greater scheme of things. If this happens you may find you can get an attractive property deal on the basis that you are adding cultural tone to the surroundings. At other times, however, a landlord will want only to maximise revenues from a development. The premises go to the highest bidder.

Involving estate agents specialising in commercial property is usually useful. Do so at an early stage. They will be able to advise you on the sort of rentals various locations command and point you in the direction of new developments in various towns. Once you have found a suitable property and are negotiating a lease, their specialist knowledge and commercial acumen will help you to get a good deal on it, although they are no substitute for proper legal advice.

Starting from scratch

One of the greatest advantages of starting from scratch is total flexibility. You are not limited to the relatively small number of specialist bookshops likely to be on the market when you happen to be looking, and you are free to consider opening a shop of any size and character anywhere in the country.

Things are seldom so simple, of course. Something or other will almost certainly constrain you, be it capital or local knowledge. The point is, however, that you need not be hidebound by the physical limitations an existing bookshop imposes.

You have a lot of serious decisions – usually pulling in different directions – to make when choosing a site for your bookshop. The site which offers hordes of customers, almost no real competition and all at a peppercorn rent has yet to be found. So your final choice is bound to be a compromise. The critical thing to remember is that if you get yourself locked into a long commercial lease you must think through all the risks and possibilities. You may find that selling on or assigning the lease is much harder than you had thought.

The ideal site

Of all your early book trade decisions, the choice of a site for your bookshop will have the most profound impact on the whole of your trading. If the site is wrong, nothing else can be right.

A five-hour visit to a town is no substitute for real local knowledge and you certainly stand a better chance of finding the right site if you stick to the places that you already know well. The more familiar you are with an area, the better you can judge its potential and assess the shortcomings.

The local knowledge will tell you which areas of a town are developing, and which have started to decline; you will also have a better feel for the shopping habits of the local people and may well know of planned developments which may raise the profile of the town or damage the town centre shopping potential. You may even be able to strike a good deal with property prices based on today's trading levels if you can spot a good development early on.

If you are forced to consider areas where you do not have this sort of detailed local knowledge you must be prepared to do a lot of research early on. This will include assessing the size of the catchment population. Study the map carefully to see what nearby towns may provide an alternative attraction for the local population.

Further information

An estate agent specialising in retail property will have detailed information about locations within specific towns. Another local route is to look for advertisements in the property pages of the local newspaper, which will often carry a selection of advertisements for commercial property.

Several trade magazines such as *Retail Week* or *Shopping Centre* regularly carry detailed comment and analysis of retail property issues and developments.

7. Bibliography

Bookselling differs from many other types of retailing in the sheer volume of product, both new titles and backlist, that is available for stock. As we have seen, there are more than 1,000,000 books in print in the UK at present, while the number of new titles published currently hovers around the 115,000 per annum mark. Such a surfeit of available product is a serious logistical burden for booksellers, who try to cope with it through the effective use of bibliography, their core tool.

Access to reliable and up-to-date bibliographic data is the key to a bookseller's first decision, which is what to hold in stock, and what to pass over. Secondly, it enables every bookseller to provide a service for customers by identifying, sourcing and obtaining the books they wish to order. Access is not the whole story, of course, since booksellers also need the skills to use the data effectively.

Fortunately there are both high and lower-tech solutions to the bibliographical tools problem. Mistakes may prove expensive, so it makes sense to take the time to ensure that you choose the right answer for your shop.

Choosing the right medium

The quickest route to providing a highly efficient bibliographic support for your bookshop is to use the high-tech solution of computerised provision, using on-line data. Whitaker provide a service called *SourceData* which offers a very high degree of flexibility and enables a bookseller good opportunities to integrate the data into their own databases. The search facilities are excellent and a wide range of delivery formats are available to suit practically any bookseller system

Using on-line access to the original source material provides a very high degree of currency of bibliographic data. This is essential if you are making extensive use of a web site in your bookselling operation, but may well prove valuable if you are a heavy bibliographic user from your retail operation. In order to run this system you would require broadband Internet access and a password protected subscription to the *SourceData* or *WhitakerWeb* system from Whitaker.

A slightly less hi-tech solution is to use data on CD-ROM. The *BookBank* system from Whitaker and *BookFind-CD* from BookData are fast, regularly (usually monthly) updated and generally more flexible (records can be downloaded for marketing purposes, for example) and accessible than other media. Bibliographic information is available for titles in print in the UK, globally or for the 1.4M titles that are out of print. Additionally substantial coverage of book jackets is also available.

Hi-tech solutions tend to be more expensive than low-tech solution, however, and they do make demands on the system resources of the computer on which they are run. Given the specification of most relatively new PCs this requirement for memory and for a CD-ROM drive are unlikely to be critical issues. Equally the wide availability of fast broadband Internet services means that on-line bibliographic support is well within the bounds of many booksellers.

Perhaps a more important consideration is that if you are going to be using one PC to cover your accounts, stock control and bibliographic activities then you may come across time conflicts which will need to be resolved for the systems to be operated effectively. It is also worth recognising that as the level of technology used to provide bibliographic support increases, so does the training issue for both yourself and your staff if the systems are to be used to a high level of effectiveness.

The lowest-tech solution is *Whitaker's Books in Print,* published annually in five handsome volumes but which because of its printed format, is not the most up-to-date reference. Still low-tech but updated monthly, however, is the microfiche edition of the same title. This system photographically reproduces 270 pages of the printed edition on a small plastic sheet that is inserted in a moveable holder into a "reader". The user selects the relevant "page" and the image is projected on to the screen of the reader. Dexterity comes with frequent use.

The microfiche system offers a reasonable compromise for the smaller bookshop. It is as up to date as *BookBank* but the subscription is lower and a microfiche reader costs very little to run. At still lower cost, you can also get hold of the microfiche edition by joining a chain process where one bookseller pays full rate for the monthly update and sells it on a month later to another bookseller for a smaller fee. Such arrangements are advertised regularly in *The Bookseller.* You miss out on the latest information, of course.

If choosing these lower tech approaches you do need to be aware not only of the degredation of the information over time, an issue that increases as the speed of change within the book trade continues to increase, but also that it is probably only a matter of time until these media are phased out by the suppliers as too costly to maintain for a decreasing user base.

Choosing the right product

You need bibliographic information in order to provide your bookshop and customers with accurate information about what titles are available. This, however, is simply the basic information requirement. If you can access the information in an appropriate format then you may well be able to make significantly greater use of the resource. Now is the time to consider this carefully.

Web sites

If you are using a web site as part of your bookselling operation then you need to consider how best to provide the sort of search engine that will be most appropriate to your customers. There are two issues to consider:

- How up to date does the information need to be?
- How extensive does the information need to be?

If there is no huge need for complete currency then it may be possible, providing you have a suitable licensing agreement, to power your Internet search engine from a CD-ROM based bibliographic product. This may mean that you generate orders for books that have gone out of print since the CD-ROM was produced and equally you may miss out on orders for books that have been published since the CD-ROM was produced. If these are significant issues then you probably need to power your search engine through a daily download from an on-line bibliographic database. You will need to make sure that your licensing arrangement allows you to use the information for your web site.

You can also decide whether you simply want to use textual information or graphics as well. There are some potentially quite substantial implications for the engineering, disk space requirements, and speed of your web site design. You should discuss this carefully with the people involved in your web site but at the end of the day you need also to be guided by what your customers are most likely to respond to. There are also likely to be implications for the costs of your bibliographic licence since the more information provided the more justification there is for increasing the cost.

The next consideration is how extensive a range of titles is to be accessible from your search engine. If you are running a niche site then the range may well be moderately compact, but a general site will require a much broader range. If you need to cover American books as well as British, for instance, your licencing costs will escalate since there is a correlation between the number of titles and the cost of the license.

Stock control

If you are running a computerised stock control system then the bibliographic details of every book on the system will have to be entered onto the computer. You may need only the most basic of information, such as author, title, ISBN, publisher and price, but even this becomes a significant overhead when repeated 20,000 times!

If you are using a manual bibliographic system you have very few options. You can buy in information to start off your system but you will need to add any new titles manually. If, however, you are using a PC based technology solution then you should actively explore the possibilities of downloading title information from your bibliographic system directly into your stock control system. This way you need only flag those titles you want added, usually by entering a list of ISBNs, and then the computer will do the rest. The result will be an enormous administrative burden lifted from your shoulders!

Marketing

There are significant benefits to your marketing function if you choose an appropriate bibliographic system. With many of the technology based solutions you have greatly improved search facilities – such as being able to search for gardening books. This can be an enormous benefit when looking to identify titles for inclusion in a promotion, and the time saving that it allows cannot be underestimated.

Choosing the right product

The various bibliographic providers present booksellers with another choice to make between their products. When deciding to use one bibliographic source over another, the critical factor is to choose what will enable you to give your customers the best level of service.

In coming to a decision, most booksellers would ask themselves the questions shown in Figure 7.1 below; you may, of course, want to add additional criteria of your own.

Scope	● How broad a base is covered? ● Are there geographical limitations? ● Are there linguistic limitations? ● What time frame is covered?
Arrangement	● What is the overall arrangement of information? ● Is it easy to use? ● Does it include listings by author and title? ● Are there listings by subject? ● Can I use the data for marketing purposes? ● Are the listings separate or combined?
Details	● What bibliographic detail is given? ● How can it be used? ● Can the information be downloaded into a PC system?
Additional features	● What additional features, such as publisher addresses, are given? ● Are readership indications given? ● Are brief details of content given? ● Will these be useful to this business?
Currency	● How up to date is the information going to be? ● What level of currency do my customers expect, or even require?
Access	● How easy is it to access the information? ● Will I need to install additional PC hardware? ● Will I need to upgrade my Internet connection?
Cost	● Can this business sustain the cost?

Figure 7.1 Criteria for choice of bibliographies

These criteria should be applied to all of the bibliographic tools that the bookshop might need. You should also recognise that most bookshops will use a variety of tools, according to the level and type of customer enquiries they handle. Only rarely, the exception probably being on-line access, will one particular bibliographic source answer all needs.

The costs involved will usually mean reaching a compromise, however, so that it becomes a question of using the "best fit" bibliographic solution.

Nielsen BookData

The merger of the two traditional bibliographic providers in the UK, Whitaker and Book Data, has resulted in a new business called Nielsen BookData and will comprise Book Data, Whitaker (including TeleOrdering) and First Edition.

As such Nielsen BookData will provide comprehensive and content rich bibliographic material for titles published UK and globally. The second strand of activity will provide a wide range of EDI and web fuctionality for booksellers, publishers and wholesalers. Nielsen Bookscan, originally known as BookTrack, will provide objective marketing research data on UK book sales.

Foreign bibliographic tools

You may not set out with the intention of supplying a wide range of foreign books but your market may develop in such a way that providing them may become profitable (imagine, for example, that a language school opens near your shop). If so, then you will probably need to invest some time and effort into finding the best ways of developing bibliographic support for the service.

Most major book-producing countries have a range of bibliographic tools comparable with Britain's, in print, microfiche and CD-ROM, although the quality and style vary considerably. Unless you have to meet very specialised orders, you will probably find *Les Livres Disponibles*, *Verzeichnis Lieferbarer Bücher, Catalogo dei Libri in Commercio* and *Libros en Venta en Hispanoamerica y España* answer most needs. For details of publishers, refer to the *Directory of Publishing: Continental Europe* (published by Cassell, the Publishers Association and the Federation of European Publishers).

Training

If you have trained as a librarian or bookseller you will find that the skills you need to make effective use of bibliographies have become almost second nature. Without training, however, they can be bewildering and frustrating tools, so that it is well worth considering a training course. It will repay your time by enabling you to provide a better level of service much more quickly.

You should also consider training your staff to use bibliographic tools and could do this yourself once you have developed your own skills to an "expert" level.

8. Buying stock

For a bookshop to generate sales, it must stock books that people want to buy. This involves risk. If books are bought and subsequently fail to sell, then the costs of carrying this stock (or the costs involved in returning it or selling it off below cost price) may put a big burden on the business. A successful bookshop has to get the buying of stock just right – taking enough risk to make the stock interesting, but not so much risk that losses are incurred. This chapter looks at some of the issues involved.

The function and purpose of stock

In practical terms a bookshop is simply a retail outlet, serving the needs of its customers in order to make a profit. To do this booksellers must buy stock, display it and then, they hope, sell it. The stock is bought at one price and sold at another, usually higher. The difference between the two prices is called the gross margin.

Sales less Cost of Sales equals Gross profit

Figure 8.1 Gross margin

This gross margin is used to cover all the running costs of the bookshop: rent, rates, staff wages, heating, lighting, the telephone, etc. There is also your own salary to take, to pay for the time and effort you have put into running the business. Anything left over after all this is real, or "net" profit.

Gross margin less Expenses equals Net profit

Figure 8.2 Net margin

Put another way, the net profit you are left with can be represented as your sales, less the cost of stock for those sales, less the running costs of the business.

The stock a bookseller buys forms the critical link between the concept of serving customers' needs, and making a profit. If the stock is bought well, then these two quite differing concepts will be met far more fully. When customers like the books that the bookshop stocks, they buy them. This greatly increases the likelihood of the bookseller making a profit. If customers do not like your stock – for whatever reason – sales will be low and profit almost impossible to achieve.

You do not necessarily have to stock just books. It is worth considering carefully the issues that are raised in Chapter 10 on stocking non-book items. This may give you an opportunity of broadening the range of customer who is potentially interested in your shop and stock. By the same token you may consider that taking the focus away from books would be a negative development for your bookshop.

Legal considerations

Booksellers are responsible in law for the content of the books they sell. Books which the state might consider obscene, seditious, liable to stir up racial hatred, or do anything else which Parliament or the courts have ruled unlawful are liable to land the bookseller in court, alongside the author, the publisher and the printer. The bookseller may similarly be cited as a defendant in a civil court libel action if a plaintiff feels wronged by a book's content.

Booksellers should note that the information given below relates to UK law. Booksellers in Ireland are subject to different legislation, but the drift is generally quite similar. If necessary, specialist local advice should be sought.

It should also be noted that this is a general book rather than a legal text. As such the information is given as guidance rather than as a specific reading of the current law. For that you need to consult with your own lawyer.

Copyright

Copyright is the name given to the right to make copies of an original work. In the case of books, the copyright normally belongs to the author, who acquires that right "merely" by the act of formulating the original text.

Copyright is a property with a separate legal existence from that of the text or of the author. As such it can be traded as any other property. In a typical publishing contract the author, without relinquishing copyright, grants a publisher the right to produce copies of the work in consideration of a royalty on each copy that is sold. Thus if 5,000 copies of a book are sold, and the royalty per copy is £1.00, then the author receives a total royalty payment of £5,000.

A further element of copyright is the development of what are known as territorial rights. These are the exclusive rights to publish a book within certain recognised territorial areas. Traditionally British rights include the exclusive right to sell to Commonwealth countries and US rights include the exclusive right to sell to American dependencies.

Complications have begun to arise in this otherwise fairly clear picture. The first emanates from European law. Continental Europe has traditionally been an "open market", where both the publisher with US rights and the publisher with British rights have been able to sell their editions without restriction. European Commission thinking, however, provides that anything that is freely traded in one part of Europe should also be freely traded in all other parts of the Union, including the UK. To date there has been no formal test of this and it is likely that any bookseller trying to sell a US edition of a book where a publisher holds British rights would be challenged and possibly penalised.

The digital environment of recent years is creating a second problem. With the rise of bookselling via the Internet there is a considerable risk of foreign editions being supplied to home markets, even though Internet booksellers have so far striven to give undertakings that the books they supply to their customers will be sourced from the "correct" supplier.

The importance of all this for the bookseller is that you could be in trouble if you import books without first checking on the copyright position. The danger is probably most significant if you are importing books from a wholesaler who may not be fully aware of any territorial restrictions applying to titles they stock.

The reverse is also worth noting, in that you could be in breach of copyright if you exported a British book to a customer in a country where a local edition of the book enjoyed the exclusive right of local publication.

Obscenity

Another important issue for any bookseller arises if there is material that is considered obscene within books purchased for resale. If so, the bookseller is potentially liable to prosecution.

Two particular Acts of Parliament apply. First, the Obscene Publications Acts of 1959 and 1964 prohibit the publication and distribution of material that is deemed likely to deprave and corrupt; secondly, the Indecent Displays Act prohibits the use of lewd images within a display. If, for instance, the jacket of a book is considered obscene, even though the contents may be innocuous, then an offence can be committed if the jacket of the book is put on open display.

There are two principal defences under the Obscene Publications Acts - *either* that publication of the article/book is justified as being for the public good, on the basis that it is in the interests of science, literature, art or learning or other objects of general concern *or* that the 'publisher' (which includes the bookseller) had not examined the article/book and had no reasonable cause to suspect that it created an offence under the 1959 Act.

Defamation

The Defamation Act of 1996 gives statutory force to the old common law defence of "innocent dissemination" – i.e. the bookseller was unaware that the book being sold contained text deemed defamatory by one or more parties. The Act requires the bookseller to prove that *'he did not know, and had no reason to believe, that what he did caused or contributed to the publication of a defamatory statement'.*

If a bookseller is put on notice that a publication may contain a defamatory statement (and this may simply be because the publication has acquired a reputation over a period of time), he/she will either have to incur the expense of researching whether or not the publication contained such a statement, or seek indemnity from the publisher.

If the publisher offers an indemnity, the bookseller must bear in mind a number of points. First, that the publisher can satisfy them that one of the established libel defences exist and they have a robust legal opinion to that effect. Secondly, that the wording of the indemnity is sufficiently comprehensive to cover the case in hand. Thirdly, that the publisher has substantial resources or insurance cover to meet any liability that may be incurred, bearing in mind the high level of damages and costs that can be awarded in such cases.

If booksellers are in receipt of any such notice of defamation they would be well advised to withdraw the publication from sale immediately; contact the publisher to discuss the matter and see if any indemnity is available; contact their own lawyer or solicitor and contact the BA as a matter of urgency.

Trading terms

Trading terms are conventionally thought of as the discount that a bookshop receives from a supplier. In fact the term covers a broader range of issues, such as length of credit, availability of marketing support, ability to return stock etc. etc. A bookshop can expect to have trading terms which differ between suppliers. There are sure to be some common features of the relationships, but they will vary widely in their details. Indeed one of the structural difficulties within the book trade is the plethora of differing trading terms. This frequently makes it difficult to remember what precise terms you have with each of your suppliers. For this reason it is important to maintain an accurate filing system, probably in a database, of all the agreements you have with your suppliers.

Publishers also tend to vary their terms between different booksellers and you may find that a nearby bookshop enjoys better trading terms than you do. Why might that be?

The primary reason is that the trading relationship between a bookshop and a supplier is largely a negotiated relationship. A number of factors historically come into play, but the relative importance of each will almost certainly vary between different suppliers.

The likely size of the business between bookseller and publisher is clearly important but, although the basic level of turnover is the "objective" criterion, there are many more criteria (often referred to as "subjective") which publishers use to decide on the discounts they offer to booksellers. The list of variables below is purely indicative. Many more exist and new factors are thought up all the time as the ingenuity of booksellers' and publishers' negotiating skills knows few bounds.

- Length of time the bookshop has been in business.
- Perceived future for the bookshop.
- Services the bookshop offers to the publisher.
- Reliability of historical payments.
- Effectiveness of window displays.
- Effectiveness of local marketing.
- Willingness to try out new titles.
- Level of returns.

The key components of trade terms are ownership, discount and credit. These respectively determine the extent of your risk, what you have to pay – and when. So we should now look in more detail at these elements which form the legal basis of the relationship between the bookseller and the supplier.

Ownership

The precise moment when ownership passes from supplier to bookseller has an importance which is usually tested only in instances of insurance claims, bankruptcy proceedings (yours or your suppliers), tax disputes and other such cases which depend upon precisely who owns what when.

An increasingly frequent component of trading terms is the so-called *Romalpa clause*. The effect of such a clause is to ensure contractually that ownership passes to the bookseller only on receipt of full payment. The intention is to protect the supplier in the event of a business going into receivership, but it seldom has much bearing on the successful day-to-day trading relationship.

It is worth, perhaps, recognising that many booksellers will find the bulk of their stock is under some sort of retention of title clause and is not necessarily their stock until all the relevant invoices have been paid. Many of the retention of title clauses used by suppliers are not legally very strong since the onus of proving the stock came from them, and not from some other source, is difficult. To this extent it is worth considering how accurately your stock control system retains information about supply routes and date of delivery.

Returns

An important area of ownership revolves around the possibility of a bookshop returning unsold stock to the supplier.

In many retail sectors the supplier is no longer concerned after a shop has bought goods. If the goods do not sell that is entirely the retailer's problem – and a cut-price sale results. Partially this is historical, but it is also because in many other retail sectors the volume of innovative ideas and new product lines is limited when compared to the book trade.

The ability of booksellers either to return unsold stock or at least to negotiate its possible return, is a comparative retail novelty. The origins of the system are immaterial; knowing how to operate it is, however, critical. The process is discussed below.

Firm sale

Part of the contractual basis for this flexibility between a bookshop and its suppliers may lie in the precise terms of trade which are used, so that it is important to understand them from the outset.

"Firm sale" is the most prevalent form of supply. Unless there has been some explicit agreement to the contrary between the bookseller and supplier, all trade orders are understood to be firm sale. This means that the bookseller becomes the owner of the books, pays for them in the usual way, and cannot later insist that the supplier take them back if they have not sold.

In this case, the bookseller's stock risk is total. The bookseller can still *ask* the supplier to repurchase the books, but cannot *require* the supplier to do so.

Sale or return

The next level of bookseller risk is "sale or return". Here the books are invoiced to the bookseller, become the bookseller's property, and are paid for as usual. The bookseller, however, has the right to return the books for credit or refund within a specified period.

This type of agreement is often used when a stand is "merchandised". Typically, a merchandising operation means that the supplier clears out unsold stock and replaces it with new titles. The bookseller, therefore, never actually invests in stock, but only pays for what is sold.

A sale or return agreement that is not attached to a specific merchandising arrangement will usually mean that the bookseller pays for the stock at the end of the normal credit period, and is generally expected to hold on to it until near the end of the specified period when the option to return lapses.

The bookseller must therefore be efficient in managing stock that is on "sale or return" and ensure that unsold stock is returned promptly for credit. To rely on a reminder from the supplier would be naïve. It should also be remembered that the return carriage costs for the books are almost always borne by the bookseller.

So while a "sale or return" agreement does reduce the bookseller's risk in stock holding, it does not eradicate it, nor provide a convenient means for undisciplined buying. It involves investment in stock and the additional costs of return. Anyone who thinks of returns as comparatively cheap should consider the following list of some – but not all – of the costs a bookseller bears when making returns to suppliers.

- Time (and cost) spent identifying titles to return.
- Time (and cost) spent listing titles to return.
- Time (and cost) spent chasing authorisation requests.
- Time (and cost) spent looking out, and packing, books to return.
- Carriage costs of returns.
- Time (and cost) spent chasing outstanding credits.
- Time (and cost) spent reconciling paperwork.

Discounts

The primary (although by no means sole) consideration of importance in supplier–bookseller trading terms is the discount, i.e. the differential between the cost price of the books and the probable selling price.

The Booksellers Association has for years urged publishers to give a minimum discount of around 35% on all orders, with no such hidden extras as carriage charges or special levies (called surcharges) if orders do not meet certain conditions. Up to a point, the BA has been successful in the campaign.

On the whole, independent bookshops are buying their hardback stock at 35%–38% discount and their paperbacks at around 40% discount at present. Larger bookshops and bookselling groups are often enjoying enhanced discounts, perhaps 40% on hardbacks and 44% on paperbacks. It is alleged that the major bookselling groups may be receiving up to 65%, or even higher, for a limited number of heavily promoted bestselling titles. This cannot, however, be considered the norm!

If bookshops use wholesalers as a supply option the discounts tend to lie within the same sort of bandings. The advantage, however, is a saving on administrative costs, since only one account has to be serviced.

Single copy orders

Many suppliers still offer lower discounts on orders for a single copy of a book, with a 35% discount on an order for two or more copies likely to fall to 25% if only a single copy is ordered. Although the supplier would put forward economic arguments to support this, the differentiation is critical and divisive from a bookseller's point of view.

Much of a bookseller's stock may consist of single copies of many thousands of different titles. This profile derives from a range of reasons: it may be due to limited funds or limited space; in part it may reflect an attempt to offer customers the widest possible choice; and in part it may be that the title only sells quite infrequently, so that holding a single copy is more justified, in terms of the desired rate of stock turn, than holding a reserve copy as well. Unfortunately, this also means that many of the orders a bookseller places are for single copies and if they routinely attract a discount of only 25% discount the bookshop will find it very difficult to generate an adequate gross margin.

Other suppliers penalise the single-line, single-copy order – that is, the order for just one copy of one title – compared to single-copy orders for two or more titles. This practice is rather more reasonable in that suppliers clearly incur costs in filling an order, and if just one book is required, then the costs must be attached to it.

A potentially simple solution to this problem may be to switch the order to a wholesaler where the financial penalty of such orders can be reduced, and possibly even eliminated.

Credit terms

The length of the credit period that a supplier will allow a bookseller is another area where negotiation can be useful.

The time is measured as the number of days following the issue of a statement of invoices supplied during the previous month when payment is due. If the period of credit is thirty days, it means that all invoices supplied to the bookshop during March will appear on a statement issued on 1 April, and will be due for payment on 30 April. For 30, 45, 60 and 90-day credit periods, the system works out as shown in Figure 8.4 below.

	Invoice date	Statement date	Payment date
30 days payment	15 March	1 April	30 April
45 days payment	15 March	1 April	15 May
60 days payment	15 March	1 April	30 May
90 days payment	15 March	1 April	30 June

Figure 8.4 Credit periods

One obvious implication of this system is that goods supplied on an invoice dated 1 March will actually enjoy nearly 60 days' credit, but those supplied towards the end of March will have a much shorter credit period. Not surprisingly, most publishers set major publication dates for the end of the month.

It is of course in any bookshop's best interest to negotiate the longest possible period of credit from suppliers, since it gives a better chance to sell the books before they must be paid for. This relationship is explored below.

Opening a new account

A new bookshop will generally have to give evidence of creditworthiness before being extended a credit facility by a supplier. The usual requirement is for two trade references and a banker's reference. The trade referees will normally be other suppliers who have given you credit and are prepared to bear witness to your prompt settlement of their bills. This can be a Catch 22, since as a newcomer to the trade you may have difficulty in providing these two references. However, you may be able to supply references from outside the book trade or references attesting to your personal integrity from your accountant or solicitor.

If a supplier is unwilling to offer you credit facilities you may be issued with a *pro forma* invoice requesting prepayment. Alternatively, you may decide it would be quicker to send a prepayment with your order – which may also help to secure better terms. The usual way to do this is to send a signed cheque made out to the supplier with an upper limit marked in the cross lines, but left open for the supplier to enter the precise sum.

Perhaps a more flexible alternative to proforma invoicing is to allow the supplier to use your credit card for payment. You will have to give a special authorisation to the supplier but you should then be in a position where your orders are processed far more quickly since the supplier knows the payment is secured. In addition to the speedier service you will avoid the administration needed to manage the cheques and you will also gain an effective credit period from your credit card company.

Wherever possible, however, you should buy on supplier credit, and the longer the credit period you obtain, the more securely based your business is likely to be. Indeed there may be the possibility of extending your credit by accepting the supplier credit terms and then settling your bill using your credit card, if the supplier will accept this.

Credit and stock turns

It is important for the long-term stability of a bookselling business to try to harmonise credit and stock turn.

Stock turn is the ratio between the sales that are generated over the year and the value of the average stockholding. Conventionally both figures are judged at retail value. The ratio provides a good picture of the effectiveness of buying, as well as showing how long, on average, books are sitting on the shelves.

A stock turn of four (a very credible stock performance) means that on average a book is sitting on your shelves for three months before it is sold. If, however, you are paying your suppliers on one month's credit, then it follows that your money is tied up in your stock for two of those three months.

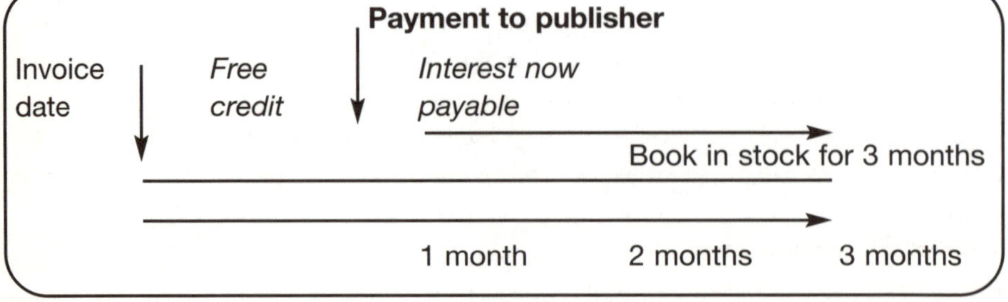

Figure 8.5 Stock turn and credit

If your stock was valued at, say, £100,000 at retail price, this means that you are having to pay interest on two-thirds of that sum, i.e. £66,000. By the same token, if you are investing your own savings in stock, you will be losing interest by having your money in stock rather than on deposit in an interest-bearing account.

If, however, careful negotiation enables you to extend your credit terms from 30 to 60 days, you will only have your money tied up for one month, and your interest payments will fall. Equally, if your rate of stock turn fails to achieve four, the value of your stock will increase, and your interest payments will rise.

Seasonal offers of extended credit may be one opportunity to exploit. You might be able to place Christmas orders or Back to School orders on extended credit. If so, it will be a useful bonus for your business, but you should beware of ordering more stock than you really need just to get the longer credit. After all, a bargain is only a bargain if you can use what you get.

A time-honoured, but unethical, method of getting a longer credit period is simply to delay paying your bills or to pay only part of them. Bigger booksellers may possibly get away with this with some smaller publishers, but smaller booksellers using the same tactic may well find themselves put on "stop" by the supplier's credit control department. This means no orders will be filled until outstanding debts are cleared. As a business needs continuous supplies of fresh stock and new titles, this is a tactic likely to cause you more problems than it may promise to solve.

If you are starting a bookshop it will be worth negotiating an extended credit period on your opening stock, which is likely to be large. You may find that individual publishers are unwilling to offer such terms, but that a wholesaler, who would be getting the whole order, might give you longer credit. This is a consideration which may make it worth your while directing your opening order, and perhaps your future business, to a wholesaler.

Publishers or wholesalers?

There is an important distinction to be made between publishers and wholesalers. Publishers usually operate a direct supply distribution system to retail outlets. This means that if you buy from a publisher you are buying direct from source, but you can only buy that publisher's books and perhaps those of one or two others for which the publisher distributes. So if you generally buy from publishers you must deal with hundreds of different suppliers, each with its own systems and terms.

Wholesalers, on the other hand, buy selected titles from various publishers, and then offer them for resale to bookshops. This means that the bookshop can buy the books produced by a variety of publishers from one source, with one system and with one set of terms.

There is also a difference in the quality of service offered by publishers and wholesalers. Most wholesalers offer a 24 or 48-hour delivery service for books that they have in stock. This means that, providing the title is available, the bookshop gets its stock back in very quickly, minimising the time that books are out of stock.

Although some publishers' distribution systems are very efficient, with the best only just behind the wholesalers', many are far less efficient. It is true that at busy times they can offer what are called "hot-line" services which provide fast turn-round. That said, however, many other publishers struggle to get books back to the bookshops in fewer than ten days from ordering. This means that if a bookshop stocks only a few copies of a book (for sound financial reasons) there is every possibility it will sell out while waiting for an order to be fulfilled. When this happens, valuable sales are lost.

All this presents booksellers with a bit of a dilemma.

A big bookshop may find that the volume of business it can direct to many publishers is such that it can get enhanced discounts by dealing directly with the publisher. The buyer may then decide that this benefit outweighs the problems associated with potentially slower replenishment of stock, and with dealing with many different accounts and ordering systems.

Small shops, however, may well find that the volume of business they might transact with any individual publisher is too small to earn anything other than the basic terms. They may even find they attract penalties because the orders do not reach the volume the publisher stipulated. In this case it may be easier to bulk orders from a variety of publishers and get the books from a wholesaler. The bonus may be that the volume of business that can be presented to one wholesaler allows for better discount terms than the individual publishers would give.

Since there are comparatively few national wholesalers in the UK they compete hard with each other – to the benefit of booksellers. The services they offer today have extended far beyond fast replenishment of stock and most will provide substantial catalogues listing titles in stock and forthcoming titles, free access to electronic ordering systems, a returns provision and the unique benefit of a single enquiry point. Additionally most wholesalers will offer their own regular promotional programmes, such as "offer of the week", to their customers whereby extra discount can be gained by ordering from promotional lists. This helps independent booksellers compete, to some extent, with the high street chains.

This is all on top of the administrative benefits of dealing with one supplier and having all your invoices appearing on one, albeit large, monthly statement. It is a much simpler arrangement than having to deal with orders routing to scores of publishers (and even with TeleOrdering you may still have to chase a lot of orders) and handling hundreds of publishers' invoices and statements.

The system at present means that for most small bookshops, and for most people intending to open a bookshop, a wholesaler offers the best starting point. It may be that as the business expands arguments develop for moving to individual publisher supply. If so, it can only be seen as a sign of success.

9. Ordering stock

Low-tech ordering

Traditionally orders were generally either given to a visiting publishers' representative (the "rep") or were posted to the publisher following receipt of a catalogue. Both methods had some advantages, but took quite a lot of time and also created difficulties in keeping track of orders placed.

Today booksellers have a far broader range of options. Most of these are fast, reliable, relatively cheap, and very efficient, but you do need to invest in some equipment to take advantage of them. The four simplest, low-tech ways of ordering, in technological sequence, are to give the order to a rep, to post it, to 'phone it or to fax it.

Representative orders

Giving an order to a rep is becoming increasingly difficult as publishers "downsize" their personnel. Many bookshops no longer see reps now, so for many it is simply a route not worth exploring. If you do, then it does involve you in breaking one of the golden rules of buying – wait twenty-four hours before actually placing the order to confirm that you still want the books once the rep's enthusiasm for the title has paled a little. You will also tend to have only a hand-written copy of the order.

Posting orders

Posting the order means either marking up a catalogue, writing up an order form, or producing a computer print-out. It is important to keep a copy of these orders and to generate an order reference. This could be a sequential number or simply your initials and a date. When you come to posting the order to the supplier dealing with a wholesaler makes it simple since it is one order to one address. If, however, you are dealing with publishers direct it becomes more complex. Posting orders is a fairly intensive process and quite expensive despite its simplicity. You need lots of envelopes and a stamp for each one.

Using the post is a comparatively slow process. When your order is delivered the publisher will have to convert it manually into an electronic order for the warehouse and invoicing system. The delays involved in posting orders should be weighed up alongside the cost, in terms of lost sales, of books being out of stock for longer than necessary.

Telephone or fax orders

An immediate solution to these delays is to 'phone your orders to suppliers. Although speedy, it is also costly, and you do not have a full copy of the order you placed. Any subsequent query – over the delivery of certain lines that you believe you did not order, for example – is likely to be difficult. Telephone bills will also rise and your customers will be unable to get through to the bookshop by 'phone while you are using it for ordering.

This leads us to probably the most effective of the low-tech ordering methods: the fax. Even the most Luddite of booksellers now accepts that the fax has arrived and is hardly more difficult than the telephone.

Ordering by fax provides all the speed of the telephone, plus the back-up security of the written order. Faxing an order will usually take less time, and so be cheaper, than placing the order verbally over the 'phone. What is more, at the end you will still have your original copy. One possible caution is that if you intend faxing computer print-outs you will need to ensure that the paper size is acceptable for your fax machine and that the print quality is sufficiently high for the order to be legible at the other end.

E-mail orders

It is eminently possible to use e-mail as a means of transmitting orders directly to suppliers. It may sound odd listing such a process under low-tech ordering options but in reality it is simply using a readily available technology to replace phone, fax or post.

Generally speaking the order would have to be for one supplier and all the order details would need to be in the e-mail, either in the body of the text or as an attachment to the e-mail message. Dispatching orders this way, provided the supplier is happy to deal with orders in this format, is probably the most effective low-tech method since you have the rapidity of communication coupled with the security of a written copy.

High-tech ordering

So much for the low-tech methods. Moving up the range, the book trade is fortunate in having a range of highly sophisticated yet relatively simple electronic ordering systems. They are accessible to every bookseller who has a computer and modem and is willing to subscribe the fairly reasonable rates set for joining them.

Indeed for all the possibilities that low-tech ordering appears to offer, it is hard to see how any but the very smallest bookseller could really cope effectively without resorting to higher-tech electronic solutions to manage the complexities of ordering and supply chain management

TeleOrdering

TeleOrdering is the book trade's original electronic ordering system. Owned and operated by Nielsen BookData, it was established in the early 1970s and today handles an estimated 50% of all UK order lines – nearly 31 million in 2002.

The basic concept is that the bookseller enters all orders (regardless of publisher) into a computer using the TeleOrdering Order Entry System, a third party order entry system or online, using WhitakerWeb. The minimum order entry requirement is ISBN, Order Reference and Quantity. The software will usually allow the bookseller to determine which orders are to be sent, and which are to be held until a certain volume is reached. The computer program then rearranges the data into a specific format and adds details of the bookseller's Standard Address Number (SAN) so that the origin and required delivery point for the fulfilled orders can be identified.

The TeleOrdering system is available 24 hours a day, 7 days a week and therefore at any time of the day or night, the bookseller's computer can automatically send the order file to TeleOrdering. TeleOrdering creates an electronic confirmation file, which can be collected immediately after transmission, containing details of order lines successfully routed/rejected.

TeleOrdering will split the bookseller's orders by publisher/distributor and place them in an electronic mailbox for collection at a time convenient for the picking operation of the distributor's warehouse. The bookshop's SAN allows for individual lines to be identified and uniquely allocated to that shop. More than 90% of all order lines are transferred electronically between TeleOrdering and the distributors; the remainder are faxed or posted first class.

Most warehouses operate a series of picking operations throughout the day as their internal systems organise the picking lists for the books required by stock location and customer. This allows for a significant improvement in the efficiency of the delivery system, since so much time is saved in preparing the order.

One of the great advantages of the way in which the TeleOrdering system has developed is that it has allowed increasing degrees of operational flexibility. A bookseller may choose, for example, to send orders during the day rather than overnight, which may tie in with the bookshop's systems if its computers need to perform other processes at night. There are also potential variations in the detail that is sent back to the bookshop by way of confirmation.

There are, of course, costs associated with ordering from publishers by TeleOrdering. As well as the set-up costs involved with computers/modems, there are also running costs. In general, however, compared with the cost of batching and posting orders manually (and dealing with the mistakes inherent in a manual operation), the TeleOrdering charges represent a cost saving over alternative methods of ordering.

For the book trade, the overwhelming beauty of the system is that the routing service is based on the Whitaker's Books in Print database; this means that if a book appears on Whitaker's *BookBank*, then it will be routed by TeleOrdering. This is not to say that if an order is placed for a title that does not appear on *BookBank* then it will be rejected. ISBNs will be routed on prefix alone if no ISBN routing information is held; assuming the ISBN is valid, it will be routed direct to the owner of the ISBN prefix. This also includes several non-UK prefixes, which are routed to major overseas wholesalers. Not only that, TeleOrdering routing can be over-ridden to route direct to your preferred supplier by using a TeleOrdering Mnemonic (Alphabetical codes up to 7 characters in length e.g. GARD). This means that it is a very broad-based system, which can accommodate practically all of the book orders that any bookshop is likely to generate.

The system is in continuous refinement and any potential user would be well advised to contact the Helpdesk (see Appendix 3 for details.

Other electronic ordering systems

Similar electronic methods of ordering books are available from a number of wholesalers, in particular Bertrams and THE. The principal system, called Buyline, allows booksellers to route their orders to a wholesaler of their preference. The wholesaler can confirm delivery by return, but the system also flags up any titles which are unavailable and the bookseller then has an opportunity to "cascade" that order on to another wholesaler on the system to see if it can supply the order.

Buyline offers the bookseller increased flexibility in achieving the primary objective: the swift supply of the book required, regardless of source. The disadvantage, however, is that the system needs very rigorous maintenance if the bookseller is to be absolutely certain that the order for the book is finally recorded somewhere. If this does not happen then the bookshop will never see the book arrive when it does become available.

Both main wholesalers run their own dedicated electronic ordering systems.

Gardners run a system called GardLink and Bertrams call theirs BertLine These systems offer all the advantages of the other electronic ordering systems, but is linked directly to supply by providing wholesaler alone. This is fine if you are using Gardners or Bertrams alone for your ordering, but may be too restrictive if you wish more flexibility in your ordering process.

E-commerce

E-commerce relies upon a technology known as electronic data interchange, or EDI. In the book trade, EDI links between booksellers and publishers are a comparatively recent development, involving individual booksellers setting up dedicated electronic links with individual specified publishers to exchange orders and invoices directly through their computer systems.

E-commerce means that booksellers must set up a whole series of these dedicated electronic links, whereas TeleOrdering requires only one. Against this, it does allow direct order placement with the publisher and the main bonus for both parties is that it also allows invoice information to be transmitted electronically, saving time and paper. Where the bookseller is running a computerised stock control and/or accounts system this invoice information can be automatically integrated into the system, bringing an improvement in speed and accuracy as well as a major saving in the costs of manual data input.

Availability reports

The ideal response to any order is for the book to be delivered to the bookshop within a day or two of the receipt of the original order. This does not always happen. It may simply be that the book is not yet published, but there are many other reasons as to why the book is not immediately available from the distributor's warehouse.

When this happens the distributor will issue a report on the book that has been ordered, telling the bookseller why the book has not been delivered immediately. The publisher will also usually keep the order on the delivery system so that when it becomes available again it will be supplied. The process is called "recording dues" and it does have its positive side. For example:

- if a book is in heavy demand your recorded dues guarantee a subsequent delivery;
- knowing dues have been recorded saves you from having to remember to reorder.

But there is a downside, too. To avoid dues, you can try stating clearly on your order "Record no dues". This device is particularly useful in the pre-Christmas rush when you clearly do not want twenty copies of ***The Best Christmas Book Ever*** arriving on your doorstep on 12 January. Some further downs are:

- dues may arrive well after you have forgotten about them;
- you may re-order, forgetting that dues are recorded, and end up with more copies than you ever wanted;
- customers may not want a book ordered for them if it turns up nine months later.

You will see now why booksellers should record the report information from publishers within the stock control system and have it handy for future reference.

Booksellers must of course understand exactly what the reports mean, if only to pass on the information to the customer who first ordered the book. Institutional customers – and especially libraries – need to know why a book has not been delivered, and when it might be expected.

Most publisher reports fall into a range of conventional responses. These are shown in Figure 9.1 below.

Report	Reason
OP	Title is out of print.
RP	Title is reprinting.
NE	Title is awaiting the production of a new edition.
OS	Title is out of stock at the warehouse.
TOS	Title is temporarily out of stock at the warehouse, but delivery is expected soon.
ND	No date available for likely reprint etc.

Figure 9.1 Publisher availability reports

Dealing with deliveries

A good many publishers operate what is called "cyclical distribution", which means they designate a specific day to deal with each grouping of orders. The grouping may be geographical or by type of shop. The system, which publishers claim enables them to deliver more efficiently, is largely a response to the growing trend amongst booksellers to order little and often. This suits the bookseller, but not the traditional distribution process.

If, for instance, orders for East Anglia are released on Tuesdays, then any orders received in the previous week will be stockpiled until the Tuesday. This is fine if you time your orders to arrive on Monday afternoons, but most irritating if they arrived on the Wednesday and had to wait almost a week for processing.

Checking the number of boxes

When you do finally receive a delivery you need to get the books on display fast in order to start selling them again. First of all, however, you do need to go through a number of important procedures.

When the carrier delivers to you, the first check – very simple, but critical – is to make sure that you are signing for the right number of boxes and that they are all addressed to you. If you sign for eight boxes and only receive seven, you are likely to end up paying for goods you have never received.

If you find that your delivery is short you should note the fact on the delivery sheet. The missing box will probably turn up the next day, but if it does not you will need to advise the publisher of the shortfall.

With luck, the invoice will be in one of the boxes which you have received (although a certain law of probability suggests this is often not the case). However, if you do have the invoice, you should mark clearly on it which books are missing. If there is no invoice, note the goods you have received so that you will eventually be able to identify what is missing from your order details.

Checking the contents

The next series of checks must be devised to ensure that what is in the boxes ties in with what is listed on the invoice; and that what is on the invoice ties in with what you actually ordered. Unfortunately, the three elements do not always correspond automatically. Checking the goods received against the invoice is simple enough, if time-consuming. Checking the invoice against your orders may be more complex.

If you use a computerised system it will probably have allocated an automatic order number. This should correspond to the number quoted on the invoice. If, however, you 'phoned an order, or a publishers' rep took it, you should have ensured that some form of unique, and recognisable, order number was given for you to check against.

If you are running a computerised stock control system then you will probably also have to input the new stock received into your system. This will have the effect of cancelling out the "outstanding orders" field and increasing the "in stock" field for the titles in question.

Discrepancies

If you find a discrepancy between the books itemised on the invoice and the actual books are included in a delivery, you must report this to the distributor as soon as possible for investigation. In most cases it will mean that you are unable to authorise the invoice for payment since there will be books you have been charged for but have not received.

If the discrepancy is due to a warehouse error a credit note will be issued. The credit note, taken together with the original invoice, should tally with the delivery you actually received.

Shelving the books

Once all of these processes are completed it is time to start sorting the books out for your bookshelves. Any customer orders should be extracted. The remaining books can then be shelved in their correct sections, in the correct sequence for each.

If there are new releases in the delivery you may need to rearrange the area on the sales floor where you display new titles in order to make room for them.

A checklist

Figure 9.2 below shows in diagram form the sequence of the various procedures involved in checking goods into the bookshop.

It is unwise to think you can cut corners. Observing these routines will pay off: they make it unlikely that your bookshop will suffer serious loss of gross margin as a result of poor goods-inwards management. You otherwise risk seeing your gross margin fall if you pay for goods which were invoiced but not received.

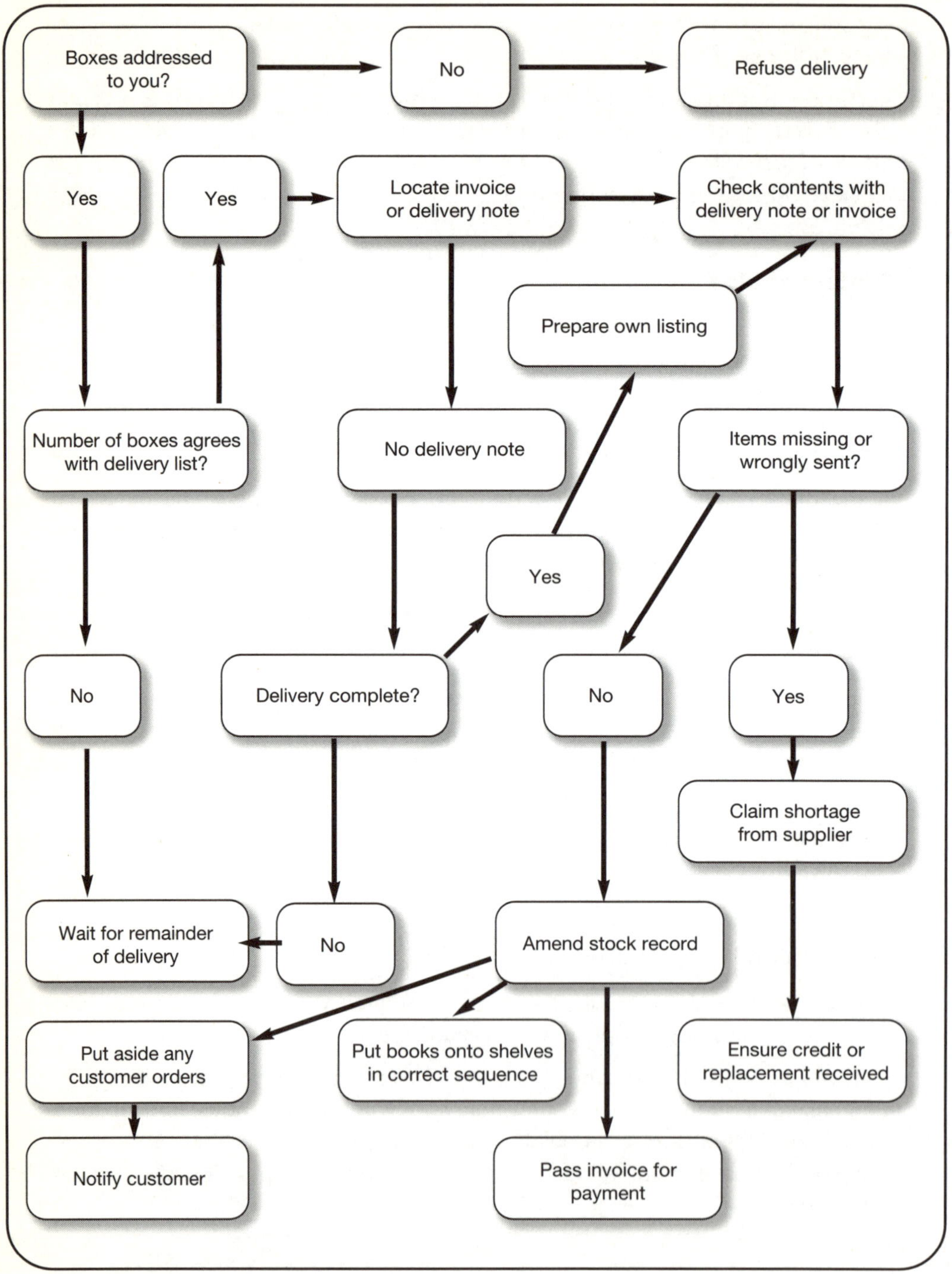

Figure 9.2 Goods inwards flowchart

Settling accounts

You have ordered the stock you require, and it has been delivered satisfactorily. This is usually signified by signing the invoice as authorised for payment. It is now incumbent on the bookseller to pay for the stock at the right time.

Distributors usually provide a monthly statement detailing all the invoices they have delivered to the bookshop in the course of the calendar month. Payment for all the invoices itemised is usually expected within either thirty or sixty days. You will need to organise a payments system to ensure that you regularly pay your suppliers within the credit terms that you have agreed with them.

First, you will have to check all the invoices against the statement to make sure you have received all the deliveries recorded, and that you are satisfied they were correctly delivered.

You will also need to ensure that you organise a cheque or a bank transfer to pay the statement, quoting all the necessary details. Alternatively, you may prefer to use batch described in Appendix 1, to organise all your payments through a single transaction.

A checklist

Booksellers risk an erratic supply of stock if they neglect payments to suppliers. Their credit control departments will simply put the bookshop on "stop" and supply no further orders until the account is settled. Gross margin suffers once again as a result of poor accounts payment management.

Figure 9.3 below gives a diagrammatic guide to the various processes involved in paying your suppliers. Followed correctly, it should ensure that booksellers' relationships with their suppliers remain cordial since financial stability is one of the main criteria by which suppliers judge their customers.

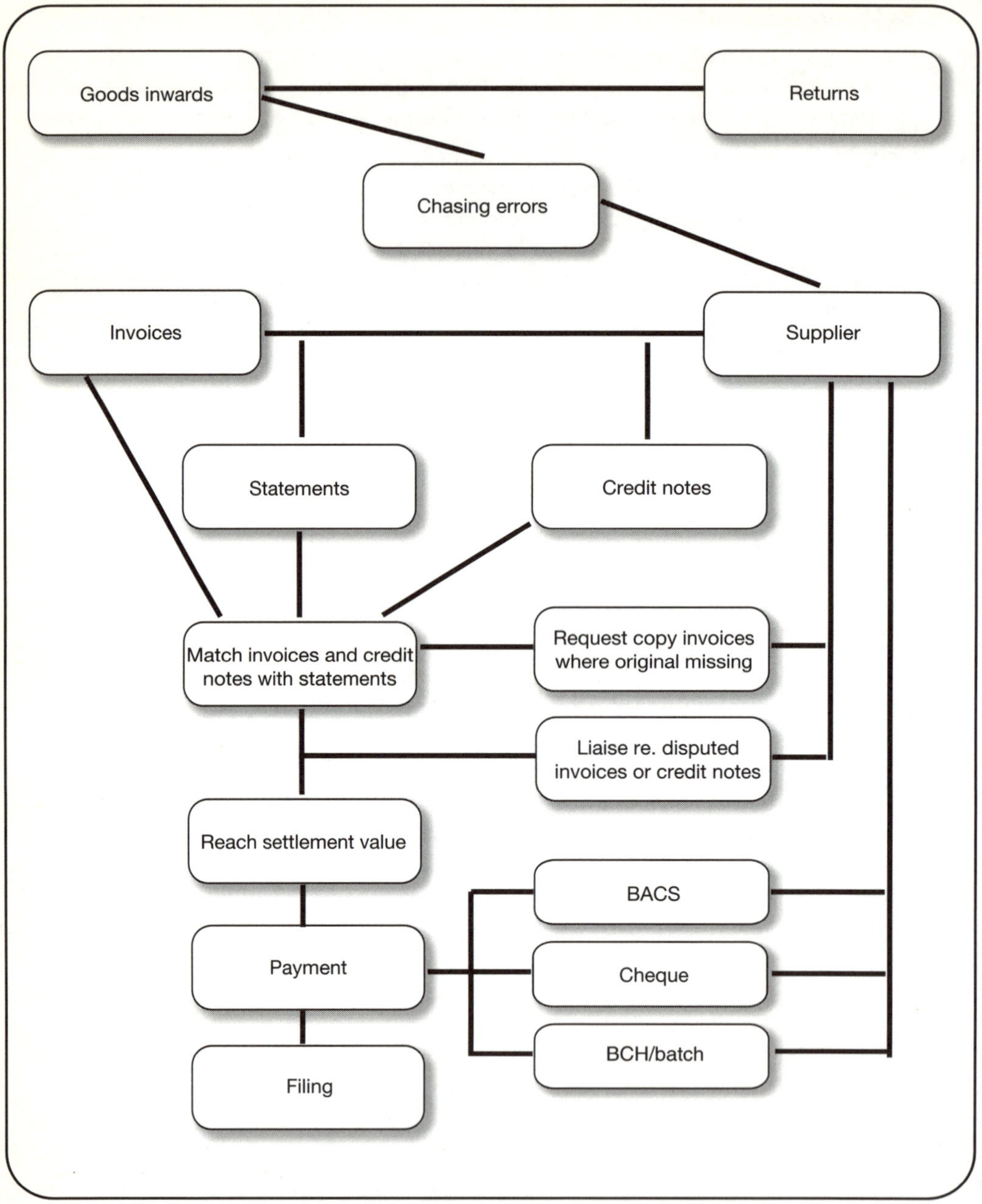

Figure 9.3 Accounts payment checklist

10. Non-book stock

Increasingly, bookshops are stocking non-book items for resale. The possibilities are wide ranging and include a specially chosen range of greeting cards, newspapers and magazines, coffee, or a selection of music. The decision to stock such products may have been historical or accidental: "We tried them and they worked so we just continued".

Taking data from the 2002 edition of the Directory of BA Members, figure 10.1 illustrates the range of products that booksellers are stocking today, and the number of booksellers who are making some additional sales to those generated by books.

Product area	Number of BA members selling
Audio books	1,430
Craft products	431
Games and toys	508
Greeting cards	2,457
Multimedia	625
Music	1,244
Remainder books	1,182
Secondhand books	413
Stationery	1,804
Video	1,350

Figure 10.1: Range of non book products sold by booksellers

If you are thinking about non-book stock for your shop, there are several factors to consider. The most important are to ask yourself first whether the new products would complement, or clash with the existing stock and secondly, whether they are likely to appeal to your existing customers – might they feel uncomfortable with these things? It is important to try and be as objective as possible about exploring this issue, since sentimentality may blur your decision making process; there are perfectly good reasons for either extending into non-book stock or for sticking just with books. You have to take the right decision for your shop!

To take an extreme example, deciding to sell kitchen furnishings at the back of the shop as an adjunct to books might leave your customers more than a bit surprised. If you alternatively went on to add a screened-off adult-only video section, you might find that your customers began actively to avoid your shop rather than risk being associated with the new products.

A post office counter might well have the opposite effect. The point is to add value for the customer and profit for the business. Greeting cards and giftwrap are quite a common supplementary product range for bookshops. Customers generally seem quite comfortable with them and there is a reasonable connection, since books are often bought as gifts. Sales will probably be quite good, provided an appropriate amount of space is devoted to them.

A considerable amount of creativity, coupled with a little sensitivity, is chiefly what it takes to decide on the products to stock, although we should also look at several other factors as well.

Space

The space that non-book products demand is a prime consideration. If you are operating from, say, 1,500 square feet, you may feel you cannot spare the space for a wide range of greeting cards units. You might, however, be able to use a small spinner.

You also need to address the conundrum as to where to site the non-book products within the shop. In order to achieve maximum impact – and perhaps fastest uptake on sales – you need the products to be situated towards the very front of the shop where all your customers can see them. This is, of course, your most valuable space and also the most influential. It would be natural to wish to keep this space for books, but it may not be the right answer!

If you site the non-book products to the back of the shop they are certainly utilising less expensive space but many customers may remain unaware of their presence in the shop, so sales may disappoint.

Possibly the best compromise is to locate the products reasonably forward in the shop, but to give good window and promotional space during an introductory period. This way you attempt to cover all the best options whilst minimising the potential downsides.

VAT

Remember that most of the additional products you may think about stocking will carry a standard rate of VAT.

At the time of writing, books are zero-rated in the UK. This means that your tills must be able to differentiate between book sales at a 0% rate of VAT, and other goods at the standard 17.5% rate. You will also have to train your staff to ring up all products on the tills under the correct VAT category. This is more than just pedantry since you may find yourself subject to a VAT inspection, and if it is thought that you may not be recording VAT sales properly then there are substantial financial and potentially legal consequences.

If in future books should be subjected to a positive rate of VAT this consideration will become more complex of course.

The margin mix

The next important factor to consider is the profit margin on any proposed new products. The margin on books for an independent bookseller is in the region of 38%. The profit margin on greeting cards is generally nearer to 50%. Figure 10.2 below shows the average profit margins on a variety of other potential stock lines, too.

Product range	Profit margin
Newspapers and magazines	25–27%
Greeting cards	50%
General stationery	around 40%
Photographic goods	35%
Toys and games	30–35%
Music	30–35%
Videos	around 25%
Coffee	around 50%
Hardback books	around 38%
Paperback books	around 40%

Figure 10.2 Some average profit margins

Adding some different products – a concept known as "the margin mix" – may well enhance the overall profit margin of your bookshop. Taking active control of the mix is important, since the success of your business may depend upon it, but never lose sight of all the other considerations.

Risk

The final consideration is closely related to the margin mix. When you extend a product range one of the potentially positive aspects of doing so is that you not only broaden the margin mix, you also spread your business risk a bit wider.

If you only sell one product, and something disastrous happens to the market for it, then it tends to affect you to the same disastrous extent. If, however, you have introduced some additional product lines successfully, you have a buffer. Your risk is spread a bit wider.

Some product options

Stationery

Stationery is a traditional product to sit alongside books and many customers find no difficulty with the juxtaposition of the products within the bookshop. Care and thought is needed if the introduction is to be a success since many stationery products need specialised display options if they are to work effectively – if they are simply displayed on utilitarian book shelving the display will deteriorate into a disorganised mess very quickly!

The range of stationery that is available is vast. As an industry it also lacks the detailed classification and structure of the book trade – so many very similar products can come from a vast range of suppliers. This means you either have to be very selective, open a vast number of accounts, or deal with a specialist stationery wholesaler. For the beginner this latter option is probably the best one since you will be able to call upon the wholesaler's specialist knowledge of the stationery market; although you will need to provide all the usual care in listening to recommendations to buy stock!

You should be aware that stationery is an increasingly fashion conscious area. If pink glittery notebooks are the rage today, you may not be able to give them away tomorrow. This means that skill and care has to be exercised by whomsoever is doing your buying. Stationery is also exclusively firm sale, so if you make a mistake it is up to you to deal with it, at your cost!

You may need to deal with a specialist card and gift-wrap supplier if you want to have access to their display units. Certainly trying to sell either of these products without the right display unit is guaranteed not to work, so you should find out what is available before you agree to stock a range.

Music

Music is potentially a good combination product to sit with books but great care and expertise is needed to make it successful. A careful look at how the market is structured reveals that there are two major variants, price and genre. You need to work out which mix may suit your bookshop. It might be budget classical music, or mid price jazz, or alternative music. You are very unlikely to be able to compete with the mainstream youth/pop/rock music market.

If you decide to introduce music you will need to identify your key suppliers, or else use a specialist music wholesaler. You will need specialised display units to properly merchandise the CDs; these might be either spinners or wall units.

A special consideration for music is security. The CD cases are a very convenient size and care needs to be taken to ensure that theft does not completely erode any potential profit. The two conventional approaches are to either take out the CDs and store them carefully in cardboard or plastic sleeves behind the counter, or else to employ a proper tagging system that seals the CD cases and rings an alarm if they are removed from the shop.

The former is cheaper, but can very easily disintegrate into chaos if the sleeves are not filed very methodically. The latter is much more expensive, but is also rather easier to operate in the long run. It may be that your shop already has a tagging system, in which case the provider should be able to offer a workable solution for CDs.

Coffee

There is a pronounced current vogue for coffee shops within bookshops. Many bigger, and some smaller, bookshops now have a separate coffee area with seating and the provision of quality coffee, and usually cakes, for customers. There is quite a variation between the two extremes of a luxury sofa-seated, nationally branded coffee shop and a coffee machine squeezed into a spare corner. You need to be aware what your customers will make of your offering.

The fundamental idea is to make the bookshop a meeting place, and to provide ample reason for customers to prolong their stay inside the shop. This can only happen if there is a sufficient quality of experience – if it is too utilitarian then it is unlikely to succeed. If this combination of coffee and books can increase their visit frequency and their likely expenditure on books, then it is also likely to do so for their friends as well.

Clearly space is a primary concern. Opinion differs as to whether the space is best prominent and central, or rather more tucked away. Logically the central position is more likely to achieve the desired results but may not always be practical. Once space has been determined the major decisions that need to be taken fall along the lines of:

- available budget
- extent of comfort provision
- buy in or do it yourself

All three points are fairly interconnected. If budget is a big problem then the whole exercise should perhaps be carefully reconsidered. The provision of a comfortable seating area together with stylish tables and counter, and all the necessary equipment is a costly exercise. If the bookshop is in a high footfall area then it may be easier to get an outside company to run the coffee shop, but much homework and great care is needed before following this route since mistakes can be very costly and damaging.

If you decide to run the coffee operation yourself, then you need to explore how you can best prepare for this since there is a lot more to making a coffee shop work than simply being able to make a decent cup of instant coffee. The market is very competitive and if your offering is felt to not add value or style it is unlikely to work very well. Whatever your decision it is likely that you will outsource any food provision since this would involve additional food preparation equipment.

Other considerations that you will need to think about are whether or not you will need planning permission, whether you will need food handling certification, and also whether toilet facilities will need to be provided.

News and magazines

Newspapers and magazines are a fairly traditional companion for books and although the margins are not high they are undoubtedly a significant traffic builder. You do need to consider carefully how you would display the newspapers and magazine and unless space is no problem you would also need to decide how you would select the titles you might stock. Your potential supplier may be able to help here, but equally may take a view that there is already enough competition for news locally. If they do take this view, and decide not to supply you, then you are unlikely to succeed in getting the regular supplies you need to make the product work.

If you do get agreement to supply you may well find yourself having to give guarantees about the volume of sales you will make. You may also have to have the newspapers and magazines on firm sale, rather than the traditional sale or return, for the initial three to six months of the contract. This can have quite a heavy financial penalty so careful investigation is needed before committing.

It is possible to purchase, hire, or perhaps even borrow, specialised fittings that will hold and display a range of newspapers and magazines. Alternatively you may decide your book shelving will suffice – do test this out first, however, since the A4 floppy size of most magazines is ill suited to traditional book shelving.

If you do go ahead you may need to consider your opening hours since many newspaper sales are earlier in the morning than many bookshops traditionally open. You may feel, however, that the sales do not warrant the extra costs and inconvenience. You will notice fairly quickly that customers for news are not prepared to stand in queues. You will have to find some way of ensuring that they are served quickly.

Sweets and cigarettes

Sweets and cigarettes traditionally sell alongside newspapers and magazines. If you are going to sell the latter then you will probably need the former anyway, but there is nothing to stop you selling them separately.

Finding a suitable and secure means of display and a good supply route are important aspects if you decide to go ahead. Sweets and cigarettes are on modest margins – sweets tend to be about 20% to 25% whilst cigarettes tend to be 10% - but they are fast turnover products and payment is almost always in cash. This can be a useful consideration.

A possible concern may be that sweets will attract excessive numbers of school children into your shop, and it has to be recognised that this may not be a positive development. You will also need to ensure that you display notices advising that tobacco products may not be sold to children under a certain age. Within the UK this is a legal requirement and you must ensure that it is enforced.

Toys and games

If you sell children's books then selling toys and games may well prove to be a very useful extension of your product range. The range is vast but there are relatively few manufacturers, so finding your way about is a bit easier than in general stationery.

One issue you will find complicated is that many suppliers require you to buy substantial quantities of each individual product – conventionally you buy a box, probably of six or twelve copies. This means that your buying tends to be quite financially intensive and you need to be confident of fairly rapid sell through if you are to make toys and games profitable. You are also likely to find serious price competition on the more popular games and toys. Since you are unlikely to be able to get the margin from your suppliers to compete on these product lines you may decide not to stock them.

Display is also an issue to consider carefully. Many toys and games are in big boxes that will not fit on shelves, but others are fairly small and get muddled up easily. Tables seem to be about the best display option.

Photographic goods

It is possible that you may feel you have a market for selling film and camera batteries. This is particularly likely if your shop is located in a tourist area. If you decide to stock these products you need to find a suitable supplier and also find somewhere in the shop where you can display the products safely and securely.

If you do have a viable market then turnover can be quite brisk in season, but you should buy carefully as the season approaches its end, since out of season sales can be very slow.

Video/DVD

Films and documentaries on video, and the more recent medium of DVD, would appear to sit quite well with books since many customers have interests that are equally communicable through books and video. You should be aware, however, that mainstream retailing is very big business and price competition is likely to be severe.

If you do decide to stock such products you need to find a specialist wholesaler; this may be the same supplier if you are dealing with music. Many of the same criteria regarding display and security for music CDs apply even more especially to the relatively higher priced videos and DVDs.

Trade shows

If you decide to diversify beyond simply books within your shop then you will probably find it useful to go to some of the various trade shows that the stationery and gift industry organise. There tend to be large annual shows in London, Birmingham, Harrogate, and Glasgow, and smaller shows at other locations.

These shows are generally massive and very busy, so if you are going you will need to book any hotel rooms very early if you are not to be disappointed. You will also need to organise your time if you are to maximise the benefit of the shows. They tend to provide good opportunities for finding new products and for also making new contact with either existing suppliers or potential new suppliers.

11. Stock selection

Buying stock involves more than the pure mechanics of purchasing, for the character of a bookshop is ultimately determined by the titles it stocks. Much – some would say, all – of the skill in successful bookselling lies in choosing that stock well.

Finding the right balance between what you personally want to stock, what your customer will buy, and what your customers aspire to buying is not easy. Your success will be measured in terms of how much your customers buy from you, and that measure can be brutal at times.

Evaluating books for stock

Evaluating a title for stock is less a matter of assessing its intrinsic merit than of trying to judge how likely it is to appeal to your prospective customers. If the business is going to survive, you should select stock on a commercial, rather than a literary basis. This is not to say that there is no place for literary evaluation or personal choice – far from it. There is room for you gently to steer your customers in the direction of books which you admire, but you must also remember that you are running a bookshop for the public's consumption rather than your own; and the cost of failure is high.

So the bookseller's role is to make available what the public wants to buy, rather than to influence public taste. That is the job of critics, reviewers, teachers and the media – almost all of whom run no financial risk in the titles they are promoting.

In the sense that the bookshop is an integral link in the distribution chain carrying books from author to reader, the bookseller's primary role is marketing, which makes a sense of the market critically important. Any failure to address the market will usually be countered by the market failing to buy from that particular bookshop.

Once you are trading, with a fully functioning stock control system, it will allow you to identify the winners and losers among the stock you have selected. This enables you to focus on the stronger-selling titles, by re-ordering them when needed and making sure you do not run out of stock. It also enables you to weed out the slower sellers, either through trying to return them, or simply by not re-ordering them after they have finally sold. The principles of stock control and the operation of stock control systems are discussed fully in Chapter 13.

Selecting new titles

Buying new titles is more of a shot in the dark. On the surface of it there is little to guide you in deciding whether to take a book or not and, if so, how many copies to order.

The experience of someone who has been an effective buyer for years is almost unbeatable. Such people make the process look easy, although they will still only get it right about 85% of the time. You cannot gain that experience in a matter of weeks, but you can learn from the processes that these experienced buyers use. They certainly rely on more than just hunch!

Again, stock control can provide useful information on sales trends within various categories and for individual authors. This can guide your choice of new titles to buy, but should be treated with care: did that last gardening book sell so well because of the author's name; the subject it dealt with; the television series it accompanied; the price and quality of the production; or because you displayed it well in the section and there were few other new titles around at the time?

With so many possibilities, your task becomes one of trying to disentangle all these variables to find out what influences your customers most.

Guides to selection

There is, however, plenty of guidance available if you care to use it. The demand for a book, at least in the short term, often relates fairly directly to the amount of publisher promotion and media attention it receives on publication. You therefore need to know what the campaign plans for the new titles are.

The regular reviews of forthcoming titles that are published in *The Bookseller* and in *Publishing News* can be a great help here. They evaluate the titles from a bookseller's point of view and draw attention to any media tie-ins with new or existing titles. *Books in the Media* is particularly helpful, too, albeit retrospectively.

The spring and autumn *Buyer's Guide* published each February and August by Bookseller Publications (available with or without subscription to *The Bookseller*) is also invaluable for its comparative listings of forthcoming titles across a wide range of subjects for the following six months. The main wholesalers issue buyers' guides for their customers, and these again highlight the titles that are likely to achieve high sales in the bookshops.

You are also likely to receive information from the publishers themselves, in the form either of catalogues or visits from their representatives. Should neither arrive, you will find that many publishers have Internet sites now, providing details of their lists. Remember, however, that they will be promoting their titles exclusively, and it will be up to you to assess their relative merits. Perhaps this bias can be overcome to an extent by referring to the Buyer's Notes that the major wholesalers distribute to their customers. This tends to be a listing of those titles that the wholesaler believes will be the better selling titles, but it may overlook some relatively important titles for you if the publisher concerned does not offer the wholesaler acceptable discounts.

The issue comes back to your personal assessment of the new books. In the end you must form your own objective view of their worth to your bookshop, while using some or all of the following sources of information:

- forthcoming titles in *The Bookseller;*
- forthcoming titles in *Publishing News;*
- listings in *Books in the Media;*
- spring and autumn *Buyer's Guide* from Bookseller Publications;
- wholesalers' notes for buyers;
- publishers' catalogues and advance title information;
- publishers' representatives;
- publishers' web sites.

Your judgement will also come into play in assessing how effective the various marketing campaigns may be. Not all of them work, and some publishers have a far better track record than others. Decide, too, how susceptible your customers are likely to be to the books and marketing in question. You can ask yourself all kinds of questions to help you reach a decision that is relevant to your bookshop. To be effective, a campaign must have an immediate impact on your customers. If your bookshop is in Orkney, television advertising within East Anglia is unlikely to have much influence, however lavish it is. The following list of questions is by no means exhaustive, but should indicate the approach to take.

- Will the book/campaign catch the public imagination?
- How much money is being spent?
- How much of it is going on press advertising?
- Is it local or national?
- Will it be discounted?
- If local, is it in my area?
- If national, is it in the sort of papers my customers read?
- How much of it is going on television advertising?
- Will it be shown in my area?
- What sort of point-of-sale material is available?
- Can I get some?
- Does this publisher have a good track record?

- Will the author be touring and, if so, anywhere near me?
- Can I hold a signing session?

In the end it is your bookshop, your reputation, and possibly your future, that are on the line. Only you can try to assess how valid the guidance is for each book as far as your own bookshop is concerned.

Competing titles

The vast duplication of titles on most subjects where there is any sort of popular interest is a perpetual problem in buying new stock (although we shall see later how it can also be turned to advantage).

Take a look at the cookery section in any bookshop and you will find a whole range of titles: regional cookery; international cuisines; entertaining; vegetarian cookery; cooking with specific ingredients. All the books provide different recipes and come in different presentational styles. Some will be by well-known cookery writers or will tie in with a television series; some will be by otherwise unknown authors.

You will also see a great range of quality and price within both paperbacks and hardbacks. The trick is to find which areas of the subject your customers are interested in, and which price ranges attract them. You also need to know what it is you are trying to do with your bookshop – are you aiming to provide as wide a choice as possible, or a selective representation; and if the latter, are you going for the top end of the market, the middle ground, or the lower end. It is much better to proactively determine what you are going to do, but if you do not find this easy then trial and error will usually reveal an answer, which you then use to judge your future buying.

If for example you have a strong market in highly priced glossy books on international cookery styles, then a new book on Thai cookery priced at £25 may well seem worth trying. If on the other hand your main sales come from paperback cookery books then the book on Thai cooking is almost certainly worth missing. Part of the fun of bookselling is to select the mix of titles that will best suit your customers from the vast and competing range. If you get it right you will win your customers' loyalty. Success comes with that loyalty.

When the mix is not right, however, you will start building poor stock which will lose value and end up costing you valuable margin when eventually you are forced to reduce the price to sell it.

Contact with publishers

Many publishers use sales representatives as a principal means of advising booksellers of their forthcoming new titles, believing that they will get the best coverage for them if the reps sell them to booksellers on a personal, face-to-face basis.

Because personal selling can be very effective booksellers should always stay very aware of their bookshop's market, and its wants and needs, letting these guide most of their buying decisions. Traditionally, one of the hardest lessons most booksellers have to learn is how to say no to a title.

A little preparatory thought should make the position clearer. There are currently around 100,000 new titles published each year. Admittedly many of these are specialist titles, but even so most bookshops could potentially buy up to 30,000 new titles a year. Of those, only somewhere between perhaps 2,000 and 5,000 titles will sell in any quantity. If the bookshop buys too many of the very slow-selling titles then creating profitability will become extraordinarily difficult.

Personal selling is clearly an expensive selling mechanism for the publisher and the rep will be expected to try to maximise any order placed during the visit. Most booksellers find that this causes little difficulty provided they deal with it professionally. Any rep who exerts undue pressure should be resisted.

The high cost of personal selling within such a widely dispersed trade is causing booksellers a different problem too, for a number of publishers are withdrawing bookshops, and particularly small bookshops, from their reps' visit cycle. This forces booksellers to rely on catalogues, advance information sheets and trade advertising. These lack some of the immediacy of a rep's visit and often fail to give full details of the marketing support that goes with the various titles.

There are alternatives available for the bookseller. The first is to move to using a wholesaler as a supplier. Most wholesalers do have a sales team supporting even the smaller bookshops for, whereas a publisher's rep is only selling one publisher's titles, a wholesaler's rep takes orders for a whole range of publishers and therefore makes a visit to a small shop pay.

Today there are further possible approaches. You may be able to get a new title presentation from a supplier on CD-ROM. Alternatively publishers' Internet sites carry up-to-the-minute details of forthcoming titles. The bookseller must of course have Internet access and will incur some cost in obtaining the information. Its quality and timeliness, however, should more than compensate for this. In time, more and more web sites will be available to interested booksellers.

If this approach is of interest it is worth building your own directory of relevant web site addresses, together with some form of schedule to make sure that you do not miss out any major publishers when you are "trawling" for new titles of potential interest to your bookshop.

Stock control considerations

Your stock will inevitably become a wide mixture of new titles and back stock. New titles will be coming regularly into the shop in response to your subscription orders. Of the remaining back stock a proportion will be titles that sell regularly, and which you have been carefully reordering to replenish stock, and those which were new titles but which have fallen into back stock by default.

Great care needs to be exercised over this latter category since it can very easily overwhelm both your space and your financial investment in stock. Without doubt a computerised stock system makes diagnostic analysis easier, but even if you do not have such a system you should still be able to estimate the relative age of your stock. The comments below should help, even if you are unable to be so precise about the proportions.

If you have a computerised stock control system it is useful to regularly review the value of stock by its age. This shows you what proportion of your stock is very new, what is very old, and of the larger mid-age section, what is being regularly reordered and what is steadily getting older. An illustrative report is shown below:

Age of stock	Value	Proportion
Less than 1 month	£8,000	7.25%
Between 1 and 2 months old	£6,000	5.45%
Between 2 and 3 months old	£7,000	6.36%
Between 3 and 4 months old	£10,000	9.0%
Between 4 and 5 months old	£12,000	10.9%
Between 5 and 6 months old	£12,000	10.9%
Between 6 and 7 months old	£15,000	13.6%
Between 7 and 8 months old	£12,000	10.9%
Between 8 and 9 months old	£10,000	9.0%
Between 9 and 10 months old	£10,000	9.0%
Over 10 months old	£8,000	7.25%

Figure 11.1 Age of stock profile

This report illustrates how in this case only 20% of the stock value resides in new books less three months old but that over 80% of the stock in the shop is more than 3 months old. Since some of these "new" books will actually be replenishment copies for back list titles it suggests that there are too few new titles coming into the bookshop.

The answer, however, is not simply to increase the volume of subscription orders since this will have a profound impact upon the overall stock investment for the shop. Rather there is a need to look at how a greater proportion of the older stock can be returned more quickly to the supplier for credit, and then using this value to create a newer title range for the shop.

If the proportion of stock that is between about three and five months old seems high then it is possible that new titles are being ordered in too big a volume, and there may be a need to modify ordering quantities, at least until the proportions have settled back to expected levels.

If the proportion of stock more than about five months old seems too high, then it suggests that returns of new titles that have not sold as well as expected has not been as robust as is needed. The corrective action has to be to look at how such titles are listed for return, and then how vigorously the return is requested from the supplier.

If the proportion of stock less than five months old seems to be OK, but the proportion more than about ten months old seems too high then it suggests that not enough chasing activity is being undertaken to make sure that the supplier is actually processing the requested returns.

12. Rate of stock turn

Before we look at the various ways of running stock control systems it is important to get to grips with one of the most important financial ratios relating to stock: the rate of stock turn, or RST. It is a core ratio which has a profound impact on the profitability of any bookselling business.

RST is an invaluable aid to help you measure the efficiency of your use of stock investment capital. It effectively denotes the number of times the equivalent of your total stock is sold each year and is calculated by dividing your total sales by the retail value of your total stock, as shown in Figure 12.1.

$$\text{Rate of Stock Turn} = \frac{\text{Sales (at retail value)}}{\text{Stock (at retail value)}}$$

Figure 12.1 Rate of Stock Turn

For example, if your turnover is £400,000 in a year and your total stock has a retail value of £100,000, then your RST is four, as shown in Figure 12.2.

$$\text{Rate of Stock Turn} = \frac{400{,}000}{100{,}000} = 4$$

Figure 12.2 Rate of Stock Turn calculation

This means that you are, in effect, selling your total stock four times a year. It also means that, on average, a book is sitting on your shelves for three months before it is sold.

If you are able to maintain your sales level, but at the same time reduce your stock holding, then clearly your RST will rise. This means that you will be using your stock investment capital more effectively than before. Should you make some bad buying decisions, however, or your sales start to fall and you are unable to reduce your stock holding accordingly, then your RST will fall, indicating the fall in your buying efficiency.

The relationship between the value of stock investment and RST is shown in Figure 12.3 below. The example takes a bookshop with book sales of £400,000 and looks at the stock investment across a range of RSTs. The Y-axis shows the cost of the stock, and an assumption has been made that the average discount is 37.5%, i.e. half sales are paperback at 40% discount, and half are hardback at 35% discount.

We see that when the RST is two, the retail value of the stock is £200,000 and this has a cost of £125,000. The chart shows how the cost of the stock needed to support sales falls when effective stock control allows a higher RST to be achieved.

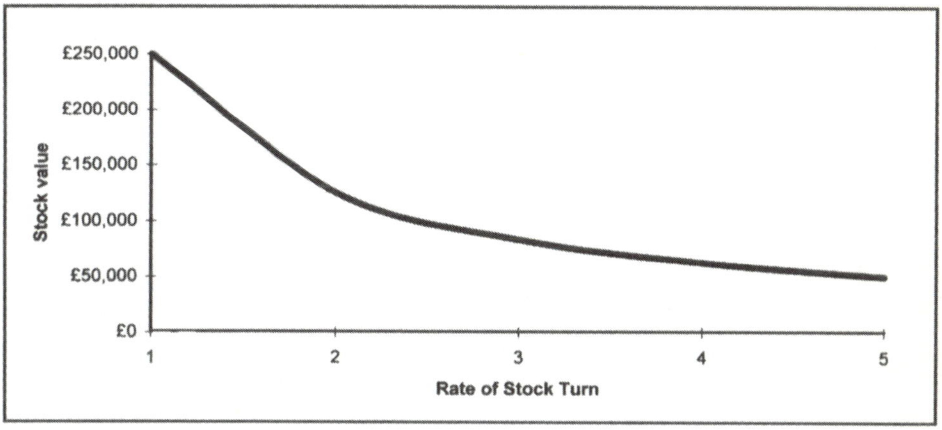

Figure 12.3 Stock investment at varying rates of stock turn

A consistent difficulty with using RST as a measure of your buying performance is that it must be calculated. Finding out the discount on most invoices is easy: you just look at them. This usually means that most booksellers will naturally tend to rely on discount – sometimes exclusively – simply because it is easier to monitor. This is not necessarily helpful for their business.

If you have a computerised stock control system it is likely that you would be looking at your RST throughout the year, since the system will tell you the total value of your stock. With only a manual system, however, the only time when you would be likely to know the precise value of your stock is after annual stocktaking.

Whatever system is in use, it is important to remember that you need to use the *retail* value of the stock, rather than its cost. Using retail value of sales and cost price of stock will give you a misleadingly high figure that is of little comparative value. The exception, perhaps, is when you are comparing different years' performance within your own company and using like-for-like measures for each year.

Interpreting results

There are several reasons why you should interpret the results of your RST analysis with care. In practice your stock levels rise and fall throughout the year, so whatever figure you use will tend to be only a snapshot of the true picture. There is nothing wrong with this, but you must recognise it as such.

A further complication may arise if a fair proportion of your sales comes from institutional sources or from special orders. This will distort your RST since these sales produce revenue without really affecting the value of your stockholding.

The RST ratio is also valuable when you look at the performance of certain areas of your stock. This analysis is only really accessible to the user of a computerised stock control system, since a manual system is unlikely to have the necessary data available.

You may decide you want to look at the relative performance of your hardback stock, your paperback stock and your children's stock. In each case you divide the sales in that area by the relevant stockholding. You can then compare the performance of your stock capital utilisation across the three areas.

An example of this sort of analysis, using real data, is given in Figure 12.4 below. This shows the total category sales in a bookshop's paperback section over the preceding twelve months, the retail value of the stock, and the calculated rate of stock turn.

Category	Sales	Stock	RST
Adult	£288	£109	2.62
Classics	£5,516	£1,505	3.66
Crime	£15,130	£4,460	3.39
Fiction	£81,869	£18,932	4.32
Horror	£7,358	£2,670	2.75
Romance	£34,035	£7,699	4.42

Figure 12.4 RST in action: comparing category sales

Assessment of this data suggests that overall the section is being run quite efficiently, but that the horror and adult sections are not performing nearly so well as the rest in terms of the RST.

Targets

Most successful booksellers would hope to achieve an RST in the region of four across their whole stock, although this does involve a lot of hard work. Many proponents of greater bookselling efficiency, including management consultants Arthur Young, who studied the book trade carefully in 1987 and produced the excellent report *Book Retailing in the 1990s,* feel that an RST of between 4.5 and 5 should be the minimum target.

Newcomers to the trade should not be surprised if they achieve a lower rate, since a new shop's opening stock represents little more than a hopeful guess at what customers will want to buy. It will almost certainly contain quite a lot of titles which they will not want.

It may seem relatively theoretical to interpret an RST in terms of how many times a year your stock turns over. In fact, there is nothing theoretical or academic about the figure: it is a matter of hard cash.

We have already seen that you achieve an RST of four with an annual turnover of £400,000 and a retail stock value of £100,000. If the sales stay the same, but your stock value increases by 33% to £133,000, then your RST will fall to three. Should your stock value fall by 20% to £80,000, then your RST rises to five.

The difference between the RST of three and the RST of five is a stock difference of £53,000. Taking this to trade prices, it represents a difference in stock investment of around £32,500. If you can achieve the higher RST figure you are saving the interest on this sum. It represents a fairly major shift in stock efficiency, of course, but the important thing to recognise is that any improvement in your RST shifts the odds of business success in your favour.

A further, useful analysis of stock performance based on a ratio called "Gross Margin Return on Inventory Investment" (GMROII) is given in an excellent monograph, ***The Mathematics of Bookselling,*** by Leonard Schatzkin. For anyone with a mathematical and analytical mind this is a fund of stimulating, very practical measures to improve the financial performance of your bookshop.

13. Stock control

It is said that anyone can sell books, but that it takes a genius to make money out of it. History tends to prove the point; why is making money out of bookselling so difficult?

A bookshop generates its cash input from the sale of books. To make the sales the shop must have a significant stockholding, and all of this stock must be paid for at some point. If the payments have to be made too long before the sales, there will never be enough cash flowing into the business to make it profitable.

Stock control is the tool that is used to link these two elements of bookselling.

Most bookshops, even quite small ones, will be selling a very wide range of titles. In a small shop the range may be across 7,000 to 8,000 titles; large bookshops may hold anything from about 50,000 titles upwards. The range gives customers the choice they want but, having ordered all these books, as the bookseller you must pay for them at the end of your credit period. All is well if you manage to sell the stock before the credit period expires, but whatever remains unsold must be financed by your business.

The reality of bookselling is that more of what you order will fall into the second category than the first and you will have to pay for most stock before you have sold it. Stock control provides you with a means to help keep the balance tipped as favourably as possible towards you. It gives you a tool to identify the titles that are selling – and ideally those which are not selling and which should be returned or sold off. It is therefore a vital aid to developing healthy sales for your bookshop.

More important, however, stock control is a vital financial control system for the shop. You are likely to have a large investment tied up in your stock and, to build a successful business, you need to control it. Stock control is a two-in-one solution, if you like. It provides you with healthy sales, plus profitability.

You should recognise the two factors – sales development and investment control – when you are looking at how you want to run your stock control. If the focus of your chosen system is slanted too much one way or the other, you will fail either to maximise your sales or to optimise your stock investment. A successful bookshop needs both.

Key components of a stock control system

You need your stock control system to show you which titles are selling so that you can ensure you reorder in good time and do not risk lost sales. Equally, even though it is bad news, you need to know which books are not selling so that you can try to persuade the publisher to take them back or else sell them off at a discounted price. You should also ensure that you do not order that kind of book again.

One of the raw truths about bookselling is that no matter how much you may try to encourage your customers to ask for a book if they do not see it, most people will simply look and go away if they fail to find what they want. This means that if a title is in demand you must try to keep it visibly in stock all the time.

Ideally you would have every book in stock that any potential customer might walk in and want. With getting on for one million titles in print, however, this is impossible for even the largest bookshop. Instead, your job is to provide what you think is the most saleable mix of titles. This will vary with time, which is where the real value of a stock control system comes in.

Although the basic purpose of a stock control system is to tell you what is selling, there are supplementary questions to ask yourself which are more than a mere elaboration of the system. They allow you to make the best possible decision on the number of copies, if any, to reorder so as to keep the business running profitably, as follows:

- how fast is each title selling?
- how many copies are already in stock?
- how long has each title been in stock?
- how many copies are already on order?

So the key components of any basic stock control system can be identified as:

- a sales record of each title in the shop;
- routines for keeping the records up to date;
- a system for alerting the bookseller when decisions are required;
- a prompt for making and implementing the decisions.

The fourth component depends on you, of course. With a computerised system, however, the implementation becomes very much easier to put in train.

Manual vs computerised systems

In these times of increasing trade complexity, and of relatively stable technology prices, it is difficult to recommend anything other than a computerised stock control system. On the surface, it is more expensive to install and run, but there are so many hidden costs, particularly in terms of staff time, in running a manual system that the higher computer costs begin to become less significant.

There was a time when booksellers could hold almost all the details of a small bookshop's stock in their heads. They would know the stock, the publishers, the prices, the distributors, the other titles by many of the authors. They worked very hard at the memory game, but in fairness to today's booksellers who may simply not believe such a story, there were only perhaps 30,000 new titles being published a year. With today's levels of getting for a million titles in print, around 100,000 new titles coming out every year, and a similar number going out of print, the complexity is too great for most people. A computerised system simply gets on with it.

Having said that a computerised system is really the only way ahead, it is also fair to add that where such a system is impossible, for whatever reason, then a manual system is clearly better than nothing. A manual system does confer some control: titles that are selling are identified, and a book's sales history can be assessed before further stock is ordered.

Relative costs

However you look at it, stock control systems cost money to buy, set up and maintain. The costs must be more than covered by the resultant savings in stock investment or by increased profits on turnover. Any system worthy of the name should achieve these ends, although the benefits of the more expensive systems may take longer to work through the business. You should be careful not to put in a system more sophisticated than you need, but at the same time ensure that what you do install is up to the job. If you do not invest, you cannot expect to reap the rewards.

The initial outlay for a manual stock control system – principally record cards and boxes in which to file them – is very low. You should not underestimate, however, the time it will take to fill in the cards in the first place and then to maintain them.

It is this hidden cost of staff time that is the real cost of a manual stock control system. It is a depressingly labour-intensive business. Worse, the sheer chore of a manual system – the endless searching, record amendment, filing and re-filing – tends to compromise it quite quickly. A less than ideal system which can be maintained through slack and busy times alike is preferable to a theoretically perfect one which collapses through neglect as soon as the bookshop gets busy.

For a small bookshop which can operate on one till, the set-up costs of a computerised system of stock control, are currently likely to be around £2,500 for hardware (consisting of a Pentium PC, an EPoS till, scanner and printer) and around £1,500 for software and licences. On top of this there are annual running costs and maintenance, of both hardware and software. These may well come to around £800 per annum.

The cost of hardware has fallen continuously in the past decade. High-specification computers are readily available on the high street, alongside the necessary printers, CD-ROM drives and modems, although you will always save yourself time and possible grief later on by consulting the software provider in advance on the performance requirements for the system you intend to use.

It is important to buy a software package that is designed specifically for the peculiarities of bookselling. If you opt for a general retail package it will have to be tailored to your needs, and without expert systems knowledge this may well turn out to be a very bad move indeed.

There are a range of bookshop systems currently on the market. *The Bookseller* periodically reviews or features some of the main systems and you should refer to the latest article (published in November in recent years). Alternatively, the Booksellers Association will be able to point you in the right general direction.

You should always make a point of talking to existing users of any system you are thinking of installing. This way you will find out some of the advantages and disadvantages of the system from an end user's point of view.

After observing stock control systems in operation for some twenty years, this author would unhesitatingly advise any potential bookseller to consider a computerised stock control system. Such a system is likely to be the only means of maintaining control over both the financial investment in stock and the practicalities of keeping the right titles in stock (and thereby maximising sales).

It is not, however, a case of only the best possible system will do. The trick is to find the system that is right for your size of bookshop, and for your likely method of working.

Manual systems of stock control

With computerised stock control increasingly replacing manual systems throughout bookselling, it may seem illogical to spend time exploring manual ways of working in some detail. However, because not all computer systems are identical (and are subject to constant upgrades) and the fundamental principles of stock control apply to both computerised and manual systems, it is sensible to look first at the manual process. Once that is understood, it is far simpler to translate it into specific stock control packages.

Most manual systems of stock control are based on a sequence of record cards, generally with one card per title held in stock. The cards may be used to create a master file, as card-in-book records, or as display stock reorder signals.

Any sort of record card can be used, but the Booksellers Association offers a custom-printed card at a very modest price. You will find that the layout of the card, illustrated in Figure 13.1 below, acts as a useful prompt to record and use the relevant pieces of information for your system.

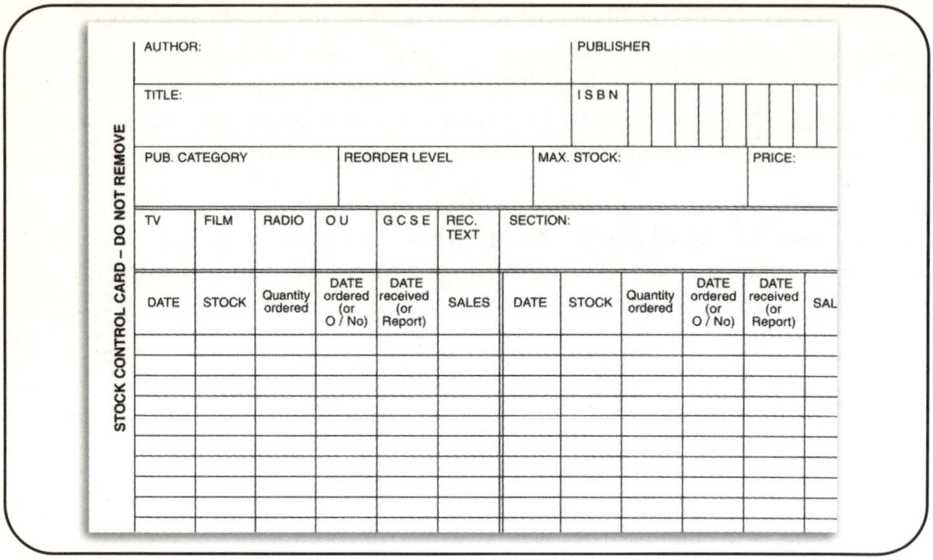
STOCK CONTROL CARD – DO NOT REMOVE

AUTHOR:	PUBLISHER
TITLE:	ISBN

PUB. CATEGORY	REORDER LEVEL	MAX. STOCK:	PRICE:

TV	FILM	RADIO	OU	GCSE	REC. TEXT	SECTION:

DATE	STOCK	Quantity ordered	DATE ordered (or O/No)	DATE received (or Report)	SALES	DATE	STOCK	Quantity ordered	DATE ordered (or O/No)	DATE received (or Report)	SAL

Figure 13.1 BA pre-printed stock control card

Master file system

A master file card system contains a unique record card for each title in the system. Typically, the information recorded on each card will include:

- bibliographic data (author, title, publisher, price);
- subject category (to indicate where the book is shelved in the shop);
- quantity in stock at different dates;
- when ordered;
- when received into stock;
- supplier (if different from publisher);
- trade terms and conditions.

It may also be helpful to include some notes on the marketing information about the title, such as details of any television or media coverage.

It is important to recognise that all the detail provided, although factual, is only information. It provides what you or your staff need to make a decision about re-ordering or returning, plus the relevant detail to allow you to take action. The card is not a substitute for your decision-making process.

There is a lot of tedious and soul-destroying work involved in setting up any card index system. With an individual card for each title, even a small bookshop might be faced with the prospect of establishing around 15,000 different stock cards, and then filing them. Generally the cards would be filed alphabetically within category or section, in the same way that the books are merchandised on your shelving.

Once the cards are all written up and filed you need to update them with regular information on the level of stock being held. Normally this would be done by section, so anyone stock-checking the Health section will withdraw the Health stock cards from the file and physically check each card against the section. The number in stock, or a zero to indicate that the title has sold out, plus the date will be entered on the card.

Organising the stock cards in sections makes it possible to stock check a manageable area within the quieter times in the bookshop. The job is rather like the proverbial painting of the Forth Rail Bridge, never-ending. Once Zoology is done, it is back to Antiques again. Clearly the more popular sections – Fiction and Cookery, for example – will have to be checked more frequently since there will be greater movement of stock there and more re-ordering needs to be done for them.

Another advantage of organising the cards by section is that if more than one person is available different sections of the stock can be checked simultaneously.

After a section has been checked, the cards must be assessed to see what stock, if any, should be re-ordered. Each card must be reviewed to see how many copies have sold since the last check. You also need to take a view on how long the supplier takes to get stock back to you. Technically this is known as the "lead time". It must be taken into consideration if you want your replacement copies to arrive before you sell out of a fast-moving title. The lead time may often be irrelevant to those using a wholesaler for stock replenishment, rather than publishers, since your books will be back in stock within 24 to 48 hours. The only time it will figure is when titles are unavailable.

The numbers you should be particularly interested in are the rate of sale that the title has achieved and, where applicable, the supplier's lead time. If you are selling two copies of a title a week, and you have three left in stock, but the normal lead time is three weeks, then clearly you have left it too late to order fresh copies from your normal supplier. You either need to consider ordering sooner for such titles or else you need to move your supply to a wholesaler which can get the book back to you much more quickly.

This is a dilemma all booksellers face continuously. To order sooner, or in larger quantities, means they are eventually caught up with quite a large volume of stock for a title that stops selling. Yet running out of a title that is selling is frustrating for all concerned, particularly when the customer may be able to find a copy in a rival bookshop nearby.

Once a decision has been made to order a title, it should be recorded on the stock card, and also on the order going to the supplier. Many booksellers using manual stock control systems now fax their orders, so the order will need to be written clearly enough for transmission on the order form. When the order is big enough to be sent it will then be faxed to the supplier.

At the end of the process the cards must be re-filed in the correct order so that the next time a stock check is run on that section the cards are all there, ready for use.

Several variants and enhancements of the master card system are also possible. A common one is to put the stock card or a separate stock slip into the back of the book on the shelf. When the book is sold the card or slip is extracted and the sale thereby identified.

As a summary, however, Figure 13.2 below outlines the routines of running a manual stock control system.

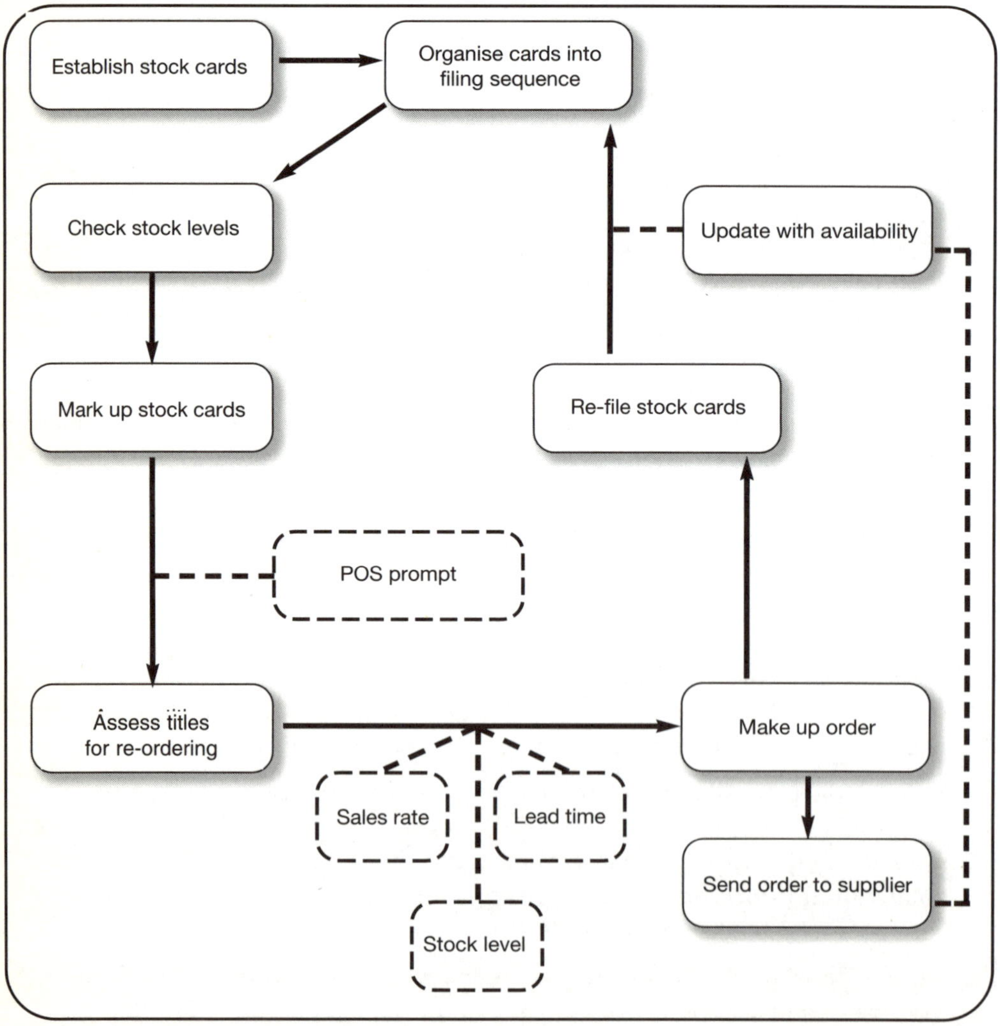

Figure 13.2 Stock control system flow chart

Of course, we have been looking here at the process involved in making up a controlled order for one title. A bookshop must do this regularly and successfully for every single title it stocks. It is little wonder therefore that computerisation has been so successful with even the smaller bookshops.

Nevertheless, before leaping wholeheartedly into the era of the computer, we should not forget that the traditional method of checking stock against cards was one of the most effective methods of building any bookseller's detailed stock knowledge ever discovered. The routines of checking and rechecking, filing and re-filing, built the stock repertoire of many. All too often today's computerised systems allow us to get away with a slack approach to stock knowledge. We and our customers can suffer as a result.

Computerised systems of stock control

The operating method for a computerised stock control system will vary from package to package, but the general principles will be very similar to those governing a manual stock card system. The advantages come from the ease with which records can be indexed and processed. Such a system also allows a more standardised approach to re-ordering patterns.

A further advantage is that it is usually possible to download title information automatically from a main database. This saves the great effort of writing out individual record cards and also ensures a clean transfer of information – providing, of course, that the original database was up to date and accurate.

Electronic point of sale data capture

In any modern computerised system of stock control, electronic point of sale data capture (more generally known as EPoS) is an essential component.

The idea behind EPoS is that as a book is sold its ISBN is recorded and the information fed back into the stock control system. In this way sales are known not just as a total of the day's cash takings, but also as an itemised listing of each sale.

The data can be collated by manually entering the ten digits of the ISBN into the terminal which acts as a cash register. This is both time-consuming and very subject to data entry error. Note also that when the ISBN migrates to a 13 digit code in January 2006 this manual operation will take 30% longer since there will be more digits to enter. As a result, it is far more usual to scan the barcode printed on the back of each book either into a hand-held terminal – say, a Psion fitted with a special laser device – or directly into the main computer system through a stand-alone scanning system. The laser beam measures the precise sequence of lines and spaces on the barcode and translates them into an ISBN format. This information is then fed back to the main stock control system, either in "real time" (i.e. as it happens) or later on.

Although adding EPoS to a computerised stock control system adds to the initial outlay cost, it also adds to the reliability of the data capture potential of the system, and saves considerable time at the point of sale. Since this is where your customers generally want your sales procedure to be as swift as possible (a long queue may even cause impulse buyers to change their mind) EPoS not only saves time, but may generate goodwill into the bargain.

Software licensing

One area involving the use of computers in business where particular care is needed concerns licensing for all software. You should have a genuine copy of all software that you use and you should arrange to file the license agreements for the software safely. If you are robust about this you will be able to know that you do not have any unlicensed software on your computer systems.

Almost every operating system and bit of software you are likely to use will require a license – which goes to pay for the development costs of the software in much the same way as an author's royalty goes toward their hard work in writing a book.

There may be some minor justification in trying out software using a copy from a friend to see if it suits you and your business, but you need to be aware just how easy it is to carry on using the copy rather than purchasing a properly licensed copy. On these grounds alone the practice should be discouraged.

If you are caught using software without the appropriate license, such as a result of an investigation by the Federation Against Software Theft (FAST) or by an anonymous tip to them, perhaps from a disgruntled ex-employee, then the results may be very serious. The ultimate responsibility for ensuring compliance generally rests with the Directors or Principals, if the business is not a limited company, and if the case was taken to court then the fines are severe.

14. Human resources

Location and stock range are critical in the creation of a successful bookshop, but no one can afford to overlook the crucial role of staff and the services they add to the shop. You only need to look along the high street or shopping mall to see the range of importance that is put on this factor. At the one end of the scale you have those shops where the staff are simply paid to put things on shelves and who seldom have (or are expected to have) much commitment to their work. At the other end you see those shops where the staff derive genuine job satisfaction from what they do. They are aware that their input is valued and that they play a real part in the success or otherwise of the business.

In a bookshop, staffing is perhaps the hardest part of the business mix to create. The level of profitability in bookselling is not high, and so if rents are high then staffing costs must be kept proportionately lower. This tends to mean either fewer good, enthusiastic staff being paid a bit more, or slightly more staff being paid less. It can be argued that paying extra for good staff will fulfil itself through additional increases in sales revenue, and is therefore worth doing. If you choose your staff well, and you are trading in an area where there is sufficient flexibility in disposable incomes to generate those additional sales, then you are winning. You may, however, find that your costs go up but that this is not accompanied by an increase in sales levels.

Each business will find its own solution to this eternal difficulty. The customer in need of help will be able to tell which have got it right.

General issues

It is critically important to comply with the legislation covering the employment of staff. There are still some quite substantial differences between the EU view of employment law and that of the UK Government. Since ultimately the UK must follow EU directives, employment legislation has become one of the major areas of legal change. Keeping up with all the minutiae is a full-time job, and you must remember that ignorance is no excuse in the eyes of the law.

Due to the continuing nature of the changes it is more useful here simply to highlight the areas of potential concern of which you should be aware. If you have concerns you would be well advised to take professional advice. A number of low cost helplines, including the excellent and free ACAS service, are available. Members of the BA can use the free Business Support Helpline, which will advise booksellers on a range of business, commercial and techinical issues. The service has proved invaluable to many members. Additionally professional help is at hand, but at a greater cost. If you do need to use a lawyer then it is important to make sure that they have expertise in the area of employment law. This book cannot, and must not, be taken as a detailed view of the current employment law. A useful source of information is the DTI website on employment regulations. This can be found on www.dti.gov.uk/er.

Ireland has its own legislative process but many of the issues will be common, if not identical, since both the UK and Ireland are part of the EU and thus come under the requirements to act upon EU Directives on employment law. An equivalent to the DTI web site providing government sponsored information on employment can be found at www.basis.ie.

Employees are entitled to receive a written contract of employment setting out key factors and terms relating to their employment. This contract should be given to the member of staff after a specified trial period. The contract would normally include details of such things as hours worked, rate of pay, notice required and holidays. Often it will also include details of any disciplinary procedures, including rights of appeal, the company may use.

As well as the statutory contract of employment it is usually seen as helpful if each member of staff can have a detailed job description. This is a document that breaks down the tasks they are expected to undertake during the normal course of their work, and also explains both what the expected outcome of the task is and what standards of work are expected. You should try to be as precise as possible but also include a general clause to the effect that "additional duties as reasonably and properly requested by the management be undertaken from time to time".

Employees have a legal right to receive full details of how their pay and any deductions from it – such as tax, National Insurance or pension contributions – have been calculated.

Staffing costs

Many small bookshops are run by a partnership team, which thereby avoids the costs incurred in taking on any extra staff. Such schemes mean, however, that at least one person must be in the bookshop for every hour it is open. For practical reasons therefore, even the smallest bookshops usually need to have more than two people involved.

A small bookshop staffed predominantly by its owners will have some advantages in controlling the costs of staff. If business becomes quiet the owners are able to take less out of the business as "salary", or drawings, but when things get busier, yet can still be managed, then their "salary" increases.

Except where voluntary staff are concerned (in some religious or charity-operated shops, for example), once staff are taken on, they usually have a contractual right to an agreed salary after a short probationary period. This means they are entitled to be paid at the agreed rate, regardless of how busy or quiet the bookshop is. Thereafter the only way to adjust the payroll according to the activity of the bookshop is either to employ seasonal staff on temporary contracts, or to make employees redundant if business falls off.

You need to ensure that the rate of pay you offer is above the National Minimum Wage, which increases periodically to cover inflationary and cost of living increases. Currently (2002) this legal minimum is £4.20 per hour for people aged 22 and over, and £3.60 per hour for people aged between 18 and 21. Additionally there should be no difference in rates of pay and conditions between male and female employees (sex discrimination) or in the pay and conditions between full-timers and part-timers (implied sex discrimination).

You may find it helpful to do some local research to ascertain the rates of pay at places of work that employ similar sorts of people to you. If you are planning to pay under this rate then you are unlikely to attract the better people to work in your shop. It may also be useful to refer to the annual remuneration survey that The Bookseller undertakes each year.

A frequent problem with temporary employees is that the bookshop is staffed with people who have an inadequate understanding of the business, whereas redundancy is generally used only in serious situations since it is a destructive and invidious process for all concerned.

Other implications arise when staff become involved in the bookshop. You will need to set up a system to run a payroll properly so that each employee (even just one person) can be paid correctly on a regular basis. There must be regulated deductions from each employee for the appropriate levels of National Insurance (to which employers must also contribute) and PAYE tax. The deductions in turn will have to be accounted for to the Inland Revenue, but are payable one month in arrears. And, as noted above, each employee must receive a full account of his or her salary and deductions.

Other staff-related costs to consider, over and above employer NI contributions, are the provision of paid holidays and any overtime rates that might need to be paid for working longer hours than contracted or for working on Sundays or bank holidays. You also need to be aware that if any members of staff, or their partners, become pregnant then you will have to deal with maternity or paternity issues. Clearly the former is more onerous, but each can have an impact upon how you run your shop. The arrangements and regulations are complex, and detailed specialist advice should be sought if this happens.

You should also be aware of the Working Time Regulations. These require that employees should not be required to work more than 48 hours a week; that they get 11 hours rest each day; that they have a day off each week; that they get a rest period in any working day that exceeds 6 hours; and that they get four weeks paid leave a year.

As the bookshop gets bigger or another branch is opened, the proportion of non-owner staffing will increase – and so will the cost of staffing. For many bookshops it is the highest single running cost for the business. As such it is an important management function to ensure that the staffing is organised effectively, with the best use made of it.

Within the main bookselling groups, where all levels of staff, from part-timers to shop managers, are employed, staffing costs will usually come out at between 9% and 14% of actual turnover. Because there is no industry-wide statistics-gathering process, there seem to be no comparable figures for the independent bookshop sector, although figures would probably be comparable. A bookshop with a turnover of £400,000 is therefore likely to be paying between £36,000 and £56,000 in wages, including the owner/manager's salary.

Sales per employee

An important measure both of staff efficiency within an established bookshop and the likely number of staff needed to help in a bookshop, is the volume of sales that are generated by each employee.

In order to make reasonable comparisons, sales per employee are conventionally measured in terms of full-time equivalent members of staff (sometimes abbreviated to FTE). To calculate the number of FTE staff, divide the total number of hours worked in the business by the number of hours in the usual working week, say, 37.5 hours.

Armed with that figure, it is then a simple calculation to divide the shop's turnover for the year by the number of full-time equivalent employees to arrive at a sales per employee ratio. So if the year's sales are £400,000 and the shop employs five full-time equivalent employees, including you as owner, then the sales per employee are £80,000. This figure can then be compared with industry figures or with fellow booksellers' if they are willing to share such information.

It is enlightening to see how the trend in sales per employee has moved over the years. Figure 14.1 below shows the gradual increase in sales per employee. It must be remembered, however, that these figures do not take account of inflation, and thus there has not been such an enormous increase in efficiency as the graph suggests.

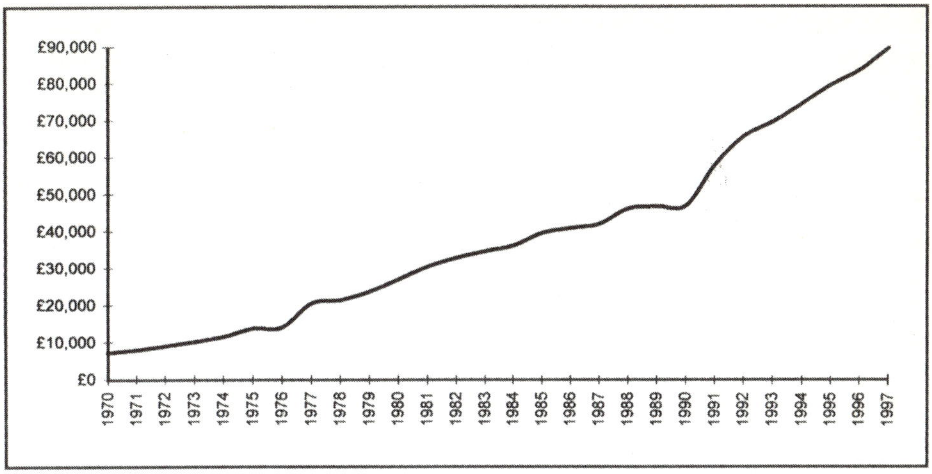

Figure 14.1 Sales per employee

It is obviously in every bookseller's interest to maximise the sales each employee generates. Any increase in this figure is likely to produce substantial profits increases since, although the additional sales will generate higher gross profits, there will not be a corresponding increase in costs.

It is generally agreed that more proficient, better trained staff are more likely to generate the additional sales that are so vital to a bookshop. Although people who can register sales on a till and put purchases in bags have a role to play, the additional services that can be provided by an interested and committed member of staff will help to increase the bookshop's sales quite substantially.

Selecting staff

Many people entering any small business – not just bookselling –for the first time have had little experience of selecting, employing and managing staff, so it is hardly surprising that many small businesses make costly mistakes in these areas. A dishonest or poorly trained employee can cost you all your profits. Equally, an unfairly dismissed employee can lead you to an industrial tribunal, with all the difficulties that might incur. Your staff are key components in your ability to generate and keep custom and as such they must be selected and treated just as carefully as your more fixed assets.

Before taking on any new staff it is important to try and create a job specification, to confirm what is involved in the job you are trying to fill, and a person specification, to decide on the sort of person you want to fill it. Some of the questions you might ask yourself are:

- to what level should the appointee be educated?
- are we looking for someone to serve customers or to work behind the scenes?
- are we looking for someone who already has book trade experience?
- are we looking for someone with supervisory skills?
- can the appointee provide references?
- how well will the appointee envisaged fit into the existing staff team?

After deciding these things you go on to advertise the vacancy, through a notice in the shop window, a card in the Job Centre, or an advertisement in the local paper.

You must also be ready to conduct interviews when people apply for the job and, if you are to get it right, it is worth taking some care at this stage. The first requirement is to give yourself space to hold the interviews; you will need uninterrupted time so that you can devote your complete attention to getting the right person for the job.

Ideally, two people should conduct an interview so that later you have the benefit of two separate perspectives, although in practice this may not always be possible. You should prepare the questions you want to ask each candidate carefully, so that the answers really can show whether the applicant is able to do the job and likely to fit the person specification you have created.

It is important that you remain mindul of Equal Opportunities and the various Discrimination Acts when you are framing your questions. You need to consider carefully how valid your reasons are for asking the question, and whether it has a real bearing upon ability to do a job. If the question discriminates, or may be perceived to discriminate, against people of a certain gender, race, disability etc., then you should refrain from asking the question. If the question is still legitimate but may be misconstrued, then you should frame it very carefully indeed.

It is useful to record in writing the main findings of the interview immediately after it has taken place. At this point your memory will still be fresh, and you may be seeing a number of people, so you do not want to get them muddled up. You need to remember that you may be required, under data protection regulations, to show the applicant a copy of any notes made, so ensure that you would be happy with anything you write being potentially used as evidence against you.

It is essential to bear in mind the full legal implications of various discrimination laws. It is not lawful, except in very specific circumstances, which are unlikely to occur in the general running of a bookshop, to discriminate against an applicant on the grounds of their sex or their race. There is also substantial legislation concerning discrimination against disabled people. You may, however, legitimately discriminate against smokers, for instance, if you operate a no smoking policy in your shop.

Remember too, an interview is not simply one-way in purpose. Interviewees should be able to use the opportunity to assess whether or not they want to join the business. With this in mind you should offer some background to the company and say how the job or jobs have become available. You also need to show that you are able to operate honestly and professionally, give interviewees the chance to ask any questions they may have and give them time to speak.

With interviews over, you should be able to decide which of the applicants you wish to employ and then offer them the position. This is often done initially by telephone, but should always be followed up in writing. It is also common courtesy to let the unsuccessful interviewees know that they have not succeeded in getting a job. The timing of these letters should be careful, however, in case the person you select for the job declines it after all – they may have been offered another job meanwhile, or they may not have liked what they heard at the interview. You may then wish to appoint your second choice, which could be awkward if that person has already received a rejection letter.

Managing staff

One of the more appealing definitions of the process of management is that it is all to do with getting things done by other people. If you are doing it yourself you are not managing, but if someone else is doing it for you, then you *are*.

It soon becomes clear that, by this definition, you must have a clear idea of what you want achieved, and how to achieve it. You then get other people to do it for you – simple. Well, perhaps not entirely, since the people who are going to do it for you need to know how they should do it, and should be willing and able to do it.

The first loop is all to do with training and the provision of clear instructions or guidelines. The second loop involves authority and motivation. We should look at both.

Training

Effective training is important if your staff are going to be able to perform their job to the best of their abilities. This is critical in helping them to extract maximum job satisfaction and also in providing your customers with the best possible service.

If you look to your present levels of expertise you will probably find a number of tasks which you can carry out effectively now without really even thinking about them. Looking back, however, there would have been a time when you did not know how to start, let alone complete the task effectively. For you to do it, someone had to tell you about the task, demonstrate it to you and practise it. Later you would receive feedback on your performance and finally you would be helped to perfect the task through the learning process of correcting mistakes.

On the basis of this experience you should appreciate that your staff will need similar help and encouragement if they are to do the tasks you want done to the standards you set. Since management is all about getting other people to do what you want done, the link between training and effective management is clear. Try never to forget this fundamental truth (as many so-called managers do).

The type of training your staff will need will tend to move through a definable pattern. It starts with induction training over the first few days of employment and moves eventually to fully professional training as their competence and responsibilities grow.

You or your manager will almost certainly carry out induction training. It should be designed to show the new member of staff how things work in your bookshop, and should cover everything from how you want customers greeted, through correct till procedures, goods inward procedures, and the way your shelves are organised. Frequently this phase of training involves working alongside an experienced colleague who is willing to pass knowledge on – commonly known as "sitting with Nelly". It is important that you make frequent checks to see that things are going as planned. "Nelly" and the new arrival may not have hit it off, so that precious little learning takes place.

The quality of this induction training, both in its design and in the way it is delivered, will have enormous impact on the effectiveness of new members of staff. If they are given valuable information in a supportive manner, you are likely to see enormous benefits over time. Dropping them in at the deep end, unless you are very lucky, will leave you as disappointed as they are.

Once the member of staff becomes more familiar with the way your bookshop works, and more proficient at the basics, it is time to move on to the next training phase. This involves passing on more specialist knowledge and can be done either in-house or through professional training.

Providing clear instructions

This author, after long experience of watching managers trying to get their staff to do things on the shop floor, believes that a principal cause of any failure is lack of forethought on the manager's part, and a failure to give clear instructions.

None of us is a mind-reader and, without clear instructions for a new and unfamiliar task, we are unlikely to be able to complete it to our manager's satisfaction. This, of course, puts a heavy onus on the manager to think the task through and identify the sequence of key stages to be completed if it is to be done to a satisfactory standard.

As a test of your ability to give clear instructions, try to complete the exercise shown at Figure 14.2 below. It will help you to clarify some of the issues involved in getting tasks done to your satisfaction. If you can master and apply this stage of the process, you will overcome many of the difficulties of managing staff.

Imagine that you want a new member of staff to spend his/her first day in your bookshop rearranging the gardening section. You can change the exercise by making varying assumptions on their level of competence.

For instance, one person might know nothing about gardening and another might be dyslexic; some people with a strong sense of design would wish to see the books ranked by size and colour; and your new employee may have been a librarian before joining your bookshop. You can go on adding whatever assumptions you find interesting to the model. Then ask yourself:

1. To what extent does your need to clarify the instructions you give influence the likely outcome?
2. How would your instructions vary if you were dealing with the handling of nuclear fission material?

Figure 14.2 An exercise in giving instructions

Authority

Now for the second loop in managing people, which involves authority. Does the person asking for the job to be done have the authority to do so, or are they chancing their arm?

In a military model of command there are clear lines of authority, so that any command must be obeyed without question and disobedience carries severe penalties. A sergeant commands a corporal, who in turn may command a private to do whatever is wanted. Training, authority and clear lines of command ensure that the process works – most of the time.

Within a civil organisation such a regimented chain of command would be unusual, but it would be a mistake to think that all sense of a chain has gone. Organisational cultures have differing ways of imposing a chain, depending on their own ideas about organisational behaviour and the delegation of authority.

The key difference lies in the way the individual who receives instructions perceives the line of authority. If your boss asks you to do something that is reasonable and work-orientated you are likely to do it. If a colleague asks you to do the same thing, you may consider it as a request rather than an instruction.

Keeping clear lines of authority within even a small organisation is an important element of letting people know where they stand.

Motivation

The final – and potentially most important – stage in the management loop is the motivation of the bookshop staff. If they are motivated but untrained, they will do their best and may even manage to achieve what is wanted, but there is little certainty about the outcome. Trained, but lacking in motivation, their success is still less likely. However, if they are both well trained and highly motivated, there is little to stop them achieving whatever is asked of them.

Motivation is a subject in its own right and everyone involved in management to any degree will have their own views on it. Certain elements seem to be common to most approaches: developing a sense of belonging is important since it lends a sense of communal purpose. Remuneration plays a clear, but often secondary role. The sense of reward/recognition that goes with a job usually matters more, since this is far more pervasive than a simple financial incentive. Providing a sense of job satisfaction is probably the real key to motivating staff. The development of feelings of self-esteem and self-worth is enormously valuable to both the individual and the organisation.

Management approaches are recognising the importance of teams and team-building in effective motivation. This is a broad area well beyond the scope of this book, but those interested in following it up would find Hilarie Owen's book, ***Creating Top Flight Teams*** (Kogan Page, 1996) instructive.

Discipline

Discipline in the working environment can be a minefield if not treated with proper professional care. Your written contract of employment should have conditions attached to it and these conditions will usually include a section on disciplinary procedures.

Such procedures need to be fair and follow the laws of natural justice. The procedures should also outline the specific steps that any proceeding will follow, and should give an indication of the severity of punishment for various situations. It is, for instance, reasonable to summarily dismiss (i.e. dismiss without notice) someone who has been found clearly guilty, after proper investigation, of stealing from the bookshop; to use the same penalty for someone caught having a cigarette contrary to your no smoking policy would be unreasonable.

The usual sequence of events would be:

- Investigation
- Disciplinary interview
- Disciplinary hearing
- Findings
- Appeal (if requested)

There should be a clear pattern of increasingly severe punishments according to the importance of the offence, or perhaps the frequency with which an offence occurs. Traditionally this follows the pattern of:

- Verbal warning
- First written warning
- Second written warning
- Final written warning
- Dismissal

Sometimes it may be legitimate to miss certain stages of this sequence out, depending upon the importance of the issues involved. It is important to ensure that there is a proper appeal procedure built into the process so that an employee may appeal against a decision if he or she feels it is wrong.

Such an appeal should be independent and should look at firstly whether the proper procedures were followed, and then at whether the correct interpretation of events was made. Finally the appeal should look at whether the outcome was warranted by the severity of the offence.

It is also usual for misdemeanors to be "spent" after a given amount of time. Thus a verbal warning may be spent, i.e. removed from the record, after three months. This means that if the same thing happens again within the three month period then the disciplinary action may be seen as continuous and, if found guilty again, then a written warning may be issued. If, however, five months have elapsed, then a completely fresh disciplinary process should be started and, if guilty, another verbal warning is appropriate.

Once you have worked out such procedures, which will also need to include certain statutory conditions, such as the right to be represented at a disciplinary interview, then you must keep to them. It is no good being judge and jury without giving the individual concerned an opportunity to explain themselves.

In bigger organisations it is usual for there to be enough senior people to ensure that any disciplinary procedure can escalate with fresh people being drawn in as needed. This means that an objective and fair view can be taken of proceedings, particularly if an employee has appealed against a decision. In a smaller shop this is clearly much more difficult. To some extent it can be overcome by carefully following a number of principles including:

- The employee should be considered innocent until proven guilty.
- The employee should be given the right to explain what has happened.
- There is a full and impartial investigation to uncover all the facts.
- Any evidence presented must be assessed objectively.
- The employee has the right to be represented at any disciplinary hearing.
- The proceedings are recorded, in at least note form.
- If fault is proven then the action taken is appropriate to the severity of the situation.
- There is an independent appeal procedure.

It may be that an independent HR specialist can be brought in to act on appeal if there is no other alternative within the company.

Health and Safety

Another area of importance that falls under the general remit of Human Resources is that of Health and Safety. There is a vast range of legislation covering this issue and it is very much a specialist area. A bookseller, however, has relatively simple issues to deal with when compared with an industrial complex.

There is a general need to provide a safe environment for people to work in so that they can complete their work with no undue risk to their health and safety. Some issues are straightforward and obvious: shelving should be securely attached to the walls, any steps or ladders must be safe to use. Other issues are more complex.

Training should be provided to all staff to show them how to lift heavy objects without risk to themselves – just think of all those delivery boxes of heavy books. A risk assessment should be undertaken for the premises to identify potential risks, such as stairs, cutting instruments in the goods-in area, loose carpet tiles etc. There are also special arrangements for anyone who regularly uses a computer to ensure that their eyesight is not being harmed and that the position of the screen and keyboard, when taken together with the height of their seat, allows them to maintain a good posture.

Professional development

As staff become more competent their training needs become more demanding.

There is a dual benefit in structured developmental training. For the bookshop it means that the member of staff will be able to put that much more into the job since they will know more about the shop's workings. This will also give you a little more freedom as you will not have to be relied upon quite so much. For the member of staff it means you are demonstrating your faith in them by helping them to become a bookseller in their own right. They will also be able to share in your feeling of job satisfaction.

If you are thinking of undertaking this training yourself the Booksellers Association's own programme, ***A Vital Thirty Minutes,*** is a very useful resource. It provides an outline for a half-hour training session for each week of the year. The format is very flexible, enabling booksellers to customise it to their own requirements.

15. Marketing the bookshop

Although marketing has apparently turned into a buzzword within bookselling during the 1980s and '90s, successful booksellers have practised it for years – quite often without recognising what they have been doing.

That said, there is little doubt that every bookseller can have a positive influence on the effectiveness of the business by applying some of the more formal principles of marketing to it.

What is marketing

The Chartered Institute of Marketing, the leading professional body in the UK, defines marketing as:

> *"... the management process responsible for identifying, anticipating and satisfying customer requirements profitably."*

One of the principal introductory textbooks on marketing develops this theme and defines marketing in terms of objectives. The rather academic definition may tend a little towards jargon, but does help to clarify the process, as follows:

> *"Marketing consists of individual and organisational activities that facilitate and expedite satisfying exchange relationships in a dynamic environment through the creation, distribution, promotion and pricing of goods, services and ideas."*
>
> ***Dibb, Simkin, Pride & Ferell: Marketing (Houghton Mifflin, 1997)***

From this definition we see that marketing is a series of activities designed to generate sales – not necessarily of goods – that are profitable for the seller and satisfy a need for the purchaser. The definition also recognises that the environment within which these sales happen is in a state of continual flux. The final idea introduced is that of the marketing mix.

The environment

Any business is influenced by a wide variety of factors, both internal and external. The external factors are usually referred to as the environment. A central concept of strategic marketing is that if a business is aware of what is happening, and likely to happen in the future, within the environment, then that business will be better placed both to take advantage of the opportunities which arise and to minimise the impact of any threats posed.

The recommended method is actively to audit the various levels of the environment in order to assess what is happening. This is a process covered in detail in any of the principal marketing textbooks, but it basically means objectively assessing what is happening through evaluating press cuttings, trends, personal observation etc, and then bringing it all together into a cohesive whole. An element of the environmental audit was covered in Chapter 6 when we looked at evaluating competitors. You may find it helpful to refer back to this section before proceeding with this chapter.

Some bookshops may find it easier to use a professional marketing consultant to undertake this exercise since they have more experience at discovering the necessary information and may find it easier to be objective and open-minded about the assessment of the information. There is, of course, a cost attached to this.

The marketing mix

The marketing mix is another central concept of marketing. Its basis is that there are a number of major variables in the "offer" which the seller projects into the marketplace, while its traditional concept is often referred to as "the four Ps". When applied to normal retail bookselling these four Ps stand for:

Product	Finding out as much as possible about customers' wants and needs and then devising a stock selection that best supplies them.
Place	Deciding where to locate a bookshop and then making the selected stock mix available in the right quantities to as many customers as possible, while at the same time keeping stor age and stockholding costs as low as possible.
Price	Determining pricing policies and setting the price of individual books within the stock mix (Price is discussed in some detail in Chapter 17)
Promotion	Telling groups of people about the bookshop and the stock mix and services that it offers.

Table 15.1 The Marketing Mix

As we see from this, there is nothing unusual about the marketing mix, nor necessarily anything particularly unique about a bookshop. A key difference with a bookshop that adopts a marketing approach is that these activities are treated in a more formal, structured way and are continuously addressed to the target customers' needs and wants. This type of approach also tends to take rather more notice of changes and developments within the environment, and reacts to how they may affect either the bookshop as a business or its customers.

The customer is an important factor to stress here. The operational aspects of bookselling demand such attention to a mass of detail that a bookseller can be driven to focus unwittingly on the product, to the exclusion of the customer. This can have a very damaging impact on the bookshop's long-term success, since it is critical to always keep the customers' requirements fully in mind. A useful discussion of how customers see shops can be found in a book by Paco Underhill called ***Why We Buy***. Further details of this book can be found in the bibliography at the end of the book.

Positioning

One key issue for all booksellers, whether they are aware of it or not, is how the customer sees their bookshop. Is it seen as an inaccessible highbrow boutique; a disorganised but welcoming place; or an authoritative and knowledgeable bookshop where customers can find what they want and get good information? The list of possibilities is endless but an important consideration is that what matters is how your customers see you rather than how you see yourself.

The whole issue of positioning a business in the eyes of its customers is complex and lies at the heart of strategic marketing. Booksellers who are interested in exploring the subject in depth should refer to specific marketing textbooks for a more detailed account.

Clearly a lot of the bookshop's activities would differ according to which market is targeted. The provision of such customer services as ordering books not in stock is probably going to be more important if the bookshop is aiming at dedicated bookbuyers than if it is aiming at more casual trade. Similarly, your target customer will influence the selection and purchasing of new titles.

Choices like this must be made very carefully since your decision may bring the bookshop into conflict with other competing bookshops. If this does happen then you might have to put far too much energy into trying to ensure that your shop does not lose so many sales that it goes out of business.

Promotion

Promotion – in the strict marketing sense – is all about establishing positive communications with potential and actual customers to tell them about your bookshop and the books you sell, with a view to their buying from you.

Promotion is not necessarily about going out into the marketplace, but it does tend to involve some form of activity beyond the confines of the bookshop. It also generally involves spending some money. This may be direct expenditure (buying advertising space, for example) or it may be the sort of indirect expense involved in getting editorial coverage on a local radio station.

Think for a moment about publishers' promotion. They may be providing bookshops with dumpbins, posters, showcards, display props and even free give-aways such as bookmarks or balloons. They do this to get booksellers to communicate their titles to the book-buying public. By participating in the promotion, at this sort of level, booksellers are helping publishers with their promotion, but not necessarily promoting their bookshops.

If, however, publishers also run co-operative advertising whereby they contribute to booksellers' costs of placing advertisements for their books, which also suggest people buy them from specific bookshops, then the booksellers are taking publishers' promotion further, and promoting their own businesses too.

So promotion involves your trying to attract customers to purchase from your bookshop. This may be done through advertising in the local paper or by putting posters up on a local college notice board. Alternatively, you may distribute flyers or customised copies of a Christmas catalogue, such as the Booksellers Association's *Christmas Books*, to households in the area. You may seek actively to promote your bookshop's web site by creating links with other sites which offer some logical connection. In all these activities you are trying to guide potential customers to buy from you.

The two strands which have developed from promotion are sales promotion and publicity.

Sales promotion

Sales promotion – where some specific activity is used to stimulate sales of a particular book or books – usually involves offering some form of financial, or other, incentive. It will probably amount to more than simply arranging an attractive display of books within the bookshop.

One prominent sort of sales promotion that has been used increasingly since the Net Book Agreement ceased to apply is discounting. In many cases the discount is offered on the recommended retail price of a new book and may take the form of either a specific price reduction (e.g. £15.99 reduced to £12.99) or a set percentage (e.g. 20% off £15.99). Alternatively a back list title may be chosen and it may be that a smaller reduction in price can be effective. It is generally felt that a discount of less than about 12 or 13% is not seen as significant by the customer.

Other popular sales promotions include:

- a "three for two" offer, when the customer may have three books, but pays for only two, getting the cheapest title free.
- two books, individually priced at, for instance £5.99, for £10.00
- three books, individually priced at, for instance £6.99, for £15.00

Not all sales promotions need be quite as overt as these. Buying a book may perhaps entitle the customer to some other discounted offer, or may involve a "give-away"' – for instance, buy three children's character books to receive an attractive free poster of the character.

Giving vouchers with a purchase opens up a variety of possibilities. They range from entitling the customer to a free coffee at an instore or participating coffee shop to themed promotions – offering discounts on holidays, for example, as part of a travel book promotion.

An important aspect of any sales promotion is to approach the matter in a structured fashion. You should decide first of all what your objectives for the promotion are – is it to sell more copies of a specific book; to generate some short term revenue boost; to publicise your shop etc. Once you have decided the objective you should decide what device is likely to best serve that end, and then work out how much the promotion is going to cost. This gives you an idea of the sort of sales you need to achieve a break-even level – if your sales fall below this point the promotion has cost you, if above, then you have made a profit. You should also consider a contingency if the promotion does not seem to be working – can you advertise, should you give more window space, should you pull the promotion? Finally you need to assess how well the promotion worked, both practically and financially, so that you can improve the next sales promotion you run.

Before becoming too enthusiastic about the many forms of sales promotion, booksellers should be aware that certain legal restrictions apply: you may not, for instance run a lottery.

Publicity

Publicity differs from other forms of promotion in that it usually means communication about the bookshop and/or the books it is selling, in the form of a news story or some editorial coverage in a mass medium at no charge. Buying an advertisement to go out alongside your local radio's books programme is promotion; getting a mention for your bookshop within the feature is publicity.

As a local bookshop you may find that opportunities to get valuable free publicity for the shop do arise. The level and quality of the coverage will tend to depend on the level and calibre of your contacts with the local news media. Achieving and maintaining the contacts may take time and effort and may often include "entertainment". This is the hidden cost of publicity.

Issuing press releases about events your bookshop is involved with can generate useful publicity. Here the key to success tends to be your ability to give a journalist a "news" story. If you can create the opportunity, then you are far more likely to get good coverage. You should also endeavour to get photographs of any potentially newsworthy events since these may well encourage a paper to publicise you. A good digital camera, and the knowledge of how to use it well, may pay rewards very quickly!

Local press advertising

Using advertising in the local press to announce your bookshop opening to the local community is something you should consider seriously. It is not cheap, but you may find that some of your suppliers (including wholesalers, if they are your choice) are willing to share costs if their books are given a specific mention. Sometimes free stock rather than hard cash is offered, but so long as you are confident you can sell the books you are given this should not be a problem. Alternatively, try the company you used to do your shopfitting.

The use of the local paper does mean you can tell people exactly where and when you are opening, rather than hope they will simply notice this, and also give them an idea of the sort of bookshop it will be. You may want to add some special event or offer to your opening programme. A signing session with a prominent local author is one idea which might help to generate some useful activity and further (free) publicity within the first few days of your trading.

Local media coverage

This leads us on to the idea of getting some editorial coverage for your bookshop in the local press, as well as simply advertising in it. Within many communities the opening of a new bookshop – particularly a local independent rather than a chain bookshop – will attract significant interest. The local newspaper may well be willing to give some editorial coverage (especially if you are also an advertiser).

If you do not have a good contact at the local paper already you should certainly try to talk to the editor. The paper may have a weekly slot for events within the community, for instance, and your bookshop opening would provide ideal copy for it. Remember that your story is more newsworthy if you can find an angle that will interest the journalist. Papers like stories; they do not like being used simply as unpaid advertising. If you can offer an interesting slant on the business – perhaps it is the first-ever bookshop to open in the area or located in a famous building – you are far more likely to get coverage. Adding a suitable photo-call is better still, even if it means you take the photos on a decent digital camera and email them to the paper.

Since local newspapers are quite often closely involved with local publications, either written by their journalists or which they may publish themselves, an offer to promote these books may prove to be a useful *quid pro quo* for coverage in the paper. It gains by having a good local outlet for its books, you gain by getting publicity and, you hope, selling lots of the books.

Evaluating advertising

An eternal difficulty with almost any marketing campaign lies in deciding whether the money you spent on advertising was worth it. There is no simple way to define success. The classical route would be to undertake market research to test levels of awareness before and after the campaign – something unlikely to appeal to many booksellers.

One relatively simple way, though it does have added costs, is to include some form of special offer voucher in your advertising and invite people to clip out the voucher and bring it in. If you have incorporated a small coffee shop into your bookshop a limited-period voucher for a free coffee may well help to show you how many people noticed the advertising. Without a coffee shop, you could try one or other of the sales promotion ideas mentioned earlier in this chapter, offering a discount on production of the voucher. You do of course have to provide the free coffee or forego the full profits, but the people who come along will also see your bookshop and, with luck, return.

Bookshop events

Provided you are both methodical and imaginative, running events is not as difficult as it looks. Most authors welcome an opportunity to meet their readers and local authors are usually even more interested since it gives them a social event as well as a chance to earn more royalties from the extra sales.

Generally an approach to the publisher of the book(s) you wish to promote is the best starting point. Provided your request is reasonable (do not expect a Booker Prize-winning novelist to turn up at your shop the day after the awards dinner), the publisher will probably be agreeable and will usually provide stock on a sale or return basis, together with posters and often a willingness to split costs on some local press advertising.

This is a good example of where the time and effort spent on developing a good relationship with suppliers is likely to pay dividends. If you have been able to create good personal relations with a number of people at a supplier and you have a reputation for doing what you say you will do, and paying your bills on a regular basis, then you are much more likely to receive positive support from your suppliers when it comes to organising events and the such like.

The simplest form of book event is a straightforward signing session. The bookshop announces the event and organises the stock; the author duly turns up; the public queues to get books signed and have a few words with the author. Simple as this sounds, it can also turn out to be a fraught occasion, since whereas it generally works with well-known authors, the bookshop can find itself embarrassed if no customers appear.

The next sort of event is more social and usually involves customers meeting the author and –one hopes – buying copies of the book, over a glass of wine. This does add to the cost of the event but, providing the advance preparation is done properly, the results can be well worth it.

Often the publisher (or the author, if local) can provide names and addresses of people they would like invited. Simply printing an invitation/announcement and mailing it to these potential customers can produce much higher attendance, which usually means that more copies of the book are sold.

The final stage in organising book events is for the bookshop to host a talk by an author, where signed copies of the book are also available for sale. This does call for some detailed and serious planning and it may involve added costs – the hire of a hall and of a slide projector, for example, if the talk is to be illustrated. Against this, a well-known author who speaks as well as he or she writes (never to be assumed, by the way) can result in a very rewarding event for all concerned. You may only cover costs with the ticket sales, but the goodwill and the very tangible publicity that has been generated for the bookshop can be invaluable.

It is important to decide what you are really trying to do when you think about book events. Are you trying simply to achieve a short-term success, making a lot of money by selling a lot of books on the night? Or are you thinking ahead and trying to develop a longer-term plan to draw attention to your bookshop?

This kind of reasoning is important both in helping you to decide how much money to invest in book events and in developing a strategy for generating long-term public awareness.

Community contacts

An independent bookshop has a major potential strength in its ability to integrate itself into the cultural life of the community. Many chain bookshops do try to do this, but may be constrained by differing local and corporate objectives.

Quite often there is an additional complication if the manager of the branch does not come from the locality and has few direct contacts within the community.

As a local independent bookshop you have the opportunity to foster strong local links. You probably have many of the contacts already, and simply need to direct attention to them to generate positive and ongoing goodwill. Those likely to prove most useful on a local basis might include:

- journalists on local newspapers;
- teachers at local schools;
- librarians;
- curators of the local museum and art gallery;
- local councillors;
- community council representatives;
- local history and arts societies;
- local authors.

With contacts established, it is easier for the bookshop to make its presence felt. You could build up the presence by advertising local events on a community notice-board in the bookshop. It might be possible to take relevant selections of books to local events for sale to the various interest groups. If this is too time-consuming, books may be supplied to local organisers who then take a 10% cut on any sales.

Another potential approach is to offer to supply a regular bestseller list or review column to the local paper. It may not be interested, but you will lose nothing by asking and many local papers are keen to explore ideas which emphasise their local nature.

Every possibility should be considered in the light of its potential benefit to the business. The trick is to identify astutely what real benefit you may get. If you want greater local awareness, it may be more effective to give up an occasional evening's leisure or give 10% on some sales than to run advertising in the local paper.

Data protection

It is likely that sooner or later you will find it very much more efficient to keep records of customer addresses on your computer system. You will need to use either a spreadsheet for this, or much more usefully a database application. Once you have started this it is likely that you will want to add various bits of information about your customers, such as that they prefer historical non-fiction, or romantic fiction.

One area to be aware of is that you are likely to need to register this activity under the Data Protection Act. There is increasing general awareness of the potential conflict between the computerisation of personal records and the human rights of the individual. By registering with the Information Commisioner, nominating a person within your organisation who will retain responsibility for the data (a Data Controller), and by following the principles of good practice shown below you will have fulfilled your obligations under the Act.

The basic rule governing Data Protection issues are that anyone processing personal data must comply with the eight enforceable principles of good practice. These principles are that data must be:

- fairly and lawfully processed;
- processed for limited purposes;
- adequate, relevant and not excessive;
- accurate;
- not kept longer than necessary;
- processed in accordance with the data subject's rights;
- secure;
- not transferred to countries without adequate protection.

You should note that personal data covers both facts and opinions about the individual. It also includes information regarding the intentions of the data controller towards the individual, although in some limited circumstances exemptions will apply. With processing, the definition is far wider than before. For example, it incorporates the concepts of 'obtaining', holding' and 'disclosing'.

You will find extensive help and guidance on these complex issues on the Information Commissioner's web site which can be found at www.dataprotection.gov.uk. Ireland operates a very similar set of rules concerning data protection and specific information for Ireland can be found on the Data Protection Commissioner's web site at www.dataprivacy.ie

Expanding your market

At some point every business finds it needs to expand. Usually it is a case of increasing the sales to provide more revenue and thereby cover ever-increasing costs. Alternatively, the bookseller might have spotted a gap in the market which could be exploited.

The kind of openings will generally depend upon your skills, your specific market and your willingness to extend the area of your activities. We can look here at some of the many possibilities.

Mail order

Although the mail order bookseller may have contact with customers by telephone, post or e-mail, or through their responses to mail shots, the critical factor is dealing with the customer at a distance, rather than in person, and this means that certain variables in the selling mix change.

You will need to set up an efficient system for dealing with orders and supplying them promptly and economically. You will also need satisfactory payment arrangements.

Today's office technologies provide booksellers with many more solutions for mail order selling than were available even twenty years ago. Some which help to make mail order easier to operate are shown in Figure 15.1 below.

Technology	Possible use
Database	Keeping track of customers and orders
Word processing	Mail merge correspondence
0800 phone numbers	Making it easier for customers to phone you
E-mail	Communicating with customers and receiving orders
Credit cards	Receiving guaranteed payment from customers
Internet	Promoting the business to interested parties globally
E-commerce	Trading securely over the Internet so that orders and payment can both be dealt with

Figure 15.2 Mail order technologies

Selling books to schools

No one disputes that schools need books, but how much money they may have available for buying them is a topic of interminable political debate. The reality is that most schools have sadly limited funds for books most of the time and so they are keen to find the best possible deal, particularly when it comes to the supply of textbooks. To achieve the best deal a number of schools may quite often combine their purchasing power to drive harder bargains on the price they pay for their textbooks.

The result is a very competitive marketplace for school textbooks. For booksellers the situation is harder still, thanks to the fact that the usual discount they receive from school textbook publishers is very low, often only around 25%.

The specialist nature of the marketplace and the constraint imposed by the low margins has given rise to a number of specialised booksellers called school suppliers. They generally deal with a wide range of schools and offer competitive discounts as a means of trying to win business; any profit comes from the economies of scale they apply to their operation.

All this means that few local bookshops are likely to find the contract supply of school textbooks to local schools an economically attractive option. It does not mean, however, that local schools should be ignored – far from it. Useful business can be done with schools. It will often have to be at some form of discount, and the bookseller must decide in advance whether the benefits of the business promise to outweigh the costs of the discount that must be given. This is primarily a financial decision, but one should not forget the importance of the community and cultural implications of dealing with local schools. There may be long-lasting negative reverberations if you decline the business.

Booksellers who do decide to tap into the schools market generally operate in four principal areas. First, many schools have a library, which often gets regular periodic funds to refresh its stock of general reading and reference books for the pupils. These funds may come from the school budget or, increasingly, from the PTA, the school's parent-teacher association. Often a teacher is asked to purchase books for the library to a certain value, and appreciates the benefit of being able to come to see books in a nearby bookshop. Some schools have similar arrangements at individual class level.

Most schools would expect some form of discount on such an order, and it is quite often given in the form of extra books – if, for instance, the teacher has £100 to spend, they may be allowed to select books to the value of £110, but are only invoiced for £100.

The next area of potential interest is school prizes, which may be awarded to pupils for good academic performance over the year. Books are a useful form of prize since they tie in well with the "worthy" aims of prize-giving. Traditionally it would be a small hardback copy of one of the classics. Although schools today are rather more open-minded, they often still prefer books to computer games as prizes. There are three frequent devices used: the school chooses books to award; the school may give book tokens; or the school may issue award-winners with pre-agreed vouchers to be spent in local bookshops. Again, the school usually expects some form of collective discount.

The teachers' need for resource materials are the focus of the third area. Its relevance to any single bookshop will vary according to what funds the schools and teachers have to spend but, if you can cultivate teachers by helping them to find the sort of books they are looking for, either from your stock or to special order, then you may find a useful, and potentially profitable, relationship developing.

Finally, we come back to textbooks and the "top-up supply" of them when a school's usual supplier has failed to deliver for any reason. When this happens the need is usually very urgent. You are probably unlikely to make any money on the deal, but you might generate genuine goodwill in the process.

Selling to libraries

Libraries, rather like schools, tend to do their bulk purchasing of books through specialist library suppliers who will order multiple copies of requested books, process them to specification and then deliver them at highly competitive prices. Again, there is great competition for library contracts, with the abolition of the Net Book Agreement and library authorities banding together to form buying consortia, obliging suppliers to offer more and more to win their business. It is no huge surprise that there has been a significant reduction in the number of specialist library suppliers over the past five years as the stronger players buy out their weakened competitors.

Unlike school textbooks, most books ordered for libraries will be supplied at higher discount terms, but the libraries will often expect a much better deal from the bookseller. They usually require special processing too, such as plastic jackets, tipped-in labels and so on. Often inspection copies will also be sent. This makes it unlikely that any local bookshop would want to become involved in contract supply to its local library (or be capable of it). That does not mean, however, that there is no potential for contact.

Most libraries will try to support their local bookshop insofar as it is possible within their budgets. A strong argument in the local bookshop's favour is that they pay rates and so should receive some support from a public library run by the local authority. The local bookshop should also be able to respond rapidly to any request, whereas a distant supplier may take longer. Such business would be at a discount but, as with schools, there is more at stake than simple economics.

To what extent a successful business relationship might develop will depend largely on the relationship the bookseller has been able to establish with the local librarian, and the history of past performance.

Selling to business

Selling books to commercial businesses is potentially a very attractive prize, particularly in a city where the concentration of businesses tends to be high. It is also, however, a very competitive field. A number of publishers operate successful direct mail programmes for their books to many businesses throughout the UK. On top of this almost every commercial organisation is Internet connected and thus is able to search globally for books from booksellers who sell through their web sites. There is a huge simplicity in this for the business recipient, who without leaving the desk gets information about specialist books relevant to their business interests. Payment, by or using a credit card, is easy and the books are delivered in a few days.

Booksellers can however find openings for selling to local businesses. Much depends on making contact and letting people know what services are on offer. This may be by local networking through organisations such as a local Chamber of Commerce, or it may be by distributing leaflets locally or even contacting local businesses by email.

The potential size of the market is hard to estimate. Many businesses will have occasional uses for reference books and may well be willing to order them through a local bookshop, particularly if they feel they can get a competitive offer. Equally there may be a case for going out into the business market with direct offers if you think there will be a positive response. The market for business books is growing and now embraces more popular titles. You may decide that certain new titles will have a wide enough appeal to be worth the sort of promotion that you might usually reserve for a general consumer book. If so, producing a flyer to distribute to businesses may be a more effective way of telling them about the books than relying on your usual window displays.

It is also worth remembering that some businesses like to give gifts to celebrate special events or if they have people visiting their premises. Many have recognised that well chosen books can make very suitable, and ethically safe, gifts. If businesses purchase multiple copies of books they will probably expect some form of discount and may look elsewhere if you are not prepared to offer one. If you have this problem with any business in your locality, try hard to get on good terms.

Internet selling

The Internet potentially offers each and every bookseller the opportunity to reach a global marketplace of book-buyers around the world, the chance to be, as one senior publisher expressed it in a letter to *The Bookseller*, "a corner shop in the global village". The reality, of course, is wildly different.

All the big players are in some way or other already established as Internet booksellers. Some have fully functional e-commerce enabled web sites where you can trade on-line, whilst others are still using their web sites as an informational publicity system. Generally they are using wholesalers to act as their fulfilment agents if they do not have the title in stock. However, it is important to recognise that the commercial and technical resources needed to establish an internationally competitive website, and an effective delivery system, are huge. That said, the possibilities for the smaller bookshop are significant.

The big internet booksellers are huge; small booksellers can look at operating their own website (expensive to develop and maintain) or consider joining a network of similar bookshops using a central template for a website, provided and backed by a book wholesaler, so that the bookseller can appear to give a fully browsable website and order fulfillment is handled by a third party. Ask your wholesalers for information about this.

In terms of straightforward economics it is unlikely that smaller bookshops will be able to offer the same level of discount and service as the international protagonists. There remains, however, great potential for any bookseller to get on the Internet and sell books successfully to a wider public.

There may well be scope for a more local approach too. An individual bookshop is far better placed than a multinational to establish a local website using links to other local sites with mutual or related interests. For example, a bookshop in the Cotswolds might well establish a website for the business which specifically featured books of local interest. Many towns and localities have now established their own Internet portals and this may well be a useful place for a local bookshop to be featured. By deciding carefully where to establish links, and how to be described on the major search engines, the bookshop may be able to acquire customers world-wide, thanks to an imaginative sequence of connections.

16. Selling

The presentation of a bookshop to the local public – its marketing – is important, but so too is the shop's physical appearance from the outside world. It must look inviting if it is to attract sufficient customers to stay in business. Setting up a bookshop with an attractive interior and a good range of stock is all very well. However, without customers inside the shop actively buying books, it can go nowhere.

The numbers game

Why on earth do people selling double glazing simply telephone out of the blue to see if we want to buy some? The answer lies in a mathematics very similar to that facing booksellers.

The people with the double glazing know that perhaps only one in fifty persons 'phoned is remotely interested in hearing more about what is on offer. Among those, perhaps one in five will actually go on to make a purchase and bring the seller some commission. Telephoning only 250 people is likely, statistically, to earn just one commission payment, whereas phoning 2,500 might earn ten (and a new car).

For booksellers the actual ratios may differ, but the principles are identical. A very high proportion of those passing your bookshop will simply walk by without a second glance. (Furthermore, it has been estimated that only one in three people entering a bookshop actually buys something.) So the more people you can persuade to come into the shop, the higher the number of potential purchasers will be. Once they have entered, the higher the conversion proportion (i.e. from potential to actual buyers), the better your sales will be.

In this chapter we shall be considering:

- some of the physical aspects of the problems of attracting enough people to buy books;
- the possibilities of active selling to customers.

Attracting people into the shop

The utopian theory is that you set up shop and people passing by come inside and buy what you have to offer. Statistically, the harsh reality is that many of the people passing your door will continue to do just that, and will not give you or your bookshop another thought. Of those who do come into the shop, many are likely to leave again without having bought anything at all.

This problem also leads us to some of the possible solutions. The more people coming into the shop, the more likely sales are to increase but, as we have seen, the costs of being on a prime pitch are higher than many bookshops can bear. So we must find ways of encouraging both more casual passers-by to come in and more people who are likely to buy books to find us.

If you have done your location research well (see Chapter 6) and opened your bookshop in a reasonably busy place then you should have an adequate number of people passing your frontage. Not all will be interested in coming in and not all who come in will be interested in buying. The shop cannot succeed, however, unless the grand total of people coming through the door is high enough to ensure that the proportion who do buy will be viable. You must therefore put a lot of effort into doing as much as possible to attract as many people as possible into your bookshop.

The first thing to consider is your front door. This may sound ridiculous, but is it easy to use? If the door is difficult to see or has an awkward handle, is heavy to push open or approached by a difficult step, then you are making it harder for people to come in.

Another potential deterrent is clutter, so make sure that neither your door nor your windows are obscured by a lot of scruffy notices giving details of locally lost cats, jumble sales, coffee mornings; or even highly professional publicity material for books or services you offer. We have seen that there is a place for such community news, and it is on a notice-board which you put up in a place to suit you – not in some of the shop's prime selling space, where it may also erode the air of professionalism you are trying so hard to develop.

The shop window

Many of your customers may make a special trip to your bookshop, but others will simply make an impulse visit as they walk past your frontage. These people will probably make up the majority of your custom over time, so it is important to look at how best you can attract them inside. They are quite often in a hurry, with other things on their mind. Your task is to seek a means of stopping them in front of the shop and tempting them to come in.

A new bookshop just opened is likely to have a freshly painted shop front and sign, so that is first base. Next comes the shop window. There are as many ideas about the effect a shop window has as there are people working on the question. The main synthesis of these ideas seems to be that the shop window is probably unlikely to sell extra copies of the precise titles featured in it, with the possible exception of an outstanding book given an outstanding display. Rather, the window is a tool for enticing people into the bookshop and a very important weapon in the armoury you must use to increase the number of people entering the shop (and thereby increase the number actually buying books).

A good shop window display is one which makes such an impact that it slows down the people who are passing. It is not likely to do this if all it displays is a vast range of books! Firstly they are too small, generally, to catch the eye of anyone not specifically wanting to look into the window, and secondly for many people it is the very range of books that is intimidating.

The hope of a good window display is also to encourage some of the passers-by to stop and pay more attention to it, so that finally they are sufficiently motivated to come inside. Once they are inside, then your internal design, range of stock and personal selling skills are allowed to come into play.

Window dressing

It may be that you or one of your staff team already have well-developed creative and practical skills at window dressing. If you do not, three possible approaches are open to you:

- hire a professional window dresser;
- attend a local course to enhance your in-house window-dressing skills;
- attend a BA training course on bookshop display.

There are some useful advantages in using a professional window dresser. Apart from having a great talent for creating eye-catching, effective windows, they may work for other shops and so have a well-honed set of useful contacts. On the other hand, their window displays may end up too stylised and look-alike. A good starting point is to talk to neighbouring shops or put an advertisement on your local art college notice-board.

The main advantage of developing good in-house skills is that it allows more flexibility to cope with changing needs. There are also cost advantages, of course. Looking at how other shops create their window displays helps enormously – try taking notes or making sketches of the better ideas. Sooner or later, however, you will need to learn some practical handicraft skills (creating tubes and covering them with material to use as display props, for example). Some form of training course is by far the easiest way to learn such things.

A fourth option is simply to try to improve your skills with time. It is possible, with practice, and if you have a flair for design it may well work, but those with limited skills in this area may meanwhile do their bookshops a serious disservice. All the time you are learning your primary advertising space is being under-used. This may be more than you can really afford.

Your principal objective is to create the sort of window displays that will stop people in their tracks. If you can succeed in doing this and thereby tempt customers into the bookshop, you are a success. However, window displays characterised by dog-eared posters peeling at the corners, supplemented with dead flies, are a waste of a valuable sales promotion opportunity.

The shop window is your permanent advertising space and it does not come free. You may be paying rent and are certainly paying rates for it, just as you are for any other part of the shop. Use the windows well – that is, use them creatively and actively to feature positive aspects of your bookshop – and you will find them indispensable. If, however, you simply stack a few shop-soiled books into the windows, you should not be surprised if the space fails to perform for you.

Practicalities

You should change your window display frequently – and obviously. A few subtle improvements are likely to go unnoticed. To many people passing your bookshop regularly, you risk becoming just part of the scenery. A succession of striking window displays can change this. You can become a focal point and grab their attention. How many people making a Christmas shopping trip to London miss the display of toys in Hamleys' windows?

With the support of suppliers you can often get good point-of-sale display material (usually known as POS). Used imaginatively, POS can provide an excellent basis for an impressive window display. A particular value of large POS material is that it is likely to be seen from further away, and also helps you to create a less cluttered window since much of your available space will be taken up with the POS material. You will also find that once you have a reputation for putting on good windows, it generally becomes easier to get what you want. POS material is expensive to produce, so publishers prefer to direct it to shops where they know it will be used to good effect.

You should also build up a collection of suitable "props" for window displays – things which you can use repeatedly. Some swathes of fabric will help change the background to the window; perspex book stands or painted wooden boxes of varying sizes will give depth and balance to displays; and dried flowers or Christmas decorations can add colour and interest when appropriate. The only limit to this is your imagination (and perhaps the storage space you have for such things). Some basics might include:

- lengths of variously coloured fabric;
- book stands;
- attractively covered boxes;

- gardening tools and plants (keep them watered!);
- paintings from a local primary school;
- mannequin borrowed from local fashion shop;
- collections of dried flowers;
- driftwood or pebbles from the beach.

Friendly contact with neighbouring retailers can be useful since many are willing to lend each other props for use in window displays, providing some form of acknowledgement is provided. You might, for instance, lend some travel books to the local travel agent or sports shop – and get a mention in their windows. Equally, you might borrow a mannequin, complete with wedding dress, from a local dress shop to support a promotion of books on spring weddings.

Taking things further

If you are forced to admit that neither you nor any colleague has much artistic talent, then you have to think again. Every time you use a professional window dresser you will incur another bill.

As an alternative, it is well worth considering taking or sending someone on a display course, perhaps locally. Do not expect an instant creative fix, but this should help you to formulate some ideas and show you how to convert those ideas into reality. Thereafter, it is a matter of hard work and perseverance: in the end, you too will be able to produce some riveting displays. The objective must always be to make potential customers waver in their automaton-like walk along the high street and to entice them into your bookshop.

Thematic displays

Where display is concerned, booksellers' great advantage over many other retailers is that there is no area of human interest that is not represented by books. A bookshop can create a display on practically any subject under the sun. This week might feature cookery books, next week might feature books on mind, body and spirit. Ideally you should use the theme for your window display, and back it up with an internal display in a prominent position within the bookshop.

Highlighting different subjects in displays also increases your chances of attracting people who might never have thought a bookshop would contain anything of interest to them. Your window displays may help to prove them wrong – to your mutual advantage.

Providing displays of books which tie in with a public preoccupation can generate extra sales and at the same time demonstrate that the bookshop is both topical and relevant. Sport might be of national interest at that point or, within the local community, there may a local flower or garden show. Another possibility is to tie in with films being shown locally or with television programmes. Links with subjects like these will help to create an empathy between your bookshop and the customers.

Providing you choose the theme carefully, with a view to seasonality and topicality, there is plenty of scope for interesting, varied themes throughout the year. Some fairly obvious examples include:

January	January sale/Burns Night
February	St Valentine's Day/travel
March	Mother's Day/gardening
April	World Book Day/Easter/weddings
May	Foreign languages (in preparation for holidays)
June	Sporting activities
July	Barbecue cookery
August	Summer holidays
September	Back to school/college/evening classes
October	Crafts (as evenings get longer)
November	Entertaining
December	Christmas gifts/book tokens

You will of course need to build your own calendar that will feature any specialisation within your bookshop, and also reflect any specific issues within your locality. This may be local festivals, historic sites, protest issues etc. Do not, however, fall into the trap of simply putting books in your window. Use props and posters to generate the interest and lead the customers' eye to the books.

Practicalities

You will need to look at your stock ordering so that you have sufficient quantities of appropriate books to support the display. Remember the purpose of the display is to generate extra sales, so choose the titles to include with your usual selection criteria in mind. Coffee-table books may look lovely, but will you sell them?

Although the choice of titles will generally be up to you, it may be different when you have agreed to do a thematic promotion with a particular publisher.

Finding strong lead titles to incorporate into your thematic displays is helpful. If you are planning to do a gardening display, to arrange it around the publication of a major new gardening title will have the advantage of higher public awareness, probably created by press coverage, and potential point-of-sale provision by the publisher. Adding a range of suitable books to accompany the lead title can only boost your sales of gardening books over the period of the display.

Do not forget the use of "props" as discussed earlier in this chapter. Many thematic displays lend themselves to these. Plan ahead for the gardening promotion and bring in props from home or borrow some from friends. Alternatively, get the co-operation of a local shop or garden centre – particularly if it is acknowledged in the window and some form of reciprocation is offered.

Selling in the shop

Getting the level and quality of personal selling within a bookshop just right is not easy.

Supermarkets put the goods on the shelf and it is up to shoppers to select what they want and then pay for it. There may be some staff around to guide you to items you cannot find, but seldom much more. At the other end of the spectrum is the high-quality jeweller, where you most certainly cannot help yourself and even browsing is generally frowned on. The service offered is very personal and usually extremely professional. Your needs are assessed; your price limit discerned, and then suitable items are shown to you.

In between these two extremes there is a lot of potential variety, with as much scope to get it wrong as there is to get it right. The mark of a good bookseller is one who can judge the balance finely.

Almost every bookshop will encourage browsing. Some do so quite actively by incorporating sofas and coffee tables into their shop design; others may even offer free coffee to encourage customers to stay in the shop and browse to their hearts' content. The rationale of this is that the longer customers stay, the more likely they are to find something they wish to buy. A few customers will abuse this "generosity" of course, but this is an accepted part of the offer that is being made. Other bookshops will prefer to hurry people along and get them to make purchases quickly. They may give the impression that opening books and studying them in detail is not what the management wants to encourage.

Again, these are two extremes. Each has some merit and it is up to the individual business to decide where it sits on this spectrum.

With a policy decision on browsing made, the next question is how customers might be approached. Should they be welcomed as they enter the shop? Should they be approached while they are browsing? Because the scope for individual choice is wide, it is useful to establish some general guidelines so that the bookshop's staff can understand what is expected of them. Doing this may generate a consistency which both they and the customers usually appreciate.

Typical guidelines might include a policy of greeting customers in a friendly manner as they come into the shop but thereafter leaving them alone unless they are clearly lost or seeking help. Many booksellers find that this is quite a positive approach, allowing customers to feel that they are not being hassled, but at the same time ensuring that they receive attentive service when they ask for it. Expecting a degree of direct eye-to-eye contact is usually beneficial, too, since it allows a measure of sincerity to enter into the relationship with the customer.

The biggest opportunity the bookseller has to encourage customers to buy more arises when a genuine enquiry is triggered, either by the customer or through the bookseller's attentive questioning and listening. Personal selling becomes critically important here. There must be the right mix of interpersonal skills – not too pushy, not too retiring – plus a high level of knowledge, the core skill of any bookseller.

This knowledge may be either close familiarity with what is in the bookshop or far more extensive, depending on the bookseller's experience. Although computer-based systems provide the access to maximum possible information, in a personal selling situation with a customer in front of you a computer screen can detract from the relationship you need to develop with the customer. Detailed personal knowledge of the field in which the customer is interested is likely to result in a long-term customer, with all the attendant benefits to the bookshop. The ability to back this knowledge up with efficient systems to confirm orders and obtain supply of the books required will cement the relationship.

The till is the second area where customer contact becomes particularly important. Customers can be won and lost through the way they are dealt with at the till. If they receive the level of courtesy and efficiency they expect then they will usually be happy.

If they are subjected to rudeness or a lack of attention they usually react in one of two ways. They may actively complain within the bookshop; or they may simply vow never to come back. The latter is more common among the British, and for the bookshop it is devastating. The active complainant inside the shop may prove uncomfortable, but does at least give you an opportunity to set things right, whereas the customer who simply walks out presents a far more difficult problem. First, they usually tell anything up to twenty friends about their bad experience in your bookshop and secondly, you will be completely unaware that anything has gone wrong.

It is impossible to spend too much time studying how carefully you and your staff deal with customers as they are buying their books. It can make the very real difference between a bookshop which becomes a heavily supported local success and a bookshop that just slips away from beneath your feet.

If all else fails... bargain sales

A time-honoured way of drumming up interest is to run a bargain sale within the bookshop. You are unlikely to do this when you are just opening, but it is something to keep up your sleeve as a promotional mechanism for later on. There is no maintenance of prices within the book trade, so you can charge what you like for books, although you must, of course, consider the impact that price changes might have on your final margin.

Booksellers can run sales whenever they so wish. An immediate post-Christmas sale is a well recognised retail tool that everyone likes; customers feel they are getting a good bargain; booksellers are helped to release working capital from slow-selling stock. Some people argue that a bookshop which does not run a book sale through January is risking adverse customer reaction when all the other shops are offering bargains.

The mathematics of running a book sale means that if you offer selected titles at half price – which is generally what customers expect – you are usually selling them below cost price. In other words, it is costing you money to sell each book.

In normal circumstances this would be akin to commercial suicide. If, however, you select the older stock which you have long since paid for and which has failed to sell at full price, some sense can emerge. Figure 16.1 below shows an all too familiar situation. You will have paid for the book within thirty days, and let's assume that not only have you been unable to sell it, but that the publisher has refused to take it back as a return.

Early March 2003	
Original selling price of book	£15.00
Book comes into stock	February 2003
Cost price	£9.30
Invoice paid	March 2003
Book does not sell	

Figure 16.1 The rationale of sales: 1

At the beginning of December you still have a book with a nominal value of £15.00, but which nobody seems to want. You have long ago paid £9.30 for it, so you are currently out of pocket. You hope someone will buy it for Christmas, but at the beginning of January it is still there. Your original payment is retreating into the past, and if it did not sell at Christmas its chances of selling are very much reduced. If, however, you reduce the book to half price, then someone might think it worth buying for £7.50. This will then give you some return on your original investment of £9.30.

Early January 2004	
Original selling price of book	£15.00
Book reduced to half price	£7.50
Book sells!	

Figure 16.2 The rationale of sales: 2

The alternative to selling at half price is probably for books to continue to sit on your shelves gathering dust. This way they make you no money at all. However, if you can sell them for half the original retail price you release some capital to be re-invested in new stock that stands a better chance of selling. You will also have managed to create some excitement for your customers by offering them some very good deals – we are all suckers when it comes to apparently genuine bargains.

17. Pricing

Until late in September 1995, pricing was a relatively minor issue for booksellers thanks to the operation of the Net Book Agreement (NBA), which ensured that the majority of books sold in the UK were sold at the same price throughout the country. With the demise of the NBA the situation changed dramatically and now anyone can sell books at whatever price they wish.

The change has brought far more fluidity – and uncertainty – into the booksellers' market. It has also meant that some awareness of the various factors in pricing theory and practice is essential for booksellers.

Average prices

The book industry has some difficulty with estimating useful average prices. This is because books cover such a wide diversity of markets and price ranges. It makes no sense to compare the average price of children's books with that of university textbooks. Yet that is how industry statistics *tend* to be presented.

Booksellers' need to understand average prices depends on the specifics of the market under investigation. For the general bookshop perhaps the most relevant markets are the children's, paperback, general hardback and non-academic reference markets. For a university bookshop the price of student textbooks and academic reference books would be far more relevant.

Average prices naturally move over time with inflation, so that any prices quoted here will become less and less meaningful as time progresses. Reference to the regular annual statistics published in *The Bookseller* (usually in February) will help to update these figures, and existing bookshops running computerised stock control systems will be able to draw their own average price data from their systems. These figures will be the most relevant, of course, because the data will relate to the books which are actually stocked and will therefore give a very good picture of average prices, both at the time and historically.

In 1989 the average price for a best-selling title was about £3.50 for a popular paperback and about £10.00 for a general hardback. At that time, of course, the NBA was still fully operative. Looking at broadly similar figures from Whitaker BookTrack data in 2000, the prices have risen to around £6.99, but discounted to an average of around £5.25 for paperbacks, and £16.99, but again discounted to around £14.00, for hardbacks.

Since 1989, the price of paperbacks has generally increased faster than the Retail Price Index, while hardbacks have broadly kept pace. Taking 1989 average prices as an index of 100, the average price of paperbacks in 1997 (the last year for which figures were available) was 143, while the average price of hardbacks, and the RPI, is 133, according to Books and the Consumer, a long-term market research project run by Book Marketing Limited.

When we look at average prices today, we must consider both the average published price and the average selling price. Data released in a review from BookTrack in early 1997 indicated that the average selling price of books in the multiple retailers and supermarkets was up to one third lower than the average selling price within typical bookshops. This trend has continued.

Public perception of prices

One element within thc Books and the Consumer project looks at the public perception of book prices.

The recent research suggests that public awareness of real price increases is quite acute. Paperbacks may well have risen faster, in proportionate terms, but the increase is still smaller than the actual increases recorded for hardbacks. To many people this suggests that paperbacks represent better value for money than hardbacks and this will quite often influence their decision to purchase.

The euro

The unit of currency generally used throughout this book is the UK pound sterling (£). It is important to recognise and acknowledge that the currency in Ireland has always been different. Previously it was the Irish punt but since 1 January 2002 Ireland has been using euro notes and coins in common with much of the European Union.

The value of the Euro and the Pound fluctuate on the currency markets. During January 2003, as the final revisions were being made to this new edition, the Pound was worth about 1.5 Euros, or put the other way around, one Euro was worth about 65p.

It is quite possible that at some point in the future the UK will join the European currency scheme and exchange the pound for the Euro. Information about the euro, and the potential issues if the UK did convert, is regularly updated on the BA website. The BA has done a significant amount of preparatory exploration and is well placed to advise members should the need arise.

How publishers price a book

To appreciate book pricing booksellers should understand what factors publishers must consider in deciding the cover price for a new book. They will include the author's royalty, the possible revenue from the sale of rights, distribution costs, trade discounts, the marketing support that will be needed, the projected life of the title and so on. The single most important consideration for the publisher, however, is the size of the print run for the book – in other words, how many copies to print.

Although this figure is frequently based on an inspired guess as to the number of copies likely to sell over a reasonable period, most publishers will be able to assess sales data from similar titles, and will often talk to major booksellers to get a better idea of the likely support a title may be given.

Inevitably mistakes do happen. There may be vast over-production of one title that fails to achieve expected sales or – equally damaging – under-estimation of demand for another, so that sales are lost while it is being reprinted or bound up. It would be fair to say, however, that the increasing professionalism within publishing and a growing ability to interpret complex sales data mean that fewer mistakes are made now than perhaps ever before. This is an important factor in the improving efficiency of the industry.

Production costs

Publishers' production costs are a mixture of origination costs and running costs. Origination covers all the expenses the publisher incurs in getting a typescript ready for printing and may include advance royalties, editorial salaries, design costs for both the text and the dust jacket, typesetting fees, general overheads and so on. These expenses will be incurred regardless of how many copies of the book are produced or ultimately sold.

Running costs differ in that they are directly related to the number of copies produced. They include the price of the materials that will be used, the printer's and binder's costs, plus the distribution costs involved in moving the book from the bindery via the warehouse to the bookseller. Most of the running costs will involve some economies of scale – the more copies printed, for example, the better the probable deal on the cost of the paper.

To get some idea of how these two elements combine to produce the publisher's final costing, look at Figure 17.1, which shows how the unit cost changes with the size of the print run.

No of copies printed	Origination cost £	Running cost £	Total cost £	Unit cost £
1,000	10,000	3,000	13,000	13.00
2,000	10,000	5,000	15,000	7.50
3,000	10,000	7,000	17,000	5.66
4,000	10,000	9,000	20,000	5.00
5,000	10,000	11,000	21,000	4.20
10,000	10,000	21,000	31,000	3.10
20,000	10,000	41,000	51,000	2.55
30,000	10,000	61,000	71,000	2.37
40,000	10,000	81,000	91,000	2.28
50,000	10,000	101,000	111,000	2.22
100,000	10,000	201,000	211,000	2.11

Figure 17.1 Book production costs for differing print runs

The figures demonstrate that for the same book, printing 10,000 copies will result in a unit cost that is about one quarter of the unit cost if only 1,000 copies are printed. This means either that the book can be sold to the end-user at a far lower cover price or that the publisher's profit figure can be massaged quite generously. If, however, only 6,000 of the 10,000 copies printed are sold, then the profits generated by the 6,000 sales will probably be undone by all the costs associated with the remaining 4,000 unsold copies.

Many publishers use a rule-of-thumb calculation to derive the likely cover price of a book from its unit cost. and multiply the cost by a set factor, currently hovering around 5.5. So if the unit cost price is likely to work out at about £2.50, the publisher will look at setting a cover price of around £13.75 – probably rounded up to the price point of £13.99.

With a cover price of £13.99, the trade price (i.e. what the publisher actually gets when the book sells to the bookshop) will be in the region of £8.40. Production costs will be around £2.50; distribution costs probably account for a further £3.65; the author's royalty will be around £1.40. These costs, together with other overheads leave a profit margin of around 85p, or about 10% of the price the bookseller pays for the book. See Figure 17.2 for the way these costs fit together.

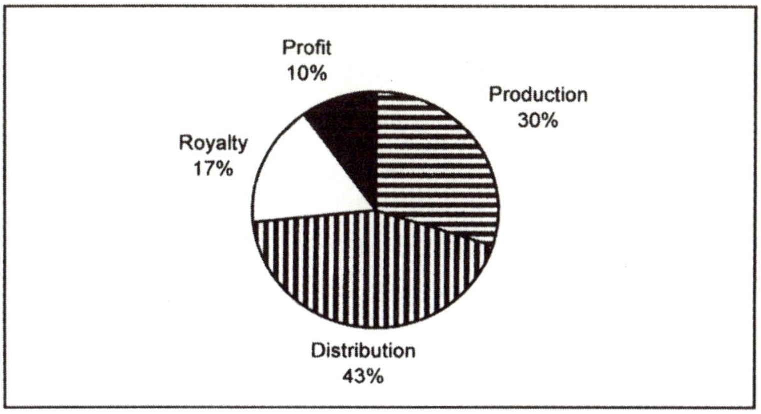

Figure 17.2 Publishers' cost structure

On this basis, with the publisher's profit margin (after expenses) around 10% of the £8.40 selling price to the bookshop, the bookseller, on a comparable basis, makes around 2% of the admittedly higher price of £13.99. However, 2% of £13.99 is still only 28p compared with the 84p that the publisher makes. It follows that you are not obliged to believe every tale of publisher hardship you may be told – some may be part of negotiating tactics.

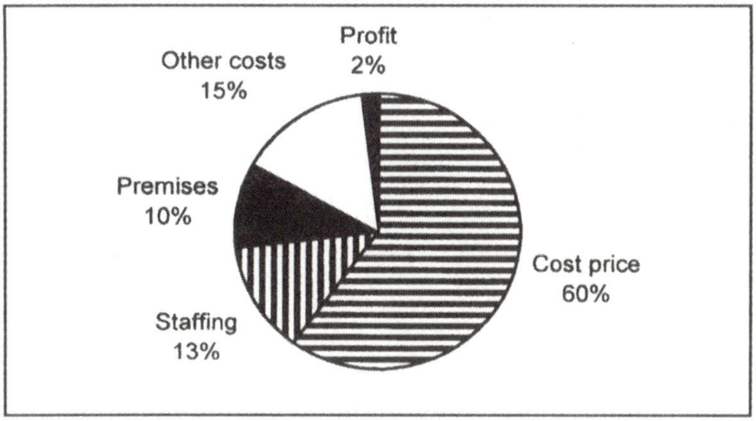

Figure 17.3 Booksellers' cost structure

A limited print run on a specialist book will of course result in a higher-priced book, since origination costs are much the same as for a more popular title. A look at your shelves will probably find you ample evidence of this.

Pricing within the marketplace

While the NBA remained in place booksellers did not generally have to consider any form of pricing strategy. The books in their shops sold at the cover price whether the bookshop was part of a large bookshop chain or a solitary independent. Without the NBA, however, every bookseller has the opportunity to sell their books at whatever price they see fit.

This is either a liberation from regimented pricing, bringing a freedom that can be exploited, or a potential danger for every bookseller, depending on your point of view. Just as you may decide to undercut competitors' prices, so they may decide to undercut yours.

Traditionally, bookselling has generally operated at a comparatively low profit margin, so that anyone actually making a profit of around 2% of sales has been at the more profitable end of the business. Knowingly to erode that limited margin by making books cheaper may not be the wisest move to make. Although volume sales may increase – one hears a lot about "growing the market" – many do not appreciate what levels of increased business they need to generate before such discounting makes sense.

This means that booksellers must now understand the mechanics of discounting and pricing before looking at a pricing strategy that will make sense for their business.

The mathematics of pricing

No bookseller can consider the mechanics of any pricing strategy properly without having an underlying understanding of the mathematics of the strategy. To see the mathematical relationship between choosing a price to sell at and the yield that will be achieved when the sale is made, we should look at some specific instances.

Consider first a book priced at £16.99, bought from the publisher at 38% discount. This means buying the book at £10.53, selling it at £16.99 and seeing a margin of £6.46. The margin falls, however, if the book is sold at £12.99. The book has still cost £10.53, but the bookseller will only make £2.46. These sums are illustrated at Figure 17.4 below.

Selling price	£16.99	£12.99
Cost price a 38% discount	£10.53	£10.53
Margin generated	£6.46	£2.46

Figure 17.4 Margin generated at full price and discounted price (38% discount)

So, to make the same margin as before, the bookseller must sell 2.6 times (£6.46÷£2.46) as many copies of the book. Selling fewer copies than this will reduce the margin generated on that book.

If the bookseller can negotiate a little more discount from the publisher the situation improves a bit. Say, it goes to 42% and the book now costs £9.85 at trade. This means that selling at £16.99 will make a margin of £7.14, while selling at £12.99 reduces the margin to £3.14. The bookseller must now sell just over twice as many copies (£6.46÷£3.14) of the book to generate the same margin. Figure 17.5 sets out the maths once more.

Selling price	£16.99	£12.99
Cost price at 42% discount	£9.85	£9.85
Margin generated	£7.14	£3.14

Figure 17.5 Margin generated at full price and discounted price (42% discount)

The relationship between the number of extra copies that must be sold to generate the original margin can be shown as a graph. Figure 17.6 below shows the relationship across a variety of supplier discounts and promotional discounting options – and demonstrates how important it is to improve the supplier margin if the bookseller is considering any serious discounting activity.

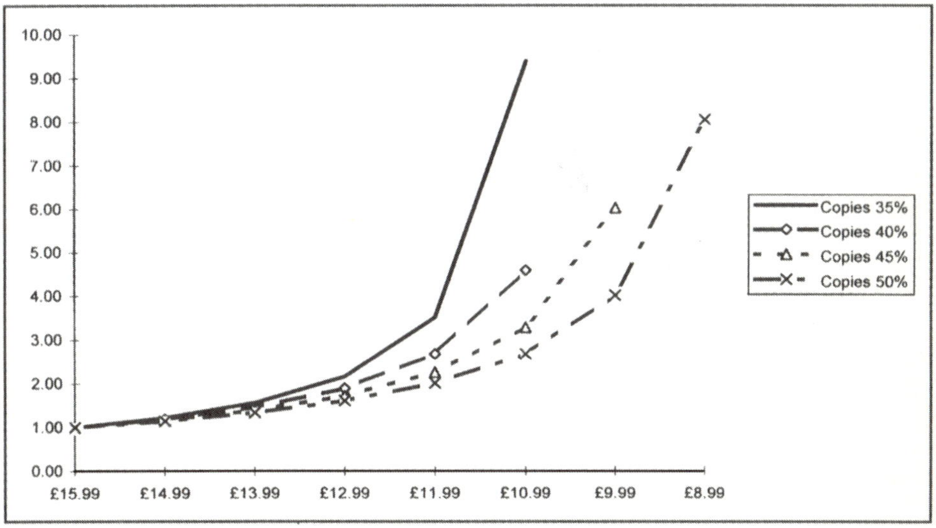

Figure 17.6 Discounting options

Conclusions

It is quite clear from the brief summary on the mathematics of pricing that the absolute prerequisite, if price is to be used as a marketing tool within your bookshop, is to maximise the discount you receive from your supplier. If you can maximise this, then you need to sell relatively fewer copies of the book at a reduced price in order to achieve an acceptable profit level.

This means you have an obligation to ensure that you are always maximising your discount. This should be done on a general level, but continually negotiating increased basic terms from your suppliers, and also on a title by title basis if it is clear that the title is going to be an important one for you.

In addition you should make sure that you are fully aware of the various offers that are going around from publishers and wholesalers. It may well be worth switching supplier for a title, range of titles or even an entire suppliers list, if it will give you a better overall discount level.

Price promises

One marketing device that can be used quite effectively to bolster consumer confidence is the "price promise", whereby the bookseller promises to match the price of a book if it can be found on sale elsewhere at a lower price. Conditions, usually defining some geographical restrictions and limiting the offer to identical editions, must of course be attached to such promises.

The promise reinforces customers' perception that the bookshop offers good value, and has no wish to "cheat" its customers but the downside is of course that if customers do find many books cheaper elsewhere and return for a refund, profitability may suffer dramatically. A price promise may also have the effect of forcing your prices to the lowest possible point, particularly if you are trading in a less affluent area where people are forced to compare prices more vigorously than they might elsewhere.

Pricing strategies

Four broad pricing strategies are generally available to booksellers. As usual, each has its advantages, theoretical and practical, and each has its drawbacks.

Full RRP

The first option is masterly inactivity: do nothing on price and simply apply the full recommended retail price on everything sold. This means that you make your full margin on all sales, but may also induce competitors to wean your customers away from you by offering lower prices.

This option is probably only realistically valid where there is little or no competition. It may be that you are operating in a specialist niche, or it may be that you are many miles from another bookshop. You do, however, need to be aware that no matter how specialist a niche or how geographically isolated you are the Internet is always there, and many Internet booksellers offer generous discounts. You may protect your margin in the short term, but against that nobody likes to be made to look a fool, and your customers may start to feel foolish if they find out that they could get their books much cheaper from other sources such as an Internet bookseller or a supermarket.

Price leadership

At the opposite end of the scale, the next option is to aim for price leadership. This is the "never knowingly undersold" option and involves building a reputation for having the cheapest prices for everything you sell. As far as bookselling goes, this means undercutting every competitor, so give it a lot of thought. Unless your publisher discounts are huge, your operating costs low; and your competition equally insignificant, this is unlikely to be a profitable strategy for booksellers (particularly those new to the book trade).

That said, there will always be retail players who will go for price leadership. If you are near such a bookseller then you have a major marketing headache on your hands. You can offer better service perhaps, but you are very unlikely to be able to undercut them. You will find increasingly customers will migrate to the other shop so that they can get more for their money, and then it is harder for you to maintain the higher level of service, since your profits will be falling.

Price matching

Half way between these two strategies comes price matching. The strategy involves matching competitor prices on a range of the most important titles of the moment and means a lot of work checking prices and then deciding which to match. It also means trying to run publisher deals to help support the price cuts you are offering. The aim is to show your customers that you are offering them just as good value as any competitor.

If you are going to be able to do this then you need to fully understand and appreciate the mathematics of pricing. You need to be working continuously to improve your supplier discounts and your credit terms. You also need to be working ahead of the game so that, to a large extent, you are able to anticipate which titles you will need to discount, and arranging suitable deals in advance.

Doing your own thing

If you "do your own thing" you offer some price reductions, but do so selectively. You choose areas, or titles, which are distinctively important to your market, but may be ignored by other booksellers with different markets. Imagine a semi-specialist nautical bookshop, for example. The bookseller knows that mass-market paperbacks are likely to be on sale at a lower price in a nearby supermarket or chain bookshop, but also knows that nautical books will not even be stocked by these outlets. The bookseller may decide that it is worth offering some form of discount on the nautical books with the aim of attracting more people into the bookshop, and the hope that they will buy some of their holiday reading there at the same time.

If you can stay imaginative and innovative then doing your own thing on price is likely to be the most successful strategy. It almost goes without saying that it is also the most labour intensive method of pricing since you need to still work night and day to maximise your supplier discounts, but also you need to be one step ahead and always thinking of fresh ways to promote your offer to your customers.

Making the choice

All booksellers will try to choose a pricing strategy to suit their particular business. Many smaller bookshops have opted for a straightforward "no discount" strategy, based on their limited margin, their offer of a high level of personal service, and perhaps less direct competition across their product range. Others adopt a broadly similar approach, but do offer some limited discounting on selected titles, so adding a perception of value to their customer offer.

The bigger bookshops have been more aggressive in their take-up of competitive pricing on leading titles. This is explained partly by the larger discounts these booksellers can negotiate, and partly by the very keen competition between them.

A study of the textbooks may help you to come up with an answer on the best strategy, but in the end the unique qualities and features of your business mean that you alone should make the choice.

18. Management matters

Management is big business. It is big business because good management allows a business to grow, whereas poor management tends to let it wither.

Because businesses must be managed effectively – by people with differing skills and abilities – a large part of management today is involved with the ability to assess your own and other people's skills, and then to seek to fill the gaps. These gaps are the areas where you can improve your business knowledge, helping your business to run more effectively in the process.

Although it is often said that the British are a nation of shopkeepers, in reality very few people are fully aware of what is involved in running a successful retail business. You will have realised by now that there is much more to it than simply presenting goods to a public eager to buy. A whole raft of management ideas must be incorporated into the business if it is to succeed.

Many management skills are latent and can be teased out with dedicated learning and intuitive practice, though there will almost certainly be areas where you will need to call on some specialist help. This book aims to cover a lot of detailed bookselling, with just a few relevant general principles. If you are not already comfortable with some of the broader management issues in running a business, then you should read rather more widely. Look in any bookshop's business management section and you will find plenty of books to give you food for thought. If you have not already read quite a few of them, then perhaps now would be a good time to start.

Basics

Keeping your business "straight" is important, not just from a tax point of view. You must always have an accurate picture of how well the business is doing, what it can afford, and what is beyond its reach. There may perhaps be times when an "ostrich" approach has much to commend it, but dealing with the finances of your business is not one of them.

You have perhaps borrowed money to start up the business, or even mortgaged your home against the loan. If the business fails, you risk losing it as a consequence. Equally, if you have raised money by issuing shares in the business then you have a duty towards your shareholders. Company law is quite clear on the privileged position of shareholders and your responsibility to them is total.

By the same token you may have employed staff to help you run your business. You might consider yourself to have a moral duty of care towards them.

Running your bookshop well may help in some way to safeguard their future as well as your own.

Simply knowing how the business is doing is not enough, but it does give you a starting point to decide what you can do about it. It is for this reason that you should consider the management element of your bookshop very carefully. One thing is certain: the shop will not run itself.

Management information

Your business planning should have enabled you to identify the areas of which you need to be continually aware. They are likely to be closely connected to the factors (usually financial) which you have also identified as critical to the success of your business.

Movement – forward, you hope, but it may sometimes be backwards – lies at the core of business. This means that to be aware of what is happening as a general trend, you also need to be able to take "snapshots" as you move along. That way, you can see the direction of travel, and take action accordingly. Some areas of information are more important than others. Knowing your daily bank balance is more likely to benefit the business than knowing how many lavatory rolls there are in the store cupboard. The former is essential business information, the latter is not.

The following list gives some fairly typical examples of measures and information which a bookshop might think were critical, and worth monitoring. It is not comprehensive and aims only to give some pointers to the sort of thing that you may feel you need to watch as part of your active management of the bookshop.

- Number of customers per day;
- Daily till takings;
- Till takings as compared with last week/last year;
- Value of daily banking;
- Value of stock (perhaps by category);
- Average sale price to customers;
- Amount owed to suppliers currently outstanding;
- Value of outstanding orders;
- Number of customer orders;
- Number of customer complaints;
- Average delivery time from major suppliers;

- Sales per square foot;
- Absence levels among staff.

Once you have picked out the areas in which you need detailed and accurate information, you should set up whatever systems are necessary to deliver that information for you.

Certain data must be gathered if you are to comply with company law and general accounting standards, so you will be well advised to watch and monitor them carefully. Other things will prove enormously useful to the running and control of the business. Knowing the value of your stock at any one time gives you a good idea of how effectively you are running your buying and selling functions; knowing how much money you are owed tells you how effectively you are running your debt collection function.

There are still further areas it might be good to know about, but in practice it could be too time-consuming to get reliable data, and the information may not be absolutely essential to the effective running of the business. You are probably best to forget this sort of thing. Try to prioritise what you do monitor and keep. If you try to keep up with too many things you will suffer from both an information overload and a lack of time to do anything with it. The bookshop may grind to a halt if you are not careful.

Control mechanisms

In the business context the term "control" has few negative connotations of repression and restraint and means something far more constructive.

You start with a plan of what you intend to do. You then break it down into a detailed set of actions that will enable you to achieve your target. Simply putting the set of actions in place does not, however, guarantee the outcome. Enter the control mechanism.

There are two parts to the mechanism. The first is a system which determines what should happen, and what actually does happen. The second is involved with devising action to help bring the process back into line.

A typical example can be drawn from financial management, and the variance report. This report generally looks at what expenditure or income was budgeted for, and then at the actual level recorded. The variance between the two figures demonstrates the extent to which actual performance has differed from projected performance, as shown in Figure 18.1.

Month	Budget	Actual	Variance
January	£35,000	£36,000	+£1,000
February	£30,000	£30,000	£0
March	£30,000	£29,000	-£1,000
April	£30,000	£32,000	+£2,000
May	£30,000	£31,000	+£1,000
June	£30,000	£28,000	-£2,000
July	£35,000	£34,000	-£1,000
August	£30,000	£31,000	+£1,000
September	£30,000	£32,000	+£2,000
October	£30,000	£30,000	£0
November	£40,000	£37,000	-£3,000
December	£50,000	£52,000	+£2,000
Year total	**£400,000**	**£402,000**	**+£2,000**

Figure 18.1 Sales performance against budget

Here the first part of the control mechanism shows how actual sales have varied, on a month-by-month basis, from the budgeted sales. The second part of the control mechanism should be designed to allow a variety of corrective actions to be taken when actual sales vary from budgeted sales by a certain sum. The bookseller may, for instance, decide that a variance of £1,000 or less per month is not significant, but that any larger variance means some action must be taken. In the example above, action would have been required in the months of April, June, September, November and December. Where sales were below expectation, in June and November, the corrective action might have been to run an additional promotion to try to stimulate extra sales. Where sales were above expectation some extra stock buying may have been needed to keep up with demand.

Devising appropriate and effective control mechanisms is an important part of any manager's job. In theory almost every task should have a proper control mechanism attached to it. Delegation of a task, for example, should always have some form of confirmation that it really has been done built into it.

As far as organising the control mechanism, you may well find that the software you are using has suitable procedures already incorporated into it. If it does not, or if you need something a bit different from what is offered, then it is relatively easy to set up a simple system in Microsoft Excel, or any other proprietry spreadsheet package. Alternatively the more ambitious may wish to establish a database control mechanism using Microsoft Access or their own favourite database package. If you have the skills then using a database application is probably more useful in the long run simply because of the many figures that can be stored, manipulated and presented.

Skills with figures

Although the dissemination of literary appreciation may sum up bookselling for some people, successful trading calls for many skills and numeracy comes top of the list. The ability to work effectively with figures has a way of turning up wherever you look.

We are not talking serious accountancy skills here. Rather, we are talking about moderate competence in mental arithmetic and estimation. At its simplest level you need to feel confident that customers are given the correct change when they buy a book. Most modern tills show you this, but if basic levels of numeracy are missing mistakes are bound to be more frequent. They tend to be costly – either your profits are being given away when customers are given too much change; or your customers will be dissatisfied and annoyed if they are short-changed. Either way, accuracy is essential.

You will also need numeracy skills for cashing up your tills, for book-keeping, and for running stock control systems. If you know that your own numeracy skills are not high, it is worth doing something to improve them. You should also satisfy yourself that every member of staff you employ has adequate numeracy.

Accounts and payroll

The procedures to use for accounting systems must be strict. You would normally agree them with your accountant in advance since this simplifies the annual audit that the business must have as part of its accounting process. A simpler audit should, with luck, be less expensive as well.

The business also needs to operate a formal payroll system for paying your staff. Pay should be worked out in accordance with their contract or with the number of hours they have worked (there might be extra pay for overtime or for any Sunday work). Depending on the terms of their contract, there may be deductions for absence and, once gross pay has been calculated, tax and National Insurance payments may have to be deducted. If there is a company pension scheme, then this is also the point at which any deductions for individual pension contributions are made.

All these payments and deductions must be recorded for possible tax inspection at a later date. It is also worth remembering that you will almost certainly have to keep proper personal records of any income and expenditure for your own income tax under the self-assessment system.

Value added tax

Although books are not subject to a positive rate of VAT in either the UK or in Ireland, most of the other goods that a bookshop might decide to sell (greeting cards, music, stationery, etc.) do attract the full rate, currently set at 17.5%.

When goods are sold subject to VAT, the selling price must be increased so that a sum equal to 17.5% of the intended selling price is added. This portion does not form any part of thc bookshop's takings.

Boxes of Christmas cards illustrate the calculation to be made. Each box costs the bookshop £1.00 and the intended selling price is £2.00, but VAT must be introduced into the calculation. Current VAT rules mean that 17.5% of the £2.00 (i.e. 35p) must be accounted for as VAT. The VAT-inclusive selling price therefore becomes £2.35. As each box of cards is sold, £2.00 is allocated to the bookshop's sales, with the 35p allocated to its VAT account.

VAT accounting is a cumbersome process, but it must be completed with rigorous accuracy or you risk both the wrath of your VAT inspector and potential financial penalties. VAT payments to HM Customs and Excise are generally made quarterly in arrears, calculated on the difference between the VAT elements of sales and purchases invoices in each quarter.

The VAT for certain overhead costs and the purchase of fixed assets can be recovered. Your accountant will be able to advise in detail, and HM Customs and Excise also offer help and advice to traders.

Security

A bookshop, like any retail operation with hopes of success, has security issues to consider. It puts attractive products on open view to the public and asks for money to pay for them. Two immediate weaknesses should be apparent.

First, although most people are prepared to pay money for the books on offer, some individuals (regrettably, they may include members of your own staff) would prefer to take them without paying, either to save themselves money or to sell them on in the black economy later and generate profit for themselves. Your stock is, therefore, at risk.

The next issue is that the money your honest customers are paying for the books they buy is even more attractive to those dishonest people who would like to relieve you of the takings. These people may be other members of the public or, again, members of your staff. So your cash operation is also in jeopardy. Let us take the two areas in this order.

Stock

You can take a number of steps to help safeguard your stock. By looking carefully at the layout of your shop you should be able to identify some areas where the books are more generally visible, and others that are relatively hidden from sight. Especially for the latter, mirrors or closed circuit television will help. It is also a good idea to site the more expensive, more attractive stock in areas that are clearly visible to you and your staff.

An increasingly popular method of deterring shoplifting is electronic tagging. You receive a supply of sticky labels, disguised as either price labels or barcodes, to put on the books, plus a set of electronic barrier gates that are installed at the shop door. Each label contains some miniaturised electronic circuitry which will activate an alarm if it has not been deactivated at the till before it passes through the barrier.

There is a possibility that once the costs of a new technology called Radio Frequency Identification, or RFID, tagging become lower, then the booktrade will move towards tagging at source. This works on the principle that the publisher incorporates an RFID tag into the book during the production process. Any bookseller who has a compatible detection system automatically then has a security tagging control over their stock.

The most effective deterrent you have, however, is probably staff vigilance. If you and your staff make a point of staying alert and watching what is happening around you, then you are more likely to deter any prospective shoplifter. You will probably fail to deter a real professional, but you may well succeed in putting off many of the opportunistic thieves.

Dishonest staff are a separate problem. You might establish a routine of random bag-checking as staff leave the bookshop. It can be perceived as a blatant lack of trust, but equally as an opportunity for your staff to demonstrate their honesty.

You may also find it helpful to talk to your local crime prevention police officers. They can often give helpful advice on the prevention of shoplifting and also offer guidance on what to do if you do apprehend a shoplifter.

Cash

Cash security involves two issues, both of which you need to consider as management matters.

The first is the development of sound cash handling rules and procedures to ensure that cash does not "vanish" between your tills and your bank reconciliation. You should remember that if you are a director of the bookshop you have a legal responsibility under company law to ensure that you do everything possible to minimise the chances of fraud within the company. This issue involves deciding what recording procedures will be used, and whether or not they will be witnessed. It also involves setting up spot-checking procedures to ensure that things are as they should be at any given moment. (If you do not feel confident about establishing such procedures your accountant should be able to advise.)

The second issue concerns the general physical security of cash. Make sure that the tills can be locked when no one is at them. This will help to reduce the chance of opportunistic till snatches. It is also worth working out a procedure to ensure that when a till contains a certain amount of money, a "till lift" is done to take surplus notes into the office for safe-keeping. This way, you minimise your loss if there is a till snatch. Procedures like this are more relevant, of course, at busy times of the year than during slack periods.

You should be discreet when gathering money from tills to take into the office, since you are potentially vulnerable to a mugging at this point. Make sure, too, that the office where you count money is out of public view, with a good lock on the door. This is where you gather cash and it becomes a cash nerve centre for the shop. Keep the door locked at all times. This will keep the "lost customers wandering around in the back shop" (known colloquially as thieves) out of the office, and at the same time keep you secure.

Security is top priority whenever you take money to the bank. Your insurance company will probably issue instructions on how many able-bodied people should be involved in the exercise. It may be fine for one person to go if the cash carried is below a certain sum, but two people may be needed for larger deposits. Always adhere to the rules, for if you break them and are then mugged your insurance cover will probably be null and void.

Once again, further advice on the physical security of cash will be available from your local crime prevention police officers.

Premises

It is worth mentioning the general security of your premises at this point. Some conditions will undoubtedly be set by your insurance company. Bookshops are not unduly at risk, although if you also sell cigarettes through a news agency you probably run higher risks than others.

The insurers will probably require you to have a burglar alarm, possibly with a direct link to a monitoring service. They will also stipulate that sound locks be installed on all external doors and windows. Make sure you follow their advice or, again, you may render your cover void.

Further advice

If you still feel that your bookshop may be vulnerable, get external advice. The obvious port of call on most aspects of physical security is the local police station. For any help you need with management-related questions start with your accountant or local chamber of commerce.

Professional help

When and whence to engage professional help is one area where every bookseller, particularly every small bookseller, has to make difficult choices.

Unless you have up-to-date accountancy skills you will need an accountant to prepare your year-end accounts. Furthermore, if you are a limited company with an annual turnover in excess of £350,000 you will also need to have the accounts audited. However, if you are a sole trader or a partnership you will not require an audit, whatever your turnover.

You do have a choice in deciding what firms to use. Here it is worth talking to several and getting a realistic idea of the scale of fees if possible. If you know the likely parameters of any assistance you are going to need, then these can form the basis of what almost amounts to a quote. It is also useful to try and talk to some of the firm's other clients to see if they are happy with the service they get. Never allow yourself to be cowed: after all, you are the customer.

It is when you move beyond specific requirements that life gets a bit harder. Professional advice is invariably expensive and it is always tempting to think one can do without it and save some money. However, the costs resulting from failing to get correct advice at the right time can be high, so strike a balance whenever you consider the question. In time, you may need to think about using the services of some or all of the professionals detailed below.

Accountants

Having accountants who do their job well and whom you can trust is an enormous boon to your business. If their advice is not sound, you may run into all sorts of tax or audit difficulties. If you feel dissatisfied your bank may be able to advise.

Solicitors

You will need a solicitor to deal with the legal part of any property transaction, either when you start up your first shop or when you open another. You may also need legal advice on such diverse things as company law, employment law or succession planning. You should always consider legal representation if you are involved in an industrial tribunal.

Architects

An architect will be useful if you find a property needing considerable conversion into a bookshop, or have one with potential for development. A competent professional should be able to come up with a variety of ideas to achieve whatever you want. Each idea will be separately costed.

Estate Agents

Make sure that any estate agents you use when you look for bookshop premises or try to sell property has full experience of commercial, and not only domestic property.

Designers

You may decide to use a professional designer to create exactly the image you want for your bookshop. Advice will usually be offered across a whole range of areas, and you should weigh up each proposal in terms of its costs and what it will achieve. A great many "add-ons" can quickly inflate the bill.

Consultants

You may decide to use a consultant to help you with some specific and more specialised areas of the business. Consultancies proliferate today and are very commonly used for marketing or computerisation, for example. Here again, you should try to find an individual or company with the most relevant experience and ideally compare notes with other people who have used their services. Try contacting the BA for information on recommended consultants.

Other ideas

There are occasions when you can get useful and free quasi-professional help. Perhaps the most notable example is ACAS, the Advisory, Conciliation and

Arbitration Service, which provides a telephone advice service (available to both employers and employees) on questions of employment law.

The enquiry most commonly put to ACAS seems to concern potential dismissal and whether such an action is likely to be construed as unfair. Its advisers expect to be given a concise and accurate picture of the issue in question, and will then offer advice on how best to proceed. There is also a range of very helpful booklets on various aspects of employment law available, as well as free usage of the business support helpline for BA members.

19. Financial considerations

This chapter aims to give what is necessarily an introductory, simple summary of the financial side of bookselling,. Whilst many things are common between businesses there are some concepts, such as Rate of Stock Turn, that have far greater importance to bookselling than they do to many other businesses.

Gross profit

Gross profit is the starting point of the bookshop's financial pepper mill. It is the first of the really important financial aspects of the business that must be fully understood, so we proceed from basics.

Books are bought from a supplier at a trade price. Normally this is lower than the price at which they are to be sold on to the customer. In terms of the business the gross profit the bookshop generates is the value of the sales made, less the costs attached to the stock that was bought to generate the sales. This is usually expressed as sales less cost of sales, as shown in Figure 19.1.

Gross profit = Sales - Cost of sales

Figure 19.1 Gross profit

The cost of sales is fairly self-explanatory, but the process of computing it is less straightforward. Two important figures are created when the bookshop does its annual stock-taking at the end of the financial year. In fact, only one figure is produced, but it serves two purposes.

The value of the total stock becomes both the closing stock for the financial year just ended, and the opening stock for the financial year just beginning. The initial raw result from the stock-taking will generally be modified to take account of any late invoices or outstanding credits for returns and it is further adjusted to reflect the loss of value resulting from any old or damaged stock.

It is then necessary to reduce the modified stocktaking figures, which will almost always be at retail price, to a cost price. Multiplying the figures by an agreed factor to reflect the average discounts that are received by the bookshop usually does this. It makes much sense at this stage to apply different reduction factors to the various classes of stock where average discount rates may vary, such as hardbacks, paperbacks and stationery, for instance. Such changes will usually be agreed with the auditor, and may have to be justified to the Inland Revenue.

The other figure that is needed to calculate the cost of sales is the total value of purchases. This will be available from the bookshop's purchase ledger. Once all these figures are produced, the calculation can be made, as shown in Figure 19.2 below.

Cost of sales = Opening stock + Purchases - Closing stock

Figure 19.2 Cost of sales

In other words, the cost of sales is the purchases plus the change in stock value, both calculated at cost price. The cost of sales is designed to match the cost of the purchases made during the year with the sales that were generated in the same period.

Assuming that the bookshop has sales of £400,000, an opening stock of £110,000, a closing stock of £115,000 and purchases of £283,250, the cost of sales is then calculated by reducing the retail stocktaking figures to cost by, let us say, 35%:

£110,000 * 65% = £71,500 and £115,000 * 65% = £74,750

£71,500 + £283,250 - £74,750 = £280,000

This means that the gross profit for the bookshop is:

£400,000 - £280,000 = £120,000

The gross profit can also be usefully expressed as a percentage of the sales. The bookshop has therefore generated a gross profit of £120,000/£400,000 - or 30%.

Profitability

It is worth exploring some simplified variations of the impact of the cost of sales on operation. Imagine three shops, all with the same £400,000 turnover and the same stock levels at the beginning and end of the year; their opening stock is £100,000 and their closing stock £110,000. The difference between the three shops, however, lies in the level of purchases they have to make to sustain their sales. This difference in purchases has a substantial impact on their profitability.

Shop 1 has purchases totalling £275,000 over the year; the purchases in shop 2 amount to £285,000, while shop 3 has purchases of £260,000. Each shop has a different cost of sales. This in turn means that each has a different gross profit. These differences are illustrated in Figure 19.3 below.

	Shop 1	Shop 2	Shop 3
Opening stock	£71,500	£71,500	£71,500
Purchases	+£275,000	+£295,000	+£260,000
Closing stock	-£74,750	-£74,750	-£74,750
Cost of sales	£271,750	£291,750	£256,750

Figure 19.3 Comparative costs of sales

The differences become very apparent when the gross profit that each shop makes is computed, as shown in Figure 19.4.

	Shop 1	Shop 2	Shop 3
Sales	£400,000	£400,000	£400,000
Cost of sales	£271,750	£291,750	£256,750
Gross profit	£128,250	£108,250	£143,250
GPM	32.1%	27.1%	35.8%

Figure 19.4 Comparative gross profit margins

An example like this is purely illustrative, of course, since all three shops have so many identical financial details. The impact of the purchases figure on gross margin is, however, highly relevant. Shop 3 has managed to spend significantly less on stock to support sales than the other two shops.

There are two obvious reasons, and one less obvious, for this. First, the discount shop 3 received from suppliers may have been larger than shops 1 and 2 received. Secondly, shop 3 may have suffered far fewer losses through shoplifting than the other two. The less obvious reason is that shop 3 has been buying and controlling stock more effectively than the other two, making more effort to return unsold stock for credit and having had less need to write off poor stock in cut-price sales. Shop 2 on the other hand has perhaps had to make serious price reductions to move some of its poor stock. Sales have been identical, but less value was generated on the titles that were sold off, so the purchases, relatively, were higher.

It must be stressed that the figures used have been stretched deliberately to illustrate the point, but by the same token it is important to understand the effect that buying can have on gross profit. Because it is first base in the bookselling game, making sure that the business generates an adequate level of gross profit is essential – and you can very easily reduce it through poor management, chiefly as a result of any of the following:

- buying at lower margins or attracting penalties on small orders;
- failing to identify and claim for invoice errors;
- failing to secure credits for every returns consignment;
- poor buying – leading to excessive write-off of stock in sales;
- suffering higher than average theft, internal or external;
- Provided you are careful to manage your stock efficiently, your shop should generate an adequate gross profit.

It is a very useful practice to review your gross margin on as regular a basis as possible. If you find that your actual gross margin is different from your expected gross margin then a detailed investigation is important. Providing you approach the matter logically you may be able to uncover why the difference has occurred, and then take appropriate remedial steps. For instance it could be that your staff have not understood the need to add VAT to the prices of stationery items – as a result you immediately lose 17.5% of your margin on those sales. If this were to be the case, then additional training would be indicated. You may, of course, find that your security has not been as good as you thought it was. True the horse may have bolted, but you can prevent the same thing happening again by introducing new rules!

Net profit

The maintenance of an adequate level of net profit is equally vital. It is calculated by deducting all the business expenses from the gross margin. Conventionally the expenses are divided into three sets of costs: employment; occupancy; and "other".

Employment costs are quite self-explanatory. They include the obvious cost of wages, plus any pension costs and national insurance payments. Occupancy expenses cover more than simple rent and rates and tend to take in energy and repairs costs, together with any service charge levied by, for instance, a shopping centre.

"Other" working costs is a vast heading and many booksellers find it helpful to subdivide it. Some obvious headings include: financial and banking; printing, stationery, packing materials and returns costs; and publicity and advertising costs. Any individual is free, of course, to aggregate the mass of expenses into some cohesive form that makes the dynamics of the bookshop more comprehensible. The thing to remember is that, however precisely you flag up and assign costs, they must be met from the gross profit.

Still using the £400,000 turnover bookshop as an illustration, the likely net profit scenario in its profit and loss account is shown at Figure 19.5.

Turnover	£400,000	
Cost of sales	£265,000	
Gross profit	£135,000	(34.5%)
Employment costs	£52,000	
Occupancy costs	£42,000	
Other working costs	£33,000	
Net profit	£8,000	(2%)

Figure 19.5 Net profit

In today's bookselling environment, this would represent a reasonable, but not brilliant, level of net profit. In financial terms it is not likely to allow the business to re-invest heavily and other injections of finance would be needed to enable it to grow significantly.

One should appreciate that the desire to expand is not universal in business and many people would see more benefit in a simple ability to remain independent. This is justifiable, but one should not forget that such a low level of net profitability leaves a business very vulnerable to aggressive competitors, since it significantly lowers the level of reinvestment that is possible.

Projecting profit and loss

An important part of your business plan is projecting your profit and loss for the coming twelve months. You should have been able to project forward your sales and, providing you have an average margin figure, this will allow you to project your likely gross margin generation over the year. By assessing your probable expenses for the period you will then reach some form of prediction of the likely result.

You should be careful that the figures you use for the projection are as reasonable as possible. You fool no one if you project impossible sales figures or expenses that are unreasonably low. The whole idea of the exercise is to get as realistic a picture as possible of how your business will perform in the next year. This will also help you to see how you might improve it. One important aspect is to carefully note any assumptions that you make. This will prove helpful later on, since you will be able to see much more clearly how your thinking was, perhaps, influenced by what has turned out to be a false assumption.

With the projected profit and loss set up you should go on to consider a control mechanism for monitoring each month's performance so that you can see how close you are to the original plan and decide whether or not you should take any corrective action.

Capital requirements

Your business will need capital, both as start-up funding when you are creating it and for working purposes when it is up and running. The capital may come from your own or shareholders' investment in the business, from the bank in some form of secured loan, or from a venture capital company.

That is the summary. Financing a business is well beyond the scope of this book and you will of course discuss the matter in great detail with your accountant, financial adviser or bank before you make any move at all.

Cash flow

Cash – the most important commodity that your business will possess – must be guarded and nurtured to ensure that it is always working for you.

Cash flow is the way accountants describe the flow of cash into and out of a business. Anyone unfamiliar with the term might find a reservoir a useful analogy in this case. A dry summer will drain the reservoir because there is little rainfall to make up for consumption. In business terms this is negative cashflow, i.e. the level of cash in the business falls. The opposite happens when a wet winter makes the water level exceed consumption. In a business this is a period of positive cash flow, i.e. the level of cash in the business grows.

In the bookshop, cash flows into the business when sales are high, but large outgoings, like rent, are low. When, however, low sales coincide with a large bill for rent or stock the cash position is drained and the business experiences a negative cash flow.

Academic bookshops illustrate the cycle well. They enjoy a good period at the beginning of term when sales are high and money floods into the business. The set books are in stock and, provided the orders were well timed, the invoices will not need to be paid until the next month. The result is that at the end of the month the shops' cash balances are much better than at the beginning.

By the next month, however, sales will begin to slacken, while all the invoices for the books sold during the previous month need to be paid. Outgoings are relatively higher than incomings, so the bookshops experience a negative cash flow.

Projecting a realistic picture of future cash flow is an important part of business planning for the bookshop, enabling the bookshop owner to predict when borrowings might be needed and what level of overdraft will be required. Your bank will expect a realistic projection from you, too. It is particularly important in the early stages of the business when you will have a lot of outgoings and very few incomings. Your initial projections will therefore show a large cash deficit for the first few months, but should also indicate how the deficit should disappear as the business begins to take off.

You should maintain a very careful eye on the flow of cash and should regularly update your projections. It is relatively easy to set up spreadsheets that will, at the very least, give you reasonably accurate cash flow projections. Clearly the more information you put in, and the more accurately it is predicted, then the more accurate the projection. The process can, however, become time consuming, so a sense of balance must be retained.

You will have some flexibility over your cash flow. For instance, whilst most bills need to be paid on time some expenditure, such as putting in new shelving, can be delayed to an appropriate time when your cash reserves are healthier.

A key outcome of such projections is the ability to predict when there is a need to advise the bank that things are not going to plan. If expected sales have not materialised, or if unexpected expenditure is required urgently, then your cash flow will be affected. There may be an opportunity to modify expenditure plans in the light of unexpectedly low sales, but this may not be possible, in which case your cash reserves will fall.

Management accounts

Management accounts are a peculiar thing – you will either love them or hate them! The idea is that you carefully measure your progress against your original budget, usually on a monthly, or perhaps quarterly, basis. The finished report allows you to see very quickly which figures have a discrepancy between reality and budget. If those figures are expenses and they are higher than expected, or if they are sales and are lower than expected, then your profitability is likely to be lower than you hoped.

It is customary to measure for both the immediate period and also for the year to date. Thus if your financial year begins on 1 January, and you are looking at the management accounts for May, you would need actual and budget figures for the period of May, and also for the combined months of January through to May. This does mean a lot of data processing but most accounting packages will make this a bit easier.

This analysis allows you then to take remedial action, or at least to think about what you might do to remedy the problem. It may involve bringing additional marketing and promotions into play. Alternatively it may involve trimming costs, or delaying projects.

As with the preparation of detailed cash flow reports there is a lot of background work needed. Figures have to be carefully analysed and categorised into the correct area of sales or expenses. Unless this is done with a high degree of attention to detail then the results may well not be worth the effort.

Open-to-buy budgeting

One area of budgeting that is becoming increasingly popular again is that of open-to-buy budgeting as a means of controlling stock levels. The fundamental idea is that over and above your stock control system you consider the amount of cash that will be devoted to stock purchases each month. This then allows you to match more closely your purchases with your sales so that you maintain your expected level of financial investment in stock throughout the year. As with all budgeting processes the detail is enormous and this may in fact undermine the practicality of such a system for your shop.

To set up an open-to-buy budget you start with the opening stock for the year, and then add to that your monthly sales budget for the year. You then choose your preferred level of closing stock for the end of the year, and your target rate of stock turn.

If we decide on a target RST of 4 this means we will anticipate holding three month's stock at any one time. Working on our bookshop with a turnover of £400,000 and an opening stock of £100,000 we may feel that the year's sales will be made up as follows:

	Jan	Feb	Mar	Apr	May	Jun	Jul	Aug	Sep	Oct	Nov	Dec
1	£35k	£30k	£30k	£30k	£30k	£30k	£35k	£30k	£30k	£30k	£40k	£50k
2	£100k	£100k	£90k	£90k	£90k	£95k	£95k	£95k	£90k	£100k	£120k	£125k
3	£65k	£70k	£60k	£60k	£60k	£65k	£60k	£65k	£60k	£70k	£80k	£75k
4	£100k	£90k	£90k	£90k	£95k	£95k	£95k	£90k	£100k	£120k	£125k	£110k
5	£35k	£20k	£30k	£30k	£35k	£30k	£35k	£25k	£40k	£50k	£45k	£35k

Figure 19.6 Open-to-buy budgeting

Row 1 is the predicted sales for the month. Row 2 is the stock value, at retail, at the opening of the month. Row 3 is the balance of stock that would be left if no purchases are made during the month. Row 4 is the closing stock for the month, at retail and based upon the target RST. Row 5 is the level of purchases that need to be made during the month in order to attain the desired closing stock level.

Using this table it becomes easy to see how your purchases should be varied across the year in order to keep your stock levels at the desired financial investment.

To set up such a system fully you need to know your opening stock, at retail value, and you also need to be able to log your purchases, again at retail value, throughout each month. These two figures, together with your monthly sales figures then allow you to monitor your progress.

If you find, for instance that your sales are exceeding your target but that your purchases have, up to now, maintained the budgeted level, you need to increase your purchases to compensate for the increased sales. If, however, your sales have not made target but your purchases have, then your stock levels will be growing and your investment in stock will be increasing. If this happens you probably need to trim back your purchases in order to regain the balance.

It would be wrong to suggest that implementing an effective open-to-buy budget system is easy. It isn't, but it can offer some considerable financial rewards if it is done. Knowing how much you have invested in stock, often a critical determinant of success, is a key management requirement. Having the tools to control it makes it a powerful weapon in your armoury.

20. Financial expectations

The two questions that are almost certainly uppermost in the mind of any prospective bookshop owner are:

How much will it cost me? and

How much money will I make out of it?

Both are almost impossible to answer. In general terms the more you put in, the more you will make; by the same token, if things go wrong – and they sometimes do – the more you stand to lose. Careful commercial assessment of the prospects and risks at an early stage of planning is the best safeguard.

Size of property, location, site, competition, proposed levels of stockholding and the affluence of the surrounding catchment area will all have a major impact on the bookshop's financial prospects. The detailed business plan outlined in Chapter 5 will have to reflect the limits you set on some of these variables. It is critically important to consider the full financial implications at the beginning of any new business. If it looks disappointing on paper and you are satisfied that your calculations are reasonably accurate, it is best to drop the project right away. This is far better than being forced to abandon it several months later, with all the attendant costs, after you find out the true picture.

You will need to consider both the projected capital costs of setting up the bookshop and the likely return on your trading. Until the business is up and running you must remember that you are only working on estimates. They may well be best estimates but, as investment companies are obliged to remind us, estimates can go up, or go down, depending upon circumstances that are not always within our control.

Estimated turnover

In Chapter 6 we looked at the range of turnover that might be generated per square foot of selling space. You should remember that these values are generally calculated from established bookshops. Your early years of trading may produce a lower turnover, even if you exceed expectations when you are established.

Turnover is estimated by multiplying the selling area of the projected bookshop (in square feet) by the estimated turnover that will be generated per square foot. As explained, you will have to estimate the level of sales density your location will be able to generate. For this example we will assume a rather smaller town location which is thought likely to generate £240 per square foot initially, but rise to around £270 per square foot in due course. So if your new bookshop is to have 1,500 square foot of selling space you might expect to generate a turnover in the region of £360,000 in the first year or so, and see this go up to around £400,000 or pro rata, depending on prevailing rates of inflation once the shop is established.

You may be more successful than this, of course, or less successful if you are unlucky. The point is that you must have some ball park figures in mind if you are to start calculating your likely financial costs.

Estimated gross margin

Not all the factors which influence gross margin are within your direct control, so that estimating it is not easy.

The figure may also be influenced by your decision on ordering either direct from publishers or through wholesalers. As a smaller bookseller you are probably best advised to use a wholesaler where most of your likely book requirements can be provided from one source. Consolidating your buying power means you will probably achieve higher discount, particularly if you look towards competitive tendering between wholesalers.

A discount level of around 38% overall would be a reasonable expectation for a single bookshop in start-up phase. Because you will lose a certain amount of margin through theft and the build-up of poor stock, a gross margin of around 33% might be a realistic working figure for your first calculations.

On this basis you would expect a gross margin of £118,800 from your estimated sales of £360,000.

Estimated net margin

It is when you come to calculate a net margin that you are likely to realise that running a bookshop is far from simple, for the likely net margin with which you are left will almost certainly turn out to be smaller than you expected or hoped for.

The estimated gross margin of £118,800 must fund all of the running costs of your business. This means property costs, staffing costs, overdraft and banking costs, advertising costs and every other kind of bill will have to be met from the gross margin you expect to generate from your first year's trading.

Realism is crucial here too. You must undertake an assessment of the likely running costs of your projected bookshop to come to any true estimate of your probable expense. We shall discuss some pointers to the likely costs later in this book. Talking to working booksellers may also help you, but bear in mind that, in a competitive book trade, some may be reluctant to divulge very much detail.

Many booksellers are pleased if they can generate a net margin of around 2.5% of sales. On the basis of our working estimates so far (i.e. a turnover of £400,000), this would mean that you might expect your bookshop to generate a net profit of around £10,000. You must now decide whether this is the sort of return you want on your money, but you should also bear in mind that a bookshop is a cultural as well as financial asset.

Of course, if you own the property or can get by with minimal paid help, your net margin may be higher. Equally, if you have had to borrow heavily to open the bookshop, then your financial costs might lower your expected margin still further.

At this stage the important thing to remember is that these are purely estimates of the likely performance of your business, designed to help you decide whether you wish to go on with the idea of a retail bookshop as a business opportunity. If you are looking for a purely financial involvement with a retail business, then you may find other retail opportunities more rewarding than bookselling.

Break-even points

An important element in the financial consideration of opening a business is the relationship between fixed costs, running costs, sales and profitability. It can be explored using the financial tool known as break-even point analysis.

The concept involved is that the fixed costs of the business, by definition, do not vary with sales. A qualification to be made here is that some bookshops located in shopping centre developments may have a lease stipulating that the basic rent will increase (usually by a fixed percentage of additional sales) when turnover reaches a certain point, but they are an exception and rent does not as a rule relate to a bookshop's ability to generate sales. Against the fixed costs there are variable costs like wages or paper bags which usually increase as the volume of sales increases.

21. Start-up costs

Some of the expenses involved in setting up a business are genuinely "one-off". These are usually known as "start-up costs" to distinguish them from the "running costs" which the business will incur year after year.

The level and extent of these costs must be carefully controlled since, by definition, they must be paid before the business starts trading. This means they are met from your own capital reserves or from a loan, and that there will be no immediate return of cash to your reserves until the business is up and running. If you under-estimate them you could find yourself running out of money before the shop even opens, which tends to be unpopular with financial backers.

In such instances you would have little option but to try and increase your loan, but you will find some resistance to this since it will make the bank wonder about the rest of your predictions. For this reason it is probably useful to try and over-estimate the likely costs and also build in the worst case scenario for timings into your initial business plan.

Premises costs

Local market factors play such a large role in property costs that it is difficult to generalise. Prices vary so much from place to place and even within a small area the difference between top price for prime retail space, and the bottom end of the market is likely to be highly significant.

Look back to Chapter 6 and its detailed consideration of location to refresh your memory of the important issues here. A knowledgeable local agent is the best person to discuss figures with once you have determined your size requirements and made a shortlist of the geographical areas that interest you.

Your choice on property is likely to be between freehold, where you own or mortgage the property, and leasehold, which is probably used more frequently since it allows access to properties in busier retail areas.

When retail property is enjoying a boom there is often a shortage of it. This means that landlords are able to seek a premium before signing up a lease. In other words, you are asked to pay them for the privilege of getting a lease. At other times there may be a local surplus of retail property, perhaps because of generally poor retail performance, and here you may be offered an inducement – a rent-free period or help with your shopfitting costs, for example – to take up a lease.

The premises element of your start-up costs is likely, therefore, to consist of a premium or a deposit, together with professional fees for solicitors and estate agents. You need proper advice because you should not forget that in signing a lease you sign a legally binding document which may run for up to twenty-five years.

You should also note that there are significant variations in the legal aspects of dealing with property between England and Wales, and Scotland. One reaches the stage of legal commitment sooner in Scotland than in England or Wales and once past this point backing out will incur serious financial penalties, if indeed it is possible.

Shopfitting

Shopfitting costs are a further variable since they depend very much on the extent of work to be done and on the quality of finish you specify. If you move into an existing retail unit with usable flooring, wiring, ceilings, lighting, etc. already in place your costs will be much lower than if you move into a newly created bare concrete shell in a shopping centre.

The bigger bookselling chains reckon on spending between around £60 and £100 per square foot on fitting out new retail premises. This figure covers structural alterations, shelving and display units, carpets, lighting, security, a new shop front and so on although, if extensive work or particularly high quality standards are required, it will rise significantly. At the other extreme, a small independent might aim to keep any structural modification to a minimum and concentrate resources on the functional aspects of the business rather than on the decorative and image side. Using this basic approach shopfitting costs reduce to only £25 to £30 per square foot. However, even this low specification means that start-up costs come out at £25,000 for quite a small bookshop of 1,000 square foot, and so must be considered carefully.

The conundrum facing small start-up booksellers is that if they cut all corners to ensure that the bookshop opens before it goes bankrupt, then the shop may look so unattractive that customers prefer to buy elsewhere. On the other hand, if all resources are put into shopfitting, leaving too little cash to finance a broad and interesting range of opening stock, customers may like the feel of the shop, but fail to find the books they want and be put off from paying a second visit.

Opening stock

The third major cost involved in setting up a new bookshop is the purchase of the opening stock. From your initial financial calculations you should have formed a picture of your potential turnover, which you can then relate to a target stock level. You should also have formed a view of the likely stock volume – in terms of stock value per square foot – that you want to target. These two figures should give you roughly the same figure, as Figure 21.1 shows.

Bookshop sales area:	1,500 square feet
Expected turnover:	£360,000
Target rate of stock turn	3.5
Target stock level	£102,857
Intended stock volume	£70 per square foot
Target stock level	£105,000

Figure 21.1 Opening stock requirements

You now have an idea of the probable opening stock value that you should have in place when you open your doors to the public. This will be at retail cost, of course. For planning purposes you need to know how much that is actually likely to cost. This is easily worked out by adjusting the retail value by the average discount, as shown in Figure 21.2.

Target stock level	£105,000
Average discount	38%
Cost price	£105,000 x (100 - 38)%
Opening stock	£65,100

Figure 21.2 Opening stock cost

You now have the probable cost of your opening stock and can add the figure to your total start-up costs.

22. Running costs

Running costs, as distinct from start-up or capital costs, are those which are necessary to keep your business on the road. They are usually regular expenses, with a degree of predictability about them which enables you to build them into your budgets and forecast your future financial position with greater certainty.

Premises costs

Unless you own freehold you will pay rent to a landlord. Rental is usually paid quarterly on specified dates throughout the calendar year. If your annual rent is £40,000 you would expect to make four payments of £10,000 each – perhaps in January, April, July and October. Prompt payment is likely to be a condition of the lease. There may also be a service charge element in your rental, particularly if you are located in a shopping centre. You will also have to pay rates to your local council, which will usually offer various options about paying, ranging from one large annual payment to monthly payments under a direct debit arrangement.

The insurance of the property often comes in here. It should be the correct type and level for the business, a matter on which a reputable insurance broker will be able to advise. If you do not have one the Booksellers Association can put you in touch with its service partner.

All these outgoings are generally fixed for a specified period of time, allowing you to take account of the payments in your cash flow predictions.

Property also generates running costs in such areas as the repair and maintenance of the building. The lease will probably require you to maintain the fabric of the building, so you will need to cost in maintenance and cover for any emergency repairs. Major repairs are usually reasonably predictable and can perhaps be seen as major items of expenditure rather than running costs. Other repairs can crop up unexpectedly and will then make surprise demands on your budget. Some level of planned maintenance can help here – if for no other reason than the fact that there may be some spare budget which can be used to deal with the emergency while the planned repair waits for another year.

Heating and lighting costs throughout the year must be allowed for, too. They depend on the size of the premises and on the level and power of the systems that are in place, as well as on seasonal variations. With time you will be able to see a pattern develop. The costs should not vary too much from year to year so budgeting is again fairly simple. If you find that costs do go up quite suddenly check the systems – a switching system may have failed or perhaps a water heater has been left on continuously. You will keep costs down if you try to ensure that all systems are well maintained and energy-efficient.

The following checklist sums up the sort of costs which you should think about under premises costs.

- Rent
- Rates
- Insurance
- Heating and lighting
- Renewals
- Maintenance
- Repairs

Purchases

The obvious continuing drain on your cash reserves is the obligation to pay for the stock you have bought as invoices become due for payment.

In reality your purchases have more to do with your cash flow than with your running costs, but they should be carefully considered as one of the costs of the bookshop.

If you stop buying new stock you will very rapidly go out of business, but the longer the credit period you can negotiate with suppliers, the more time you give yourself to try to sell the stock before payment is due. Equally, the higher the discount you negotiate on stock, the less you have to pay in relation to its resale price.

We saw in Chapter 13 how effective stock control can be used to make the maximum sales from the minimum investment in stock. This way you make the best use of the resources put into purchasing stock. If, however, you do not buy as effectively as you might, you will find that your purchases rise as a proportion of your sales – a development which can have dramatic consequences for your bookshop.

Wages costs

Your staff will expect to be paid for their efforts. They have a contractual right to be paid at the rate agreed, in full on the due date.

The number of people working in the bookshop and the total wages bill generated are matters that you control, so be careful to keep the wages costs within your original budget. It is very easy to feel that you must have more people since there are so many different jobs to be done in a bookshop, ranging from unpacking the books to running stock control systems and serving customers to keeping accounts and changing the window display. The pressure on everyone's time can be intense.

It is useful to consider the wages budget in terms of a set percentage of sales. To arrive at this figure you should first assess roughly how many staff you think you need and then work out how many you think you can afford. The truth probably lies somewhere between the two. If you then divide that figure by your anticipated sales you will come up with your wages budget as a percentage of sales. The figure will probably be somewhere between about 9% and 14%. If it is not, it may be worth looking at the numbers again.

If you find that sales are increasing faster than you had expected, you are probably wise to increase the wages budget. When you have worked out your wages budget as a percentage of sales, this becomes fairly simple.

You should remember that you can make the most flexible use of this budget by employing people for the hours at which the bookshop really needs them. The early part of the day is often quite quiet and you may be able to get away with fewer staff, saving them for the times when the shop becomes busier.

Remember that the wages costs include such extras as national insurance, pension contributions and directors' emoluments.

Distribution costs

Distribution costs usually include such items as the bookshop's postage and mailing expenses, any packing materials used, and the cost of the paper and carrier bags for customer purchases.

Paper bags call for some thought, since the cost can vary considerably according to the sort of design and quality you plan to use. It also depends on whether you wish to be seen to use recycled paper as a "green" issue.

Any motor vehicle (a company car, for example, or if you charge mileage, etc.) or travel and entertainment costs are also included under the distribution heading, as follows:

- postage;
- carriage costs for returns, etc.;
- packaging costs;

- paper bags;
- carrier bags;
- travel and entertainment;
- motor vehicle costs.

Administrative costs

Costs in this area tend to build up if they are not watched closely since almost any cost that is involved with the administration of the business is considered here. You need to make a careful assessment of the likely cost for each item over the year, work the figure into your budget and then adhere to it. The following list shows you what a variety of costs you will need to consider:

- Stationery.
- Advertising.
- Display materials.
- Training.
- Trade subscriptions (e.g. BA membership).
- Telephone.
- Hire of equipment (tills, etc.).
- Cleaning.
- Professional fees.

Finance costs

This is the area where most people end up hating the banking industry in general. You will incur costs on almost everything you do, so it is a serious mistake not to take them fully into account when you are thinking about running costs. Some typical expenses are shown below.

- Bank charges.
- Credit card charges.
- Bad debts.
- Depreciation charges.
- Gains or losses on foreign exchange (if you sell overseas).
- Book Tokens charges.

This brief summary should have demonstrated that there will be charges coming at the bookshop from every corner. Step one is to assess these likely costs realistically. Thereafter you need to do everything possible to generate sufficient sales to cover them.

There will be times when you will need additional help to cope with periods of negative cash flow. You should talk to your bank to find out the best way of covering such times with a suitable overdraft arrangement.

23. Information technology

Computers are no longer "new technology". They are here to stay and it would be rash to choose to ignore their potential impact on business. A single computer and operator can now perform tasks that used to take for ever and use up almost every resource in the shop. What is more, most programmes are now so user-friendly that almost everyone in the business is capable of using the system after minimal training.

That said, before you rush to install the latest configuration, it is wise to spend some time working out a sensible balance between what you want to put into your system and what you want to get out of it.

Costs

One of the beauties of a sophisticated computer system is that it can do almost anything you want it to – after considerable analysis and programming, as well as processing time and disk space. Each requirement will drive up the cost of the system, often by a tidy sum.

It is also generally true that it is much better, and cheaper, to define the requirements of the system properly at the start than it is to continually go back to the developers with new ideas. This does mean a very rigorous analysis of needs, but the process will pay dividends.

As a result it makes sense to take a management decision on the probable use of any desirable element in the system at quite an early stage. If something is vital to the effective day-to-day functioning of the bookshop the cost of it must be accommodated somehow, whereas an element which falls into the "wouldn't-it-be-nice-if-we-could ..." category may have to be set aside pending future prosperity.

Data overload

Another element to consider carefully is the level of detail which will be output from the system. Data is useless if it cannot be interpreted and if you are not careful the sheer quantity of data will overwhelm the decision-maker. Producing a print-out of all book sales across a calendar year – on a one line per transaction basis – results in a doorstep of print which is rarely looked at; it is just too daunting to try and accommodate the depth of data, yet alone make any useful interpretation of it. You have data overload.

A summary, on the other hand, may cover such a wide variation of performance that it really does not give a true picture of what is happening. If this is the case then the danger is that decisions will be made on the basis of inadequate data.

So the challenge is to see that the system is designed to provide adequate data for sound business decisions to be taken. This means defining what decisions will be needed and then matching the level of information to them. It also becomes incumbent on the decision-makers to know the limitations of the data they are presented with. Few people get entirely accurate information all the time – the trick comes in knowing how confident of the data you can be.

Data handling should be made easier as a result of the data warehousing software that is beginning to become more widely available (the system called PowerPlay produced by Cognos is a current example). The warehousing concept works on the basis of recording data on almost everything imaginable and constructing what are known as "data cubes" from it. The analysis software is then used to interrogate and summarise this data across various dimensions. It effectively allows three-dimensional analysis of the data instead of the two-dimensional analysis of a conventional database.

The critical feature of such systems is that the operator is able to "drill up" and "drill down" through the various levels of data in such a way that trends can be identified far more easily than usually. Furthermore, the depth of data held means that these trends can be tested across an array of options. The computer resources required are considerable, but may well reduce as the technology continues to advance.

Electronic data interchange

EDI, as electronic data interchange is generally known, owes its development to the parallel advance in sophisticated communications systems and complex data handling systems. The combination now enables serious amounts of data to be passed between computer systems with no interference from an operator.

EDI addresses what has traditionally formed the basis of most business-to-business communication: the transfer of huge amounts of data (usually pieces of paper) from one company to another. It reduces the physical aspects of the transfer, with consequent cost savings all round.

In the book trade the traditional method means that a publisher gives a bookseller an order form; the bookseller completes the form and returns it to the publisher; the publisher generates an order and sends it to the warehouse; the warehouse produces a picking list for the books, a delivery note, and an invoice, sending one copy of the invoice to the bookseller and one to the publisher. The bookseller records the books' delivery. At the end of the month the publisher issues a statement to the bookseller. The bookseller matches the invoice to the statement and, if they agree, sends a payment to the publisher. The same sort of thing happens with any returns the bookseller makes to the publisher. It is a complex, convoluted system, even when it goes right. If there is an error anywhere along the line further letters flow. Rain forests get destroyed in the process, and costs mount.

The concept of EDI is that many of these communications can be coded in such a way that they can be sent electronically between the businesses involved, cutting out printing time, paper costs and time spent filing it, and the costs of any additional keyboarding. It also allows data to be automatically processed by all parties for their own system's use.

It does of course mean that all the participating companies must have effective computer systems and modem links with the telephone system, or other Internet provision means such as ISDN or Broadband cable connection. They must also agree various data protocols: if an electronic message is to make sense to both sender and recipient both parties must be working to the same code book. Fortunately for the industry, such protocols are increasingly gravitating towards those which Book Industry Communication (see Chapter 3) has established on a trade-wide basis.

EDI and the small business

It would be easy to assume that the development of EDI is only relevant to large businesses with a huge volume of transactions. However, every business has significant amounts of transactional data to process and if efficiencies can be found, then savings can be made. As the cost of computer processing power continues to fall and EDI becomes more widespread, the benefits it confers will become more readily available to businesses of all sizes. The small business may even be able to make more significant savings in time as the process of balancing statements, invoices and deliveries becomes automated.

If you feel that EDI might benefit your bookshop, the best initial approach is probably to a large publisher, which will almost certainly run EDI for some of its other customers. Before you commit yourself, however, you would be well advised to talk to a number of suppliers as well as to BIC and the Booksellers Association for further advice.

TeleOrdering

We looked at the operation of Whitakers' TeleOrdering when considering high-tech ordering options in Chapter 9 and it only remains to stress here that the establishment of a trade-wide electronic ordering system has been one of the most important steps in enabling the retail book trade to develop as it has. The system has been continuously developed to keep it in line with the industry's changing needs and further improvements are currently planned, so that it seems set to remain one of the central tools for booksellers.

Nielsen Bookscan

Part of the Whitaker stable of book trade support tools, Nielsen Bookscan is a system which electronically collates retail sales data directly from some 1,500 general bookshop outlets. The information, which is kept in a completely anonymous form, is used to produce accurate details of the number of copies that are selling from the bookshops on a weekly basis. A total of 5,000 titles is tracked each week to give total sales, the average selling price, and the value of the total weekly sales of the books across the participating bookshops.

Contributing booksellers are sent a weekly update on both the 5,000 titles selling across the whole sample and the 5,000 titles selling across their own shops. This allows for accurate bestseller identification across a far broader band than the usual top ten or twenty titles which feature in other lists. It also allows booksellers to track any titles that they have missed.

Because the sample of bookshops which contribute data is known to Nielsen Bookscan, the system can extrapolate the likely number of copies sold throughout the UK. This makes it an enormously useful tool for any bookseller since it reflects sell out data on an objective basis.

Batch

Booksellers Automated Transaction Clearing House (batch) is a Booksellers Association service, full details of which appear in Appendix 1, which allows members of the BA to pay suppliers electronically. It allows booksellers to clear their payments through batch monthly, saving administration, time and money.

Accounts packages

Buying one of the off-the-peg accounts packages that are widely available now may simplify book-keeping and accounting for many booksellers and release time that could, perhaps, be more usefully spent elsewhere.

The two principal packages likely to interest small booksellers are those offered by Sage or Quicken. These allow the bookshop to set up its book-keeping data in various ways to suit itself, while enabling it also to set up the requisite formal ledgers, as follows:

- nominal ledger: details of all transactions affecting the business;
- purchase ledger: details of all buying transactions;
- sales ledger: records of all goods sold;
- payroll: with all relevant regulatory criteria built in.

The package must also be able to produce formal management and audited accounts.

Before setting up any system, however, it is important to consult your accountant, whose detailed knowledge of the capabilities, and any possible shortcomings, of such packages may well prove invaluable.

Using the internet to reach customers

With the number of households owning sophisticated PCs with attached communications systems growing annually, society is becoming increasingly technological in the UK. Without much doubt the greatest attraction for many people is access to the Internet.

Although much of the activity on the Internet is "leisure-based", there is greatly increasing interest in the concept of home shopping where the hassle involved is no more than going to a retailer's home page, ordering what is wanted, and paying for it.

As we saw in Chapter 15 when looking at marketing, the Internet offers booksellers the chance both to sell to distant customers and at the same time to use the Web page as a form of publicity – for advertising forthcoming events or new titles, for example. This is particularly appropriate if the bookshop specialises in a specific interest area.

A further advantage that can be exploited is that, provided a suitable link with an efficient wholesaler can be set up, stock need not be held, but simply ordered from the wholesaler as orders come in. This kind of system leaves the bookseller open to the risk of letting customers down if the book ordered does not arrive promptly (or at all), but in terms of financing the business the opportunities have to be attractive.

Seeking advice

Unless you already have all the necessary skills, you are strongly advised to seek specialist advice before investing in any form of information technology. The field is changing continuously and you risk wasting money by investing in technology that is limited, superseded, or simply unsuitable for the purpose.

Your local Chamber of Commerce or the Booksellers Association may be able to help, either directly or by pointing you in the direction of suitable sources of expert advice.

Backing up data

Those who are familiar with the temperamental nature of computer systems may find this section redundant. For others, however, including anyone who has not yet suffered the devastation of a computer crash, it is essential.

"Backing up" is the general term used for the critical practice of ensuring that the data held on any computer system is regularly copied to a remote source. This way, should anything happen to the original data the system can be restored with minimal loss. The concept is that if the shop burns down, a copy of the programmes together with all the data will be safe. The hardware can usually be replaced quite easily and quickly, with the insurance company footing the bill in most cases. The copies of the software can then be re-installed and your system is up and running again almost immediately. Of course, the value of the back-up data will only be as good as the age of the data. If the back-up is a week old, then you may have lost a week's data; but if it was done last night then you will have lost very little, if any, data.

The frequency of backing up will depend on the stability of the data. In general terms, the actual programmes need to be copied only once initially, and once again after any programme changes. The copy should be kept quite separately, in a totally different location from the main system – at home, for example, provided you do not live over the bookshop, in which case your bank or a data security warehouse are possibilities.

Where data changes more frequently, the need to make back-up copies is more frequent. On most systems data is changing on a daily basis, so that copies must also be made daily and, once again, removed to a remote location.

With almost every back-up system some data – that which changed since your last back-up – will be lost. Provided you have stuck to your back-up routine, and the copies are not corrupted, you will have to re-create, at most, one day's data. If you are lax with the routine or neglect to establish a proper procedure your difficulties could be immense, and even threaten the future viability of the business. Backing up really is important.

Depending upon the volume of data you need to back up on a regular basis there are a variety of options open to you. If your data is below about 250Mb you can back up onto high storage Zip-Disks. These are a type of floppy disk but with a much greater capacity. If your data comes closer to about 600Mb you can back up onto CD-ROM using a CD rewriter. If your data needs are higher than this you are best using a tape streamer to hold the necessary data safely.

A further alternative is to use an online data warehouse where you download copies of your data over a fast Internet connection to a secure off-site server. In the event of needing to restore your data you simply download over the Internet.

Escrow agreements

A final consideration may be setting up an Escrow agreement if you are using software supplied by a third party. Under such an agreement (which has full legal validity) a copy of the software code is kept by a further party, called the Escrow agent, and the original supplier undertakes to keep the copy fully up to date with any changes that are made to the system. If the original supplier later goes out of business, this coded copy is released to you, enabling you, or a new software provider, to have access to the original code.

24. To grow or not to grow?

You have worked hard and made sensible decisions. Your bookshop has become a success: your customers like the choice of books and services you offer them and are buying in significant quantities, so that you now see your monthly sales exceeding budget. All your initial hopes and dreams have become reality and the bookshop is thriving – thriving so well that you need room for expansion to cope with the burgeoning demand.

The downside, however, is that you never have any free time for other activities and perhaps your health and/or marriage are suffering as a result. You have created a success, but that very success may be about to take you over. You now have decisions to make that may be as far-reaching as your initial decision to open a bookshop.

Economies of scale

One feature of the book trade is that, like many other retail industries, it is dominated by the economies of scale that can be achieved. A bookshop which can sell 100 copies of a book becomes far more important to its suppliers than one selling ten. Publishers begin to take more notice and to consider the bookshop for marketing expenditure. They may also take demands for improved trading terms more seriously.

The bookshops which can achieve phenomenal turnover from remarkably small premises exist, of course, but they are comparatively rare. Most shops do quite well to achieve an average turnover from the space available and any increases (at least, significant increases) must usually come from increasing the selling space in several possible ways, as follows:

- increasing the physical size of existing premises;
- moving to new and larger premises;
- opening a second shop to run in conjunction with the first.

If you feel that the time has come to open another shop remember that you will also have to expand your control systems to accommodate it. This may mean either replicating everything you already do or seeking expansion to existing computer programmes. It will certainly mean that the volume of administration with which you already have to deal will increase.

Moving up from six shops to seven will be less dramatic and disruptive than moving from one to two, but there are still many issues to be considered before making each successive step. Increasing the number of shops you run does clear a path for substantial increases in the potential turnover of the business. It also, however, increases your statistical risk of getting a few things wrong.

Each option offers both benefits and pitfalls. The prize to keep in mind is that every successful bookshop chain had to start somewhere – and you may have the entrepreneurial flair to make the newest name on the bookselling scene.

Trusting a manager

Perhaps one of the hardest steps any owner-manager must take is the decision to employ a manager. Until then, control of your operation is entirely in your hands. If you want to do it, it happens, and *vice versa*.

As soon as you employ a manager some degree of hand-over becomes necessary. You must start to trust someone else's judgement – and there are some people who find it enormously difficult to start letting go of control. They will point to other instances when trust was given and then abused, and no one can deny that this is easily possible. Yet it is also impossible for you to be in two or more places at the same time. You need to have holidays, too, quite apart from some time in which to develop the business.

Begin by identifying someone as potential manager material. This person should ideally be someone you know fairly well, or at least have worked closely with. You need to train your manager-elect to operate and think in the way you want, but at the same time allow the individual to develop in his or her own right. You can start by delegating some of the more ordinary processes and then move, at your own speed, towards handing over some of the more important work. Many booksellers allow the process of building trust to begin very gently. The potential new manager's skills and judgement should be given time to develop, so that a view can be taken on the effectiveness of their decision-making. Remember that, although constructive criticism can be enormously useful, making it is a skill in its own right, a skill that may not be given to you.

As time moves on so mutual confidence should begin to emerge, and this is the bedrock for your future professional relationship. A manager given the right training, guidance, motivation, opportunity and support will prove a valuable asset to your business.

It does not always work out so well, of course. The person selected may well have their own ideas as to how your bookshop should be run and they may not match yours. You should be able to notice this kind of disparity early on, and take a decision on the future sooner rather than later.

Equally, the person may prove highly talented and adapt to the new demands with alacrity. He or she may also be ambitious and may be expecting a larger salary than you can afford. In this case you may find that they leave for another job with better prospects and pay. Hard as this may seem, you should not give up; it is too easy to come to the conclusion that training is a waste of time because once trained – at your expense – people move on. Some people always will, but others will not. Faith, though hard to maintain at times, usually brings rewards in the long run.

Taking a strategic view

The strategic view on growth proceeds from the usual principle that a business must make a profit if it is to survive and invest in its future. The costs of running a business will always appear to be rising rapidly: it is almost unknown for rents or heating bills to come down; and salary bills tend always to get bigger. The conclusion is that any business needs to maximise the margin it generates from sales.

A bookseller does well to produce a gross margin of around 35%. This means that, if this high margin is achieved, all the expenses of the business must be met from the 35%. Anything left over can be re-invested in the business or redeployed elsewhere.

Some notional figures will make the point. If your bookshop has an annual turnover of £300,000 you will have to meet all your bills from the £105,000 gross margin you generate and only then re-invest any residue, which is unlikely to be a large sum. This will probably mean that you are unable to generate adequate onwards investment to help the business grow. After all, a new computer system for even a small bookshop is likely to cost in excess of £7,500.

If, however, you ran three bookshops, each with a turnover of £300,000, you might be able to put yourself in a better position. By straight mathematics your total gross margin triples to £315,000 but, assuming you are able to run some of your costs across the three shops (quite possible with good management practice), your total costs should not triple. In this way you begin to benefit from economies of scale, so that re-investment in the business becomes a more realistic possibility. On top of this your increased turnover should allow you to negotiate some higher discounts with your main suppliers.

Clearly there is a downside: you are putting risk into three leases and three locations; you have more employees; and you will need good control measures to ensure that security is up to scratch. On balance, however, the odds seem to be stacked rather more substantially in favour of those booksellers who manage to run a small group of two or three bookshops, rather than a single one. The figures simply give them a better chance of survival so long as they manage their growth process successfully.

Now that you are well motivated by the prospect of future success, it is time to remind you of what is involved in the final stages of opening your very first new bookshop.

25. Preparing to open

Having made up your mind to open a new bookshop, arranged the finance and found your desired location you now need to start the detailed planning to enable the bookshop to open to the public as soon as possible. With a thousand and one things to be done, it saves time and money if you do them in the best possible order.

The complexity of the project will almost certainly force you to make some compromises, which in turn means you will also have to prioritise some matters. Having an overview of the whole process will help you make the best decisions.

Planning

The advantage of planning in detail for the opening is that you are more likely to get a realistic view of the timescale you are working to, the likely costs, and the amount of help you will need to organise.

If you already have project management software, such as MS Project, on your computer, it would be sensible to use it to control the processes involved and give yourself a clearer picture of how things are actually progressing. Otherwise, do your planning on paper. It will generally take the form of a sequence of interlinked lists of things to be done and will probably include some flow charts to help ensure that everything is done in the best possible sequence.

Correct sequencing is important. The purpose of the planning process is to try to ensure that on the day that the bookshop opens everything is properly in place. This means ensuring that all the opening stock is properly merchandised and priced; window displays are attractive; staff are trained and ready to go into action; systems are all up and running. To do this, you must have all the building blocks in place – you cannot merchandise your opening stock if the shelving has not been finished, and you cannot sell any books if the tills are not set up.

The conventional way to plan involves working backwards from the desired objective. You want to open the bookshop with your stock properly merchandised on your shelving. An example of a much simplified Gantt chart plotting some of the steps required to achieve that position is shown in Figure 25.1.

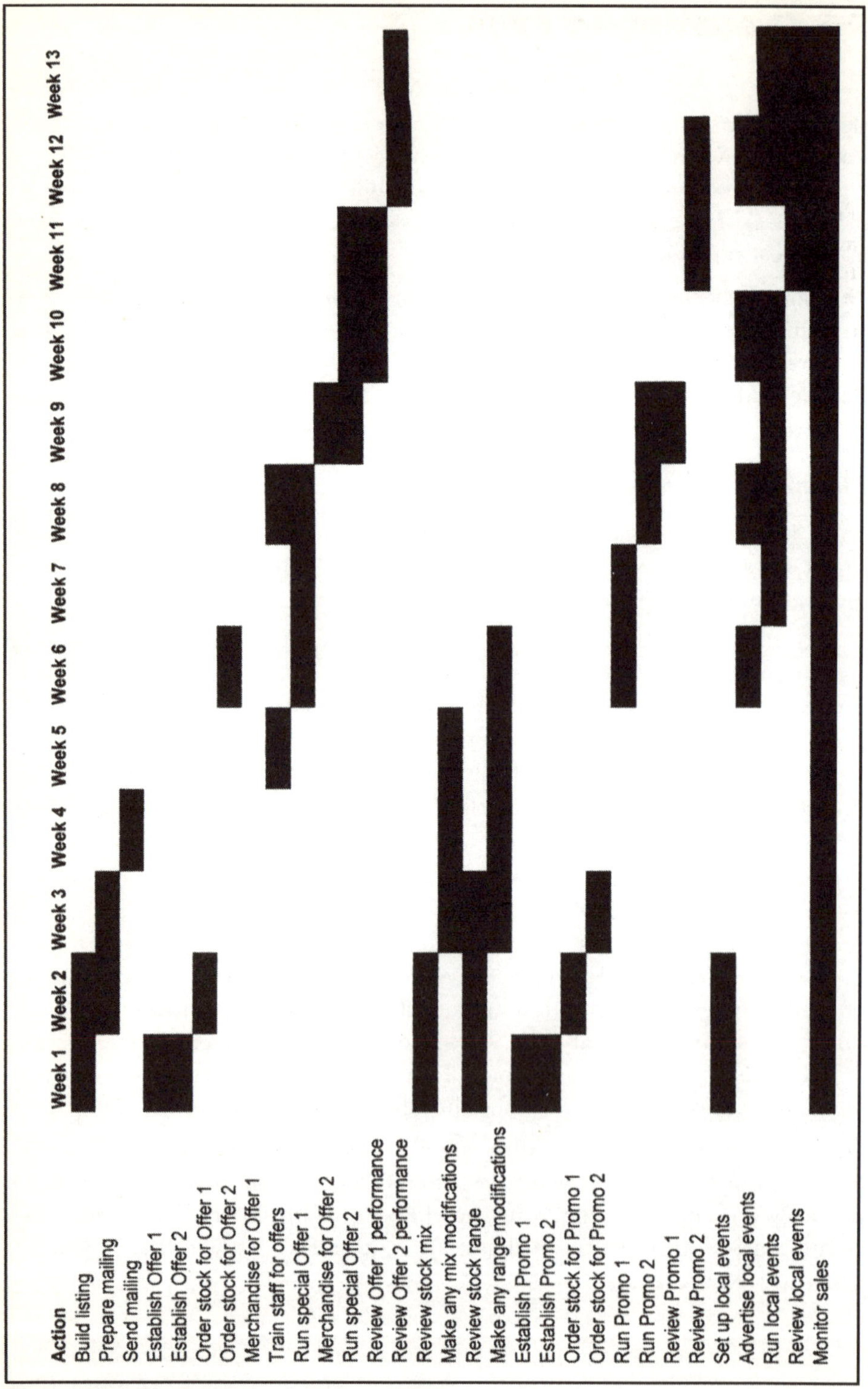

Figure 25.1 Illustrative planning chart

As well as working out what needs to be done, you should also build in some control measures to ensure that you are satisfied that each task has been completed properly before the next is started. It is rather like the test a good teacher runs at the end of a term, reassuring when pupils do well but also serving to ring an alarm when they do not. In project management, the idea is that certain key stages in the project can be readily identified as critical steps, to be completed by a certain date.

So controls are also necessary to ensure that the project runs to schedule. Here project management uses a useful concept known as "milestones", which are the combination of the critical step with the critical time. Within the planning exercise illustrated above, the milestone stages might be identified as:

- successful establishment of the local events programme by the end of week 2;
- successful completion of the material for the mailing by the end of week 3;
- successful establishment of special offer 1 at the beginning of week 6;
- successful establishment of promotion 1 at the beginning of week 6;
- successful establishment of promotion 2 at the beginning of week 8;
- successful establishment of special offer 2 at the beginning of week 9.

If you have planned your project efficiently and the milestones have been met, the project is likely to complete on the agreed date. Failing to pass the milestones at the right time means you risk missing the completion date, so you should consider some contingency plans to either deal with the delay or speed up the subsequent work.

Building work

Your chosen premises may need some building work to convert them into a bookshop. With luck, the extent of the work might be minimal, consisting of such simple maintenance as the repair of gutters and down-pipes to be carried out before the shopfitters arrive. The surveyor's report on the property should tell you the scale of work to be undertaken.

On the other hand, you may have to organise some extensive building work to take down internal walls and create an effective selling space, for example. This may be because the premises have not been used as a shop before, or it may be because you wish to create more space and a better environment. You should involve professional advisers like architects and quantity surveyors if the work is more than you can supervise adequately yourself.

Before work begins, make sure that you apply for any necessary planning permission and/or building control permissions. If the fascia of the bookshop is to be changed you will also need specific permission from the local authority. There may well be a required period of notice to be posted to allow the public to make any objections. You should make sure you build this into your timetable.

It is usually a mistake to underestimate the length of time the building work phase will take. Almost without exception it will be longer than you had thought. To an extent you can protect yourself against rising costs through penalty clauses in the contract you agree with the builders, but you cannot cover yourself so easily against further costs caused by delays in the building. Your planning will need to recognise this.

You must also allow for clear-up time after builders and craftsmen have finished. Any mess will have to be sorted out before more work is started, so include cross-overs in the planning. Some of this –like getting the painting done before the new carpet goes down – is obvious, but other elements are easily overlooked. Will you need dust sheeting to protect existing stock and fittings; have you organised the hire of industrial vacuum cleaners (and perhaps some extra staff) to clean up the dust builders inevitably create? It all takes time and money.

The target is to have your bookshop looking as you want it, and for the bills to fall within your estimates. This is never easy but it will become impossible unless you work hard to rise to the challenge.

Staff

By this time you will know the size and have a good idea of the scope of your proposed bookshop, as well as an indication of the turnover it is likely to generate.

This indicative turnover figure will, in turn, have given you a pointer to how many staff you may need to help run the business. Using the suggested figure of around £80,000 sales per employee, you should get an indication of the likely number of full-time equivalent employees you will need.

On this basis an indicative annual turnover of £400,000 gives you yourself, as owner-manager, together with four more full-time equivalent employees. They may be full-time staff with some extra help for Saturdays, or you may find it works out better with a mixture of full and part-time staff, plus some extra help for weekends and holidays.

Experience suggests that you should try to get by with as few staff as possible at the opening stage. This is because you will have a better idea of the accuracy of your initial projections after you start trading. If turnover promises to be higher than expected you can always take on more help, but "letting staff go" if turnover does not match your estimate is not a pleasant experience.

You should now plan what jobs you will need help with; what sort of people you will need; what pay and conditions you will offer; and how you will go about recruitment.

You should also think carefully about initial training for staff. Even if you intend to employ trained booksellers and have specific people in mind, they will need to know how you plan to run your particular bookshop systems. For any staff who lack the basic bookselling skills you will need to develop a form of training to instil these skills, as well as providing a detailed working knowledge of your own systems. A basic induction training programme for new bookshop staff in a bookshop would include:

- emergency procedures for fire;
- till procedures;
- customer orders.

It is easy to overlook or even dismiss training when there are so many other pressures, but it is a mistake to do so. The staff you choose have to make the right impression on your future customers – and it is first impressions which count. Make sure your staff receive good training from the word go, and you stand a much better chance of building up a long-term success from your bookshop opening.

Sunday Staffing

If you plan to open on Sundays (and your bookshop is in England or Wales) you must make sure that you understand the staffing implications of the Sunday Trading Act. It specifies that staff cannot be forced to work Sundays and allows them formally to "opt out" of working that day. Anyone who does so is officially protected from harassment but if they are subsequently subjected to any kind of least-favoured treatment an industrial tribunal is likely to rule for automatic unfair dismissal.

The section on trading hours below discusses further conditions imposed by the Sunday Trading Act.

Systems

Every business needs systems, whether they are low-tech systems for keeping a manual record of daily sales or high-tech systems for making payments to the bank via an electronic link.

By the time you open the bookshop you should have all your systems thought out and ready for use. You can make changes later if necessary, but it is good to be set up for action. There are several basic areas, of which you should by now be fully aware.

First, your accountant or book-keeper will have pointed out the systems you need to operate in order to keep your financial records in good order. These are the essentials, enabling you to both keep an eye on the state of the business and fulfil statutory requirements for your taxation payments. Cash security systems should be built in, too.

Payments systems come next. They include measures to ensure that your staff are paid properly (less necessary deductions) and that you pay your suppliers, which means that invoice-handling and reconciliation systems will be needed.

Then there are stock ordering and control systems which must also be ready to go from day one so that you can track sales and do the relevant re-ordering.

As the business develops and things start to settle down you will find you need a few extra systems too. Some of these will help you comply with numerous bits and pieces of legislation that affect every business. Health and Safety regulations are one example, and a semi-formalised system for regular reviews of such issues will help to keep you out of trouble.

Shopfitting

Shopfitting a bookshop means far more than simply putting shelves on the walls and building a counter to sit the till on. With luck you may be able to use what was there before, but you may have to undertake structural alterations and rebuild the shop front, put in false ceilings, install security devices, new lighting and so on.

Do not overlook the local authority and/or landlord permissions which may well be required before work can start. There is a multitude of regulations – building control, fire safety, planning permission, advertising controls etc. – to comply with.

Assuming four broad approaches to shopfitting, each costs more than the one before but is quite possibly more effective. Each approach has its merits. Your choice will depend on your skills, your experience and your access to capital.

Do it yourself

This is the bargain basement of shopfitting but provided you are confident enough of your own design, building and decorating skills you can draw up your own plans, buy in whatever fixtures you need and then install everything yourself. Unless you are exceptionally skilled, however, you risk ending up with a bookshop which bears little relation to your first plan. In the competitive marketplace of today there are remarkably few gaps for the well-meaning but amateurish bookshop.

Assisted DIY

The next approach is to instruct local builders to carry out work to your specifications. The plans and design will be largely yours and you are free to buy in shelving and whatever you need independently, but the builders do most of the installation, decorating and so on. This is likely to be quicker, and costs will still be very manageable. With well-chosen builders you should have a good job done, but the finished bookshop may lack the professional polish that experienced shopfitters can give.

Specialist shopfitters

Using specialist book trade shopfitters will enable you to install fully designed shelving developed over years of experience. You can look either in *The Bookseller* or you can go onto the Booksellers Association website and refer to their online directory called the BA Guide to Retail Services & Accessories. This gives a listing of a variety of firms and services that may well be of significant help to you. Usually these companies can supply a total shopfitting service, designing the complete layout using their own products.

Costs will be significantly higher, but the end result is usually attractive, effective to use, and robust enough to cope with the pressures of everyday bookselling. There is always the added advantage that it will be easy to modify or expand the shelving at a later date. You may find, however, that you do not get the absolute maximum out of the space you have.

Design consultants

At the very top end of the scale come the design consultants. You can expect to pay a good deal, but equally the result you get will probably give you the best long-term value for money, with the maximum use made of the available space. Good design enhances the appeal of your shop, which will show through in improved profitability year after year.

The interior

Regardless of how you set about the shopfitting, there are general matters you should consider carefully, and it pays to do this at the outset rather than muddle through making changes as you go.

Consider first of all the ambience to be created inside the bookshop. For example, do you want something traditional, or modern? The choice is wide and on the whole, provided designs are applied carefully and consistently, most are successful. You can come unstuck if your customers perceive your bookshop as an uncoordinated mix of different designs. This may hold an eccentric charm for some, but the people who find such designs attractive are growing fewer all the time.

Remember that security has a bearing on design. Choosing a cosy interior full of nooks and crannies or using high gondola units to allow maximum shelf space within the bookshop makes life very easy for shoplifters. A design that provides clear visibility throughout the bookshop will enable you to keep a much closer eye on your stock, and thereby limit pilferage. An alternative strategy – admittedly rather costly – is to consider installing a closed circuit television system to provide security cover for the hidden areas. Any such system should be linked into video recording equipment so that if a theft is identified the police can be shown the video tapes. You need to remember, however, that in the light of the Data Protection Act you have to advise customers that images are kept for security purposes.

The fascia

We have examined the importance of the bookshop's appearance from outside. For people who know your shop and are familiar with your aims, the shop front, or fascia, will help to convey something of this. For others, the shop front is there to help entice them over the threshold. It is for this reason that the fascia design is so critical. Its colour, the architectural balance, and the type of lettering used all convey certain images – reliability, modernity, etc. – to people on the street. You have the opportunity to make your mark on them.

It follows that visibility is all-important. The shop name should be easily readable from as many different angles as possible, which means choosing lettering that is legible and large enough to be read from the other side of the street. If the words "books" or "bookshop" are not part of your trading name then you should consider adding some kind of subtitle to the name to indicate what you are selling. To give your bookshop added visibility from further along the street, use a projecting sign as well (making sure to get planning permission for it first).

We looked in Chapter 16 at the role of shop windows in attracting potential customers into the shop. You should consider the practicalities of your windows, which ideally perform the dual function of allowing people outside to see inside and be tempted to come in, while giving the bookseller some space to feature selected books such as brand new titles or put on a more generic display.

Stock

If this is your first bookshop, choosing the stock to open with is particularly difficult. You have no past stock records to guide your initial purchasing. Bookselling experience within the town (with another bookseller) will give some people guidelines, but if you are completely new to the area or the trade then you need to seek help on the range of titles and the appropriate quantities to order. A good wholesaler can be useful here. Those opening a second bookshop can base their opening stock broadly on the sales patterns of the first shop, amending it to reflect any changes in the market between the two.

One important factor in placing an opening order for the bookshop is that the order is likely to be the largest single set of orders you ever place with your suppliers. This may give you a good opportunity to organise some rather better than usual trading terms on these orders. Getting, let us say, an extra 5% discount or an extra thirty days' credit on your opening order will help your cash-flow situation in these early days. Negotiate hard to get the best possible deal.

Security

You should not open the bookshop without having set up systems and procedures to help minimise theft, either of your stock or of the shop's takings and some pointers were given in considering management matters in Chapter 18. Remember that in both cases the thieves can be either internal (i.e. fraudulent staff) or external (i.e. shoplifters and criminals).

Shoplifting

There are three principal ways of helping to minimise losses through shoplifting.

First, we have seen how the layout of the shop should allow as much visibility as possible, to deprive shoplifters of the privacy they need to take and hide items. Installing convex all-round visibility security mirrors or experimenting with a closed circuit television security camera system to cover blind spots may be helpful, although both options mean extra costs of course.

Secondly, train all staff to be vigilant and to know how to identify potential shoplifters through their behaviour. They should, for instance, be suspicious of "customers" who seem to pay more attention to where the staff are than to the books on the shelves. The staff should also know what to do if someone is caught shoplifting. The following checklist sets out essential facts and procedures to pass on when training your staff to deal with the situation.

- You must actually see the shoplifter take at least one item.
- In England and Wales there need be only one witness to the act of theft, but under Scottish law two independent witnesses are required.
- Leave no gaps in your observation, so maintain clear lines of visibility at all times.
- It will probably be necessary to testify to the police or to a court that the goods stolen have actually come from your shop.
- If possible note where the shoplifter hides the item. If it is hidden it makes it much easier for the police to prove intent to steal.
- Watch for the item being passed on to another colleague or being "put back" on the shelves. If you challenge the shoplifter and there is nothing on the suspect you may be open to a charge of wrongful arrest.
- Although a suspected shoplifter can be apprehended inside the bookshop, it is better to allow the person to leave the shop before you do stop the suspect.
- Be polite but firm. Do not touch a suspect since this might be construed as assault. Ask the suspect to accompany you back to the shop. Then call the police.
- Try to ensure that two people remain with the suspect at all times until the police arrive.

The third way to minimise losses is to merchandise your bookshop so that the more vulnerable items of stock are on the shelves that are most visible to staff. Certain sections of stock are more vulnerable than others. Antiques guides command a high "second-hand" price and children's annuals and sports books usually find a ready market at local pubs. Highly priced art books are another obvious temptation. Shelving books of this kind at the back of the shop is foolish; they will surely vanish into a sports bag – taking your profits with them.

Fraud

An important part of initial staff training should deal with identifying fraudulent transactions. These can range from the presentation of counterfeit notes to the use of stolen credit cards.

Call the BA for basic information on combatting fraud or visit the BA website, www.booksellers.org.uk Your bank, local Chamber of Commerce, or local crime prevention officer can also offer advice.

Cash

The cash your bookshop generates – so important to you – interests others too, so your opening plans must allow tills to be positioned in such a way as to make it difficult for a customer to reach over and empty the cash drawer. Ensure, too, that the till drawer can be locked whenever the till is not staffed.

Tills are less vulnerable to the activities of "till-snatchers" if high value notes and any build-up of other notes are removed, but see that you have somewhere the cash can be stored more securely elsewhere in the shop. If cash is being put in a drawer in an unlocked back office, then it is probably safer left in the till.

Plan carefully for general cash security within the shop as well. Bookshops are not hugely popular with armed robbers, but that does not allow you to get away with being careless. Money should always be counted behind locked doors, preferably with two people present to reduce the risk of temptation.

If you take the money to the bank alone always exercise proper caution and never allow a behaviour pattern to build up. Some sensible rules are shown below.

- Do not go to the bank at the same time each day.
- Do not use the same route each day.
- Carry the money discreetly and securely.
- Be alert.
- Work out in advance what you will do if threatened.
- Ensure you comply fully with insurers' requirements.

Internal security

Internal security is a sensitive area for any bookshop. Everyone wants to think that their staff are totally trustworthy and the evidence proves this is so. The difficulty comes with the few who are not, since they can do so much more damage to your business through their privileged access to your stock and cash.

Your first line of defence should be always to take up references for new staff. This way, you are less likely to take on anyone who has a history of doubtful practice.

As we have seen, your induction training must include till procedures. All staff dealing with tills should be told to follow the procedures you have laid down and be made aware that any deviation from them may lead to disciplinary action.

It makes sense to build internal security systems into your financial systems. They need not be obtrusive, but they should serve to put temptation out of your staff's mind. You should have formal book-keeping procedures to ensure that the sum of money in the till at the end of the day's trading matches the total sum rung up on the till. In theory the two amounts should match exactly, but they are seldom precisely the same. If the difference is significant, however, you should be able to get an explanation. You ought also to make sure that the day's banking corresponds with the sum expected from the day's takings, and agree procedures for dealing with Book Tokens to prevent any being "redeemed" twice.

It always seems a good policy to allow staff discount on their personal purchases, since this makes it less likely that they will steal. Some bookshops also permit some form of staff borrowing of stock, providing books are returned in mint condition for re-sale. Both mechanisms should, however, be subject to control.

Taking things further

Sadly, it is almost inevitable that at some point during your bookshop's lifetime something will go wrong. You may become aware of rather too many differences between the day's takings and what actually gets banked or find that your gross margin is lower than expected at the end of the financial year.

If you suspect that these differences are coming from within the business, take very cautious action. There is seldom an obvious culprit, so you may have to investigate by yourself – quietly. This is always difficult since you must not show any lack of trust, but you must find a way of isolating what may be happening. Usually the best approach is to try to assimilate as much information as you can and then to look for patterns. An obvious one (usually seen too late) is a till showing losses regularly, except – miraculously – on one person's days off.

Once a situation has been identified you will have to decide whether to call in the police or to deal with the matter yourself. If you prefer to deal quietly with it, remember that any dismissal becomes unfair if the rules of natural justice are not followed. If the employee has two years' service or more you may find yourself taken to an industrial tribunal for unfair dismissal. In a situation like this you would be well advised to seek professional help from a body such as ACAS which can provide the detailed assistance you need if you are to keep on the right side of the regulations.

Trading hours

If your bookshop is within a shopping centre your lease may oblige you to open for certain "core trading hours", regardless of your personal or business preference. Sometimes you are able to open for longer, but often the core hours cover the entire period when the centre is open to the public.

Outside shopping centres you are likely to have far more freedom over the hours you choose to remain open. Usually the best starting point is to match your neighbours' opening hours, since it can be difficult to attract additional customers if you are the only shop still open well after everyone else has closed. Equally, you risk alienating customers if you are closed when other shops remain open. If you do want to extend trading hours consider carefully what the security implications of doing so may be.

Sunday opening

Sunday opening is increasingly frequent in most sectors of retailing. Trading on a Sunday is unrestricted in Scotland, but the Sunday Trading Act applies to England and Wales and imposes a number of important basic restrictions – the staffing implications were mentioned earlier in this chapter.

The size of the business premises is an important factor for booksellers wanting to open on Sundays. Provided the bookshop's sales floor has an area of less than 280 square metres (around 2,800 square foot), it may be open for as long as wanted on Sundays without any external permission. If, however, the shop is larger than this the bookseller must advise the local authority of the intention to open, and trading will be limited to a maximum of six hours each Sunday, which may be chosen, as convenient, between the hours of 10 a.m. and 6 p.m.

Countdown to opening

You must expect the final few days before opening to be hectic. You will probably need all the help you can get, as well as all your own energy. Whether you rely on strong coffee to keep you going or soothing herbal teas to calm you down (or probably both), you will need them in quantity.

You will also need unlimited tolerance, decisiveness and a determination to succeed – all of which makes these days an excellent introduction to the everyday world of retail bookselling

3

Part three

Appendices

The appendices which follow are intended to provide a useful resource for both experienced booksellers and newcomers to the profession.

Appendix 1
describes the work of the Booksellers Association and should allow first-time booksellers to gain a full grasp of the services offered (and any lapsed members to think again perhaps).

Appendix 2
explains the structure of one of the basic building blocks of today's book trade, the International Standard Book Number.

Appendix 3
lists a range of book trade-related organisations which will often be able to provide helpful information on request. Telephone numbers and fax numbers are given, together with e-mail addresses where these are known.

Appendix 4
is a glossary of selected terms used in the book trade, often important where the trade's application of terminology may differ from that of other businesses. The glossary also includes a number of the acronyms and abbreviations that are increasingly used within the industry.

Appendix 5
details books and publications which have been referred to in the text and which may be found helpful as further reading around the subject of bookselling specifically, and the book trade in more general terms.

Finally, it is hoped that the index will help to give the book more lasting value for its readers as a reference tool.

Appendix 1

The Booksellers Association

"To deliver to all member booksellers, regardless of their size, specialisation, location or experience, a valued and beneficial resource which is seen to be active, accessible, and in touch, and represents and promotes the interests of those members."

This is the mission statement of the Booksellers Association of the United Kingdom and Ireland Ltd, otherwise known throughout the trade as "the BA". For most booksellers, whether independent or part of a chain, the BA provides a valuable focus for the active representation of their views to government, to national and international bodies, to publishers in general, to the media and to members of the public.

To fulfil such a broad brief the BA must be active in many areas, which members and potential members alike should find it helpful to understand in their full scope.

The BA structure

The Booksellers Association is a trade association governed by a Council whose primary function is to determine BA policy. It answers to the annual general meeting, to which all members are invited.

The BA role

It is the Council which is responsible for determining the overall role of the BA, which it has defined as follows:

- helping members to increase sales;
- helping members to reduce costs;
- helping members to increase productivity;
- communication;
- representing members' views.

Helping to increase sales

As a trade association answerable to a voluntary membership, the BA must help members to increase sales if it is to merit their annual subscriptions and thereby continue to operate. It devotes a great deal of sustained creative effort to providing this help through a number of channels.

Book Tokens

As a sales-generating scheme, the Book Token idea is built around encouraging the giving of books as gifts. For booksellers it has the added appeal of creating new readers among those who might not otherwise venture into bookshops. The initiative has proved so popular that a number of the chain booksellers have set up their own store-specific schemes in recent years, but Book Tokens Ltd, a wholly-owned subsidiary company of the BA, remains the market leader for independent retailers. Only members of the Booksellers Association are eligible to sell and exchange Book Tokens – an additional incentive for joining the BA.

Although research conducted by Book Tokens Ltd shows new customers are attracted into bookshops, both to buy and exchange tokens, the scheme is not intended as an alternative to selling a book and is simply a device to enable a sale to be made where difficulty of choice or limitation of stock might otherwise have prevented it. The research also suggests that on average an extra 20% is added to the value of the token when customers redeem it.

Book Token vouchers are available to booksellers in books in values of £1, £5, £10, and £25 and to booksellers in Ireland in euro denominations of 2, 5, 10, 20 and 30. They are supplied on a sale or return basis, subject to satisfactory references being given. Alternatively, the bookseller can operate a monthly account or simply purchase a supply of vouchers outright. Promotional display material for use in the bookshop is provided free of charge.

The vouchers themselves are inserted into any of the range of free colourful Book Token wallets that are produced with detachable bookmarks to add extra value to the gift. Plain envelopes for the wallets are supplied free of charge. Customers select the wallet of their choice and the value of the vouchers required, which can be in any combination of the values above. The bookseller then removes the vouchers from the book and puts a shop stamp or sticker on the back of each voucher in the space marked "Issued by". The vouchers and wallets are bar coded and can be set up to be scanned into an EPoS system if required.

The selling bookshop makes a 12.5% commission on all voucher sales. Against this, a 1% service charge is levied on all vouchers supplied to booksellers, as a contribution to the running costs of the Book Tokens scheme.

Customers can exchange the tokens at more than 3,000 BA member bookshops in the UK and Ireland. To realise the cash value of the vouchers you have exchanged you send them directly to Book Tokens Ltd on one of the quarterly settlement dates, or on a monthly basis if you have a monthly account. When settlement is made, a discount of 12.5% is deducted from the face value of the exchanged tokens and this sum is paid to the bookshop which sold them originally. In every case the exchanging bookseller receives 87.5% of the face value of the token, and the selling bookseller 12.5%.

In summary, the benefits of the scheme are:

- Books can be sold even when customers do not know what to buy;
- Book Tokens encourage transactions in quiet periods;
- When Book Tokens are redeemed an extra 20% (on average) is added to their value;
- Virtually no capital is needed, as Book Tokens are usually supplied on credit;
- Less than one square foot of selling space is needed to display Book Token wallets;
- Attractive display material is supplied free of charge.

Marketing activities

The BA's practical marketing support for booksellers includes ***Christmas Books***, a Christmas catalogue which is a showpiece of co-operative marketing. The catalogue usually features a range of some 200 children's and adult titles, and is produced for sale to booksellers for onward distribution to customers as a reminder of the enormous value that books provide as Christmas gifts. The catalogue is supported by most major publishers and many booksellers.

BA Marketing is also involved in administering some of the high-profile **book prizes** mentioned in Chapter 2. As well as providing some tangible rewards and recognition for the authors without whom the book trade would wither, prizes do keep books very much in the public eye. Providing booksellers work to maximise their impact (and publishers keep winning titles available) sales will usually follow such awards all the way to the bookseller's bank.

BA Marketing is also closely involved with all trade-wide book promotions, the most high-profile of which recently has been **World Book Day**. Devised in 1996 as a celebration of reading, World Book Day has developed into a firmly established part of the trade promotions calendar, and includes the distribution of millions of £1 Book Tokens to every school child in the country. World Book Day is supported by all major publishers and most BA members.

For 2003, the BA is closely involved with the development of a BBC-related promotion of books, **The Big Read**. The BA is committed to representing booksellers' interests in any such promotions and will always aim to provide materials to booksellers where at all possible.

Training

The BA does not currently operate a training department, having closed it down in 2002, due to the uneconomic costs of running it. The BA does, however, manage a database of training offers from other organizations, and can offer details on individual tutors and consultants, and will help booksellers to source training for their own businesses. The BA plans to keep a watching brief on training provision within the industry and at some point may offer a training programme.

The BA can also offer all members a fully equipped training room at the association's London headquarters, for use for their own courses or meetings.

Lobbying activities

In a more abstract, but no less real sense, the BA maintains a continued, determined pressure on the government of the day to retain a zero rate of VAT for books. Books within the UK have been allowed a zero rate because of their cultural and educational role within society. The BA has been instrumental in ensuring that these arguments are not forgotten and by so doing, it has helped to maintain lower prices for books. With VAT as high as 25% elsewhere within the European Union, the battle will continue.

Helping to reduce costs

The BA's prime target of reducing costs for members is a natural reflection of the fundamental business truth that effective cost control underpins any profit to be made from retailing. Some of the ways in which the BA aims to do this follow:

Batch.co.uk and the Booksellers Clearing House (BCH)

Batch is a key member service. This wholly owned subsidiary of the BA is an electronic clearing house for both payments and information. Batch also includes the Booksellers Clearing House (BCH), which is an entirely manual system. Batch and BCH enable booksellers to pay multiple suppliers with a single cheque. This creates substantial savings for members.

Booksellers using batch on-line can view invoices as they are raised, verify deliveries, notify suppliers of discrepancies, even print copy invoices directly from the system.

Booksellers who do not currently use the Internet can receive a single consolidated paper statement detailing all transactions from numerous suppliers. All a buyer needs to do to authorise payment is put a tick in a box next to an invoice. This can be over a secure Internet connection or on the paper statement. Credits can also be taken. A cheque can be sent for both Batch and BCH that needs to arrive by a specified day (usually the 20th of the month), or the batch payment can be taken by Direct Debit on the last working day of the month in which the payment is due.

The payment to the suppliers is made in cleared funds on the last working day of the month.

There are no charges to booksellers who are members of the BA and many bookshops are finding that there are substantial benefits for their businesses saving time and money. It is possible to link batch with proprietary accounting and stock control systems removing the need for manual keying of data.

The suppliers on Batch are keen to have as many of their customers as possible using Batch as they are then able to deal electronically with buyers of all sizes. The suppliers fund Batch through a charge. More suppliers and bookshops are joining Batch all the time and there are more exciting developments in progress. Further information is available on the Batch website at www.batch.co.uk

Information on suppliers

As Chapter 8 made clear, the complex range of publishers' terms is an enormous burden on any bookseller.

Help is at hand, however, in the shape of the ***BA Directory of UK & Irish Book Publishers (including distributors, sales agents and wholesalers)***. This invaluable annual provides full contact details (including personnel) for almost every publisher, an outline of each company's terms to booksellers, and details of any returns mechanisms operated. It is through the intelligent use of the Directory that booksellers will discover how to avoid many of the pitfalls of low discounts on small orders or the added costs of returning books to the wrong supplier.

Dedicated stationery

The standardised multi-part stationery that the BA produces offers members good savings, too. In most cases items can be economically over-printed with the bookshop's name and address – and the cost of originating stationery (particularly on low volumes) can be high. Standardised stock cards (see Chapter 13 for an example) and a range of bags are also available.

Special rates for members

BA members can also reduce their costs by taking advantage of the special rates the Association has negotiated for credit and debit cards, insurance schemes, parcel services and so on. Contact the BA for the latest details.

Helping to increase productivity

To be productive, every business must ensure that all its resources – staff, stock or computers – work effectively to generate maximum sales at minimum cost. The BA works at trying to ensure that its members have every possible way of achieving full productivity open to them.

Stock

The effective performance of stock depends on a complex mix of proficient staff and a stock control system that can cope with the demands made on it. Staff in the Trade & Industry team can advise on the various stock control systems on the market. The BA is also involved from time to time in arranging exhibitions where selected system providers are available to give hands-on demonstrations to BA members.

Computer systems

The increasing concentration of the book trade and the greater sophistication of technology in recent years have combined to produce a two-edged danger: at the same time as smaller businesses risk getting left behind in a technological sense, the bigger companies may all follow their own routes and thereby create a technical communication wilderness with very little common ground.

The BA has recognised both dangers and set about addressing them by trying to ensure that information flow within the book industry is both open to all and structured into widespread usage of common standards. To this end it is a founder member of Book Industry Communication (BIC), the trade body described in Chapter 3 which is dedicated to the development of industry-wide standards for electronic data interchange.

Supply chain

The book supply chain is another critical area of productivity. With such a multiplicity of supply sources for booksellers to deal with and so many outlets for the sale of books there will always be scope for inefficiencies – and a temptation for any individual link in the chain to disclaim responsibility or control.

The BA, in conjunction with the Publishers Association and other book industry bodies, is tackling the problem with an ongoing review of the book supply chain aimed at trying to increase efficiency across the board. The objective is to identify both specific areas where savings might be made and trade practices that might be modified to make them more effective overall. The report commissioned from management consultants KPMG which emerged in spring 1998, ***Supply Chain Challenge,*** identified potential savings of £150 million to be made from an estimated total of £750 million which the trade spends on supply.

The BA's rationale for its involvement is that any improvements in the supply chain will have an impact on members' productivity and can be actively pursued and promoted. Equally, any proposals which threaten to have a negative impact can be monitored and diverted.

Communications

Communications – both with members and with the world at large – are a particular concern for any trade association. They are, after all, the main reason for forming such groups in the first place. The BA accordingly puts great care and effort into ensuring that its communications are timely, accurate and effective. It is a complex network, with a long reach, which includes the following:

Annual conference

The principal forum that the BA provides for mass communication between members and the rest of the book trade is the annual conference. This two or three-day event usually takes place in late April or May. The location varies so that all members may feel they have combined ownership of the meeting.

The format for the conference is usually mixed, to allow different issues to be presented in an appropriate style. As a result, there are formal plenary sessions when various experts (from within and outside the book trade) give their authoritative view on issues held to be of key importance to the industry as a whole, while smaller, workshop-style meetings air opinions about matters which concern particular groups of the membership.

The conference also provides a platform for the BA annual general meeting, which is always open to all members whether they have paid to attend the whole conference or not.

The strong social element within the conference provides good opportunities both for meeting new contacts, and for developing formal and informal relationships with fellow members of the trade.

BA groups

The BA Council recognises a number of specialist areas of bookselling involving specific issues which may be of paramount importance to participants but are less relevant to those outside the specialisation. As a means of providing both support and a forum for specialist discussion, the Council has established a number of groups.

Each group will normally elect its own committee to look after the group's affairs, and to also organise meetings for its membership.

The Council has the authority to establish such new groups as it sees fit, according to the demands of the membership and the trading environment at any given time.

- Academic, Professional and Specialist booksellers
- Children's booksellers
- Christian booksellers
- Export booksellers
- Internet booksellers
- Library suppliers
- School suppliers

Branches

Another mix within the membership which fosters useful communication is the geographical location of BA members. The result is a series of regional BA branches to which all members who trade in that area belong, regardless of any specialisation. The branch committee sets up meetings to which guest speakers are invited and where matters of local involvement may be discussed. The chance to meet socially like this is an effective means of combating the sense of isolation that some specialist traders may experience.

Liaison with UK book trade organisations

The BA has an obvious special responsibility to represent members' views and interests to other organisations involved with the book trade. It therefore maintains formal and informal relationships with the Publishers Association, the Library Association, and all manner of bodies involving books, authors and agents.

National press

Because the Association is a natural calling point for journalists writing about issues which involve the book trade the BA plays an important role in putting the industry viewpoint for book retailers. All kinds of issues relating to the supply of books, such as censorship and VAT on books have featured lately.

Through the cultivation of good contacts within the industry the BA is able to give informed comment on almost any trade-related enquiry put to it. The membership can often find this a great relief, since misinformed comment can have a dramatic impact on the fortunes of those working in the industry (no one likes a bad press), whereas sound, authoritative comment can be most beneficial in developing public understanding of complex issues.

London Book Fair

As a part of its industry-wide remit to foster good communications, the BA is a major sponsor of the London Book Fair, which functions as a principal meeting place for booksellers and publishers.

Refer to Chapter 3 for a brief outline of the event. Booksellers are encouraged to participate through both the offer of special discounts from publishers and the provision of free entry tickets to the fair.

International liaison

John Donne's dictum that "No man is an island" was never truer than in the world of books. The UK is only a part of an increasingly global business. The BA participates formally in several book industry forums both within Europe and on the wider international scene, where it represents the views of the UK book trade and likewise reports back on developments likely to have an impact at home.

Contact is not restricted to formalities, however, and the BA also has innumerable informal links with booksellers' associations all over the world.

It is always ready to help any member intending to make any business arrangements, formal or casual, overseas.

Representing members

In addition to making the UK Book industry's voice heard among international trade bodies, the BA takes on a large role in representing members' views to the government of the day, both within the UK and in continental Europe.

Individually, members have very limited access to government departments; the procedures by which one acquires it are often arcane and heavily reliant on having the right contacts. However, the BA has developed extensive contacts within these fields over the years and can often find the right approach to raise the specific issues which concern members. It also monitors the many directives emanating from Whitehall and, increasingly, Brussels to identify any possible impact on members. Which individual member would care to take on the European Commission on the subject of the harmonisation of VAT?

Joining the BA

It should by now be clear that every bookseller, established or aspiring, would be well advised to consider becoming a member of the BA. The value of the benefits that are conferred on members, if sensibly deployed, will far exceed the cost of the annual subscription.

The fee structure is based on a small percentage of new book turnover for each member, levied on a sliding scale, and subject to a minimum subscription.

For details on joining, contact the Membership Department at the BA for an application form. It asks for, among other things, details of the services you provide (or intend to provide), the value of stock holding (actual or estimated), and the most recent or projected sales levels. Help and advice can be given if any aspect of the application causes a problem.

Confirmation of acceptance into membership will be usually within a few weeks.

Appendix 2

How ISBNs work

Currently, 2003, an ISBN consists of ten digits divided into four parts. The first part is a single digit which identifies the language group from which the book originates. Thus ISBNs starting with "0" or "1" originate within the English language group; "2" signifies French; and "3" signifies German. The next part, which is of variable length, indicates the publisher of the book. This is usually known as the publisher prefix. The third part is the title number, which identifies the title and edition within the publisher's list. The last part is always a single digit, which serves as a check digit to authenticate the ISBN. This digit can be any of the Arabic numerals 0–9 or the Roman numeral "X".

From January 2006 the length of the ISBN code will be increased from ten to thirteen digits. The new three digits will include the EAN prefix 978 (see below) so that the ISBN will match the EAN. A new prefix, 979, will also be included for books which will double the available capacity and meet predicted demand.

The ISBN is conventionally written with a space (a hyphen is incorrect, although it often appears) between each of the four parts. This is how you will find the ISBN reproduced in books and in publishers' lists. Within computer databases, however, these spaces are often omitted to overcome any potential format difficulties.

You will generally find a book's ISBN printed on the title page verso, or occasionally at the foot of the title page itself. It also appears on the back cover of the book. When on the back cover, it is usually at the bottom right hand side of the cover, and appears in three different forms. These are shown below in Figure A2.1.

ISBN 0-415-17508-9

9 780415 175081

Figure A2.1 ISBN presentation

The ISBN appears first in regular print; next in an optical character recognition font (OCR-A); and then in the form of a barcode. The OCR-A and barcodes are machine-readable and can be accessed by laser scanning devices attached directly to the computer systems which are used for stock and sales monitoring.

The main convention for barcodes originates from the International Article Numbering Association and is known as the EAN-13 protocol, based on 13 digits. This is achieved by prefixing the ISBN with the number 978 which identifies the product as a book, and then recalculating the final check digit accordingly. The EAN-13 code thus has the basis of the original ISBN embedded within the barcode. The associated computer system will then decode this number and re-generate the original ISBN, complete with correct check digit, for use within the stock and sales monitoring system.

Although all this sounds unduly technical, a grasp of the mechanisms used in the ISBN is important because it is this code which is central and fundamental to almost all of the automated bookshop systems that are increasingly becoming a critical part of any bookshop's operation.

Appendix 3

Useful addresses

Advertising Standards Authority
2 Torrington Place
London WC1E 7HW
Tel: 020 7580 5555
Fax: 020 7631 3051
www.asa.org.uk

The Antiquarian Booksellers Association
Sackville House
40 Piccadilly
London W1J 0DR
Tel: 020 7439 3118
Fax: 020 7439 3119
www.abainternational.com

The Arts Council of England
14 Great Peter Street
London SW1P 3NQ
Tel: 01207-333 0100
Fax: 0207-973 6590
www.artscouncil.org.uk

batch.co.uk, incorporating Booksellers Clearing House (BCH)
272 Vauxhall Bridge Road
London SW1V 1BA
Tel: 020 7802 0802
Fax: 020 7802 0803
www.batch.co.uk

Book Industry Communication
39-41 North Road
London N7 9DP
Tel: 020 7607 0021
Fax: 020 7607 0415
www.bic.org.uk

Book Marketing Ltd
2-4 Idol Lane
London EC3R 5DD
Tel: 020 7398 0705
Fax: 020 7626 3660
www.bookmarketing.co.uk

Book Tokens Ltd
Minster House
272 Vauxhall Bridge Road
London SW1V 1BA
Tel: 020 7802 0802
Fax: 020 7802 0803
www.booktokens.co.uk

Book Trust
Book House
45 East Hill
Wandsworth
London SW18 2QZ
Tel: 020 8870 9055
Fax: 020 8874 4790

Books in the Media
Endeavour House
5th Floor, 189 Shaftesbury Avenue
London
WC2H 8TJ
Tel: 020 7420 6178
Tel: (Helpline) 020 7420 6133
Tel: (Subscriptions) 01795 414955
Fax: 020 7420 6103

***Books* Magazine**
Publishing News
39 Store Street
London
WC1E 7DB
Tel: 020 7692 2900
Fax: 020 7419 2111

Books Ireland
11 Newgrove Avenue
Dublin 4

Ireland
Tel: (00) 353 1 269 2185
Fax: (00) 353 1 260 4927

The Bookseller
Endeavour House
5th Floor, 189 Shaftesbury Avenue
London
WC2H 8TJ
Tel: (General) 020 7420 6006
Tel: (Subscriptions) 01795 414953
Fax: (Subscriptions) 01795 414555
www.thebookseller.com

The Booksellers Association of the United Kingdom & Ireland
Minster House
272 Vauxhall Bridge Road
London SW1V 1BA
Tel: 020 7802 0802
Fax: 020 7802 0803
www.booksellers.org.uk

The British Council
Bridgewater House,
58 Whitworth Street
Manchester M1 6BB
Tel: 0161 957 7182
Fax: 0161 957 7168
www.britishcouncil.org

The British Library
Bibliographic Publishing
National Bibliographic Service
The British Library
Wetherby
West Yorkshire LS23 7BQ
Tel: 01937 546585
Fax: 01937 546586
www.bl.uk

British Retail Consortium
21 Dartmouth Street, 2nd Floor
London SW1H 9BP
Tel: 020 7854 8900
Fax: 020 7854 8901
www.brc.org.uk

BTBS - The Book Trade Charity
The Foyle Centre
The Retreat
Kings Langley
Herts WD4 8LT
Tel: 01923 263128
Fax: 01923 270732
Helpline: 0808 1002304
www.booktradecharity.demon.co.uk

Children's Book Circle
c/o Lucy Firth
David Higham Associates
5-8 Lower John Street
Golden Square
London W1F 9HA
Tel: 020 7434 5915
Fax: 020 7437 1072

Christian Booksellers Convention
PO Box 148
Uckfield,
East Sussex TN22 5GR
Tel: 01825 840254
Fax: 01825 840068
www.cbcltd.co.uk

Data Protection Commissioner (Ireland)
Block 4
Irish Life Centre
Talbot Street
Dublin 1
Ireland
Tel: (00) 353 1 874 8544
Fax: (00) 353 1 874 5405
www.dataprivacy.ie

CLÉ (Cumann Leabharfhoilsitheoirí Éireann)
43-44 Temple Bar
Dublin 2
Ireland
Tel: (00) 353 1 6707 393
Fax: (00) 353 1 6707 642
www.publishingireland.com

Comhairle nan Leabhraichean / The Gaelic Books Council
22 Mansfield Street
Glasgow
G11 5QP
Tel: 0141 337 6211
Fax: 0141 341 0515
www.gaelicbooks.net

Copyright Licensing Agency
90 Tottenham Court Road
London WIT 4LP
Tel: 020 7631 5555
Fax: 020 7631 5500
www.cla.co.uk

Direct Marketing Association (UK) Ltd
DMA House
70 Margaret Street
London
W1W 8SS
Tel: 020 7291 3300
Fax: 020 7323 4165
www.dma.org.uk

Edinburgh Book Festival
The Scottish Book Centre
137 Dundee Street
Edinburgh EH11 1BG
Tel: 0131 228 5444
Fax: 0131 228 4333
www.edbookfest.co.uk

European Booksellers Federation
Chaussee de Charleroi 51b
Boite 1
B-1060 Brussels
Belgium
Tel: (00) 32 2 223 49 40
Fax: (00) 32 2 223 49 38
www.ebf-eu.org

The Federation of Children's Book Groups
The National Secretary
2 Bridge Wood View
Horsforth
Leeds
West Yorkshire LS18 5PE
Tel: 0113 2588910
Fax: 0113 2588920
www.fcbg.org.uk

First Edition
12/13 Riverside Business Centre
River Lawn Road
Tonbridge
Kent TN9 1EP
Tel: 01732 783 533
Fax: 01732 783 557
www.first-edition.co.uk

Information Commissioner
Wycliffe House
Water Lane
Wilmslow
Cheshire
SK9 5AF
Tel: 01625 545 745
Fax: 01625 524 510
www.informationcommissioner.gov.uk

International Booksellers Federation
34a rue du Grand Hospice
B-1000 Brussels
Belgium
Tel: (00) 32 2 223 49 40
Fax: (00) 32 2 223 49 41
www.ibf-booksellers.org

Irish Book Publishers Association
43-44 Temple Bar
Dublin 2
Ireland
Tel: (00) 353 1 6707 393
Fax: (00) 353 1 6707 642
www.publishingireland.com

Logos
Whurr Publishers
19B Compton Terrace
London N1 2UN
Tel: 020 7359 5979
Fax: 020 7226 5290
www.whurr.co.uk

London Book Fair
Oriel House
26 The Quadrant
Richmond
Surrey TW9 1DL
Tel: 020 8910 7815
Fax: 020 8910 7930
www.lbf-virtual.com

Malcolm Gibson Marketing
18 Pentland View
Edinburgh EH10 6PS
Tel: 0131 445 1639
malcolmgibsonmarketing@blueyonder.co.uk

Nielsen BookData
Globe House
1 Chertsey Road
Twickenham
Middx TW1 1LR
Tel: 020 8843 8600
Fax: 020 8843 8744
www.bookdata.co.uk

Nielsen BookData
Woolmead House West
Bear Lane
Farnham
Surrey GU9 7LG
Tel: 01252 742500
Fax: 01252 742501
www.whitaker.co.uk

Nielsen BookScan
Woolmead House West
Bear Lane
Farnham
Surrey GU9 7LG
Tel: 01252 742555
Fax: 01252 742556
www.nielsenbookscan.co.uk

Office of Fair Trading
Publications
PO Box 366
Hayes UB3 1XB
Tel: 0870 60 60 321
Fax: 0870 60 70 321
www.oft.gov.uk

The Publishers Association
29B Montague Street
London WC1B 5BH
Tel: 020 7691 9191
Fax: 020 7691 9199
www.publishers.org.uk

Publishing News
39 Store Street
London WC1E 7DS
Tel: 020 7692 2900
Fax: 020 7419 2111
www.publishingnews.co.uk

Publishing Training Centre at Book House
Book House
45 East Hill, Wandsworth
London SW18 2QZ
Tel: 020 8874 2718
Fax: 020 8870 8985
www.train4publishing.co.uk

Retail Week
33-39 Bowling Green Lane
London EC1R 0DA
Tel: 020 7520 3538
Fax: 020 7520 3529
www.retail-week.co.uk

Scottish Arts Council
12 Manor Place
Edinburgh EH3 7DD
Tel: 0131 226 6051
Fax: 0131 225 9833
www.sac.org.uk

Scottish Book Trust
The Scottish Book Centre
137 Dundee Street
Edinburgh EH11 1BG
Tel: 0131 229 3663
Fax: 0131 228 4293
www.scottishbooktrust.com

Scottish Publishers Association
The Scottish Book Centre
137 Dundee Street
Edinburgh EH11 1BG
Tel: 0131 228 6866
Fax: 0131 228 3220
www.scottishbooks.org

Standard Book Numbering Agency
Woolmead House West
Bear Lane,Farnham
Surrey GU9 7LG
Tel: 01252 742590
Fax: 01252 742526
www.whitaker.co.uk

Whitaker Group (Head Office) Now Nielsen Books
Endeavour House
5th Floor, 189 Shaftesbury Avenue
London WC2H 8TJ
Tel: 020 7420 6000
www.whitaker.co.uk

Appendix 4

Book trade glossary

One characteristic of the book trade is that for many years it has evolved within its own circles. Booksellers did not see themselves as just any old retailers: they were special. Similarly publishers considered themselves a head above other manufacturing industries. The book trade revelled in being known as the trade closest to a profession.

As a result it has tended to develop its own language to describe what it deemed important. Although the same terms are sometimes used in other industries they often denote slightly different things, giving rise to confusion and misunderstanding. In the course of adopting more modern management techniques, bookselling has also borrowed liberally from the management cult of developing acronyms and abbreviations. This is not always a device to bewilder outsiders – although it can be – it is also a kind of "shorthand speech", adopted to speed things up. Whatever the thinking, the result is quite a large special vocabulary.

The glossary below attempts to decipher some of the terms which are in common (and occasionally less common) use in today's book trade. Some terms are more or less unique to the book trade, others are in general use, but also have specific book trade meanings. It is hoped that the glossary will prove as helpful to those already steeped in the trade as it will be to new entrants.

ABA: American Booksellers Association. www.bookweb.org

ABA: Antiquarian Booksellers Association. www.abainternational.com

ACORN: An acronym (A Classification of Residential Neighbourhoods) for a demographic information tool which divides households into distinct categorisations based on an assessment of lifestyle and other characteristics.

Administration: *Legal/Accountancy:* Process whereby a business which is technically insolvent is protected from its creditors in order to maximise the potential return for creditors and share holders by selling the business as a going concern, rather than just winding the business up.

ADSL: *Computing*: Asymetrical Digital Subscriber Line. A fast type of internet connection using special copper wiring. www.adslguide.org.uk

APACS: Association for Payments Clearing Services. www.apacs.org.uk

Appraisal: Process of assessing individuals and giving feedback on performance.

ASN: Advance Shipping Notice.

Assets: *Accountancy*: Property, buildings, stock, cash or anything else owned by a business and recorded on the balance sheet.

Assign: *Legal*: You assign a lease when you sell it, with the land lord's agreement, to another party. In many leases, particularly older English leases, you may still be held responsible if the party to whom you assigned the lease ceases to pay the landlord. See "privity of contract".

Audit: *Accountancy:* An external inspection of a company's accounts by a firm of independent accountants to verify that they give a true and fair view of the business.

Average stock: (Opening stock + Closing stock) ∏ 2. Sometimes used in calculation of Rate of Stock Turn. Gives a slightly more accurate picture of the RST.

BA: The Booksellers Association of the United Kingdom and Ireland Ltd. www.booksellers.org.uk

BACS: Banks Automated Clearing System.

Balance sheet: *Accountancy*: Statement of the company's assets and the various claims over those assets at a particular date. The balance sheet is the most important financial statement and, although apparently complex, it is simply a list of a business's assets and liabilities together with their value.

Barcode: A coded label consisting of a series of precision-printed vertical lines of varying widths and with varying spaces between the lines, usually black on white. This label can be picked up by a laser scanner. The scanner then decodes the sequence of line widths and spaces to produce a numerical representation which can be utilised by a computer system.

Bargain book: Another name for a remainder, or sometimes a promotional book.

BATCH: Booksellers Automated Transaction Clearing House. www.batch.co.uk

BHTC: *Historical*: Book House Training Centre, the publishing

	industry's main training provider. BHTC was renamed the Publishing Training Centre at Book House in 1997. www.train4publishing.co.uk
BIC:	Book Industry Communication. www.bic.org.uk
BML:	Book Marketing Limited, a specialist market research organisation within the book trade. www.bookmarketing.co.uk
Book Token:	A voucher scheme operating within the book trade where by customers can buy vouchers for set values which can be exchanged in other bookshops. Book Tokens may only be operated by members of the Booksellers Association. www.booktokens.co.uk
Book Trust:	Book Trust was founded in 1926. It is an independent, educational charity working to bring books and people together. www.booktrust.org.uk
Bookseller, The:	Weekly booktrade journal. www.thebookseller.com
Break clause:	*Property*: A clause in a lease which allows for a lease to be terminated by the tenant at a set point in time, usually without penalty.
BRC	British Retail Consortium. www.brc.org.uk
Broadband:	*Computing*: Very fast Internet connection using telephone, satellite or cable television network wiring.
Budget:	*Accountancy*: The annual plan of sales and profits which must be met by a business (or part of a business) if it is to achieve a satisfactory performance.
Cable modem:	*Computing:* Specialised modem to connect a PC to a broadband cable connection.
Capital:	*Accountancy*: Funding for business. Often used simply to denote equity, but can also involve loan capital.
Cashflow:	*Accountancy:* The change in a firm's cash balance over a period. A critical measure of a firm's survival ability, both short and long term.
Catchment:	In physical terms a town's catchment is the surrounding area from which the majority of the town's shoppers come. Thus the catchment of a town may be a circle with a two-mile radius from the town centre. It is often also used to describe the actual number of people that live in the catchment.

Category killer: Large store with very wide stock holding. A competitive device intended to wipe out local competitors holding a smaller stock.

***Caveat emptor*:** *Legal*: "Let the buyer beware". In other words, there are no specific rights protecting your purchase – so make sure that you know what you are buying before you part with money.

CD-ROM: *Computing:* Compact Disc-Read Only Memory: a disc on which the data it contains can be read, but cannot be modified.

CD-RW: *Computing:* A CD drive that is able to write to CD-ROM as well as read them. It requires special CD-ROM media to write on to.

CILIP: Chartered Institute of Library and Information Professionals. www.cilip.org.uk

Clé: Clé. The Irish Book Publishers Association. www.pub lishingireland.com

Closing stock: *Accountancy:* The value of the stock at the end of the trading period.

Confirmation: A statement that an order has been received, usually giving details of the specific titles ordered and their availability.

Corporation Tax: A tax based on the profits that a company has generated over the year.

Cost of sales: *Account*ancy: The costs involved in generating the sales that have been recorded. Cost of sales = Opening stock + Purchases - Closing stock.

Cost price: The invoice price of goods intended for re-sale, excluding VAT.

Covenant: *Legal:* A written document under seal, also known as a deed. It contains a promise to act in a certain way, which is signed, sealed and takes effect on delivery. A bank will often require a covenant to cover a business loan; such a covenant will specify what specific performance measures (i.e. gearing to be within set parameters) will be used to judge the continuation of the loan. If these conditions are not met the loan may be withdrawn.

Credit card: A plastic card with a unique account number and coded magnetic information. When a customer uses a credit card the retailer is paid by the credit card company, which then bills the original customer. The retailer must pay a small percentage fee for this guaranteed payment. Check current BA rates since these may be better than your financial services provider can offer.

Credit control: The active management of the amount of credit allowed to customers. When the amount of credit passes an agreed limit; when the supplier is unhappy about the level of credit that has been extended; or when adequate payment has not been received within an agreed period, then a supplier may put the customer on "stop".

Credit period: The time after the issue of a statement when payment is expected by a supplier. This period is usually negotiated at the commencement of business. A common credit period is 30 days. Sixty days is becoming more frequent, and some businesses are able to negotiate 90 days' credit.

Creditor: *Accountancy*: Someone to whom you owe money.

CRM: Customer Relationship Management.

CTN: Confectioner, Tobacconist and Newsagent.

Current asset: *Accountancy*: Items owned by the business that will be used up, sold or converted into cash within twelve months. They include stocks, debtors, bank balances and cash.

Current liability: *Accountancy*: These are debts owed to outside organisations that must be repaid in the short term, usually in less than twelve months. They include creditors (suppliers), bank overdraft, dividends due to shareholders and taxation.

Cyclical distribution: Distribution system whereby orders are not dealt with as they come in, but are held back to be processed on fixed days, either by region or by bookseller, depending on the system parameters.

CV: *Curriculum vitae*, a résumé of past educational and career history requested from a job applicant.

Database: A system of holding large amounts of related data together in a format whereby the relationships between data can be sorted and interrogated. Usually computer based, e.g. Microsoft Access.

Debit card: A plastic card with a unique account number and coded magnetic information. When a customer uses a debit card the retailer is paid by the debit card company, which then treats the payment as an electronic cheque charged against the customer's bank account. The retailer must pay a small fee for this guaranteed payment. Check current BA rates since these may be better than your financial services provider can offer.

Debtor: *Accountancy*: Someone who owes you money.

Depreciation: *Accountancy:* The amount by which an asset's book value is deemed to have fallen each year. Charged as an expense on the profit and loss account for that year.

Dividend: *Accountancy*: Each year the directors of a company must decide how much, if any, of its profits will be re-invested in the company, and how much, if any, will be paid out to the shareholders. Once the proportion of profits to go to shareholders is decided, that amount is divided equally by the number of shares issued by the company. It is known as a dividend. Frequently a company will pay an "interim dividend" half way through the year, with the remainder at the year end as a "final dividend".

DTP: *Computing:* Desk Top Publishing. A computer-based software operation to produce text and graphics on the page. Replaces the traditional "cut and paste" job involved in design and layout on paper.

Due diligence: An investigation by, or on behalf of, an intended buyer of a business to check that the assets, turnover, profits and various other factors are as required by the buyer or claimed by the seller.

Dues: Books which could not be supplied at the time of ordering are often recorded as "dues" to be supplied when they become available.

DVD: Digital Versatile Disc.

e-book: *e-commerce:* Electronic commerce. Current terminology for trading through EDI processes.

e-mail: Electronic mail.

EAN: A standardised barcode format, derived from the International (*formerly* European) Article Numbering Association system. www.ean-int.org

EAN-13: The principal EAN protocol in operation for books.

EAS: Electronic Article Surveillance

EBF: European Booksellers Federation. www.ebf-eu.org

EDI: Electronic data interchange.

EDIFACT: Electronic Data Interchange for Administration, Commerce and Transport. www.unece.org/trade/untdid

EDItEUR: Pan European Book Sector EDI Group. www.editeur.org

EFTPoS: Electronic funds transfer at point of sale.

EPoS: Electronic point of sale data capture system.

Equity: *Accountancy:* Funding by shareholders in the form of shares, in return for which the shareholders are entitled to part of the company's assets.

Escrow agreement *Legal*: Effectively, put on ice. In an Escrow agreement two parties sign a contract, but do not want it to come into effect until something happens. The contract is then handed to a third party to hold until the condition is satisfied. A common application would be with a customised software programme where the originator does not want the bookseller to have original coded software, but where the bookseller needs to have that code should anything happen to the originating company.

Euro The unit of currency under the European Monetary Union system. Ireland uses the Euro ( ) but the UK still (2003) uses Sterling (£). www.europa.eu.int/euro

Exclusivity clause *Property:* A clause in a lease stipulating that the tenant shall have an exclusive right to sales within certain product groups, usually within a managed shopping centre. This in effect means that there will be no direct competition from within the centre, but there may be competition from other shops in the town.

Expense: *Accountancy:* An operating cost, rather than capital expenditure, which relates to a particular accounting period.

Fiche: Abbreviation frequently used for "microfiche".

Firm sale: Goods bought on firm sale are non-returnable. The total risk in the purchase lies with the bookseller.

Fixed assets: *Accountancy*: Items owned by the business that will generate income, such as property, equipment, furniture, vehicles etc. Without these assets the business would not be able to operate.

FTE: Full-time equivalent employee. Used to calculate the sales generated by each employee.

Franchise: The right to sell branded products (or services) in an approved format. Often operates under tight rules designed to ensure consistency of product offering to consumers.

Freehold: *Property:* Ownership of the total rights to a property, i.e. the property is not rented from a landlord.

Gearing: *Accountancy*. Debt divided by equity. High gearing can mean high risk.

Gigabyte: *Computing:* One thousand million bytes.

GLN: Global Location Number. www.e-centre.org.uk or www.sanagency.co.uk

Goodwill: *Accountancy*. Goodwill that arises when a firm buys another for more than its net "book" value. The excess amount is goodwill.

Goodwill: *Customer service:* The deliberate abrogation of seller's legal rights in order to satisfy a customer who has a valid com plaint, but not one which is covered by his/her legal rights.

GPM: *Accountancy:* Gross profit margin.

Gross profit: *Accountancy:* What is left after the cost of sales is deducted from the value of sales (seldom as large as expected!) Gross profit = Sales - Cost of sales

Gross profit margin: *Accountancy:* The gross profit expressed as a percentage of sales. Sometimes known as GPM.

Hardware: *Computing:* Hardware denotes the physical components of a computer system, as opposed to software *(q.v.)*.

Heads of lease: *Legal/Property*: A summary of the lease conditions used in the initial stages when property is in the process of being sold, to give an idea of the extent of the property and the likely costs. It is not intended to be other than a description to allow potentially interested parties to decide whether they wish to view the property.

Hot-line: A special ordering service designed to give a very rapid response time. Often used by publishers at peak times to get books into bookshops quickly.

Impulse purchase: A purchase made on impulse, as opposed to a pre-determined and planned purchase.

IMTA: International Map Trade Association. www.maptrade.org

Industrial tribunal: An official body dealing with matters generally relating to employment such as unfair dismissal or discrimination.

Insolvency: *Legal/Accountancy:* A business is insolvent if it does not have sufficient financial resources to pay its bills when they are due.

Interest: The amount of money charged by a person or institution that lends a sum of money to a borrower. Usually expresses as a percentage.

Intranet: *Computing*: A private secured internal network within an organisation. Does not usually allow any external access other than through password protected entry from specified locations.

Invoice: A bill requiring payment for goods or services provided.

IPG: Independent Publishers Guild. www.ipg.uk.com

ISBN: International Standard Book Number. A unique reference number for each title and format published. http://isbn-international.org

ISDN: *Computing*: Integrated Services Digital Network. A fast type of internet connection using special telephone wiring

ISMN: International Standard Music Number. http://ismn-international.org

ISSN: International Standard Serial Number. www.issn.org

Issued share capital: *Accountancy*: Money put into the business by the owners and shareholders. In return for their investment they receive dividend payments (a sharing of the profit), the amount being in proportion to the size of their shareholding.

JIT: Just-in-time. A system of minimising stock by having fresh stock delivered at the exact point in time when it is needed.

Kilobyte: *Computing:* One thousand bytes.

LAN: *Computing:* A local area network.

Laptop: A small portable PC. Frequently used by publishers' reps.

Lead time: The time between placing an order and its delivery.

Lease: A written agreement between a landlord and a tenant whereby the landlord allows the tenant to occupy premises for a defined period, and usually with certain conditions attaching, in return for the payment of rent.

Level playing field: *Historical*: The concept (fundamentally flawed) that trading should be even-handed regardless of the size of individual companies involved – i.e. everyone should get an even chance.

LBF: The London Book Fair. A major UK book exhibition, organised by Reed Exhibitions and sponsored by the BA. www.lbf-virtual.com

Long-term liabilities: *Accountancy*: Debentures or other long-term loans, such as mortgages, where the debt repayment is not due within the next twelve months.

Loss leader: Strictly, something selling at below cost to attract extra business. Often used more loosely to describe goods sold at below-average profitability, but not necessarily at a loss.

Mail-merge Word processing programme which merges a database of names and addresses into a standard format letter, so producing personally addressed letters.

Management accounts: *Accountancy*: A tool to aid managers in the control and forward planning of their business. The accounts will usually focus on previously specified key criteria.

Margin: 1. The difference between the selling price and the cost price.
2. An alternative, loose, term for "gross profit" or "net profit", depending on context.

Margin mix: The range of margins across the variety of products stocked by the bookshop. The more high-margin product, the stronger the margin mix.

Mark-up: A set percentage by which a cost price is increased in order to determine the selling price. Providing the mark-up is followed correctly, a pre-determined gross margin will be generated on the sale.

Marketing mix: Product, Pricing, Promotion, Place. For services, People, Physical evidence and Process are usually added to the formula.

MBA: Master of Business Administration. A second degree with full academic Masters status.

MBO: Management buy-out, the sale of a business by its owners to the management for a consideration (usually cash).

MBS: Mind, Body and Spirit. Books on alternative lifestyles.

Megabyte: *Computing:* One million bytes.

Microfiche: A small (about 6" x 4") sheet of plastic with multiple pages of text reproduced in minute form. Allows large quantities of text to be kept in minimal space.

Microfiche reader: A machine used to read microfiche. Consists of a powerful light source, mirrors and a lens which together project a full page of text on to the front screen of the reader.

Modem: *Computing:* A device which allows messages and files to be conveyed between a main computer and a remote computer using a telephone line as a link.

MOSAIC: A geodemographic coding system run by a company called Experian. Similar in nature to ACORN *(q.v.)*.

NBA: *Historical*: Net Book Agreement *(q.v.)*.

NE: Publishers' report on a book, denoting that a new edition is in preparation. Variants may include an indication of its likely publication date (NE/Oct).

Net assets: *Accountancy*: Net fixed assets plus net current assets. This shows the net value of the business once short-term debts have been repaid.

Net Book Agreement: *Historical:* The legal instrument that was in force between 1900 and 1995 governing the price at which books could be sold by bookshops. No longer valid.

Net current assets: *Accountancy*: The amount by which the total value of cur rent assets exceeds the total value of current liabilities.

Net profit: *Accountancy:* What is left of the gross profit after all expenses are accounted for. In Partnerships and Limited Companies final accounts, the Net Profit figure is given before tax charges have been deducted.
Net profit = Gross profit - Expenses.

Network: *Computing:* A network is used to link more than one PC together so that they can either communicate with each other or share central data.
Business: Maintaining contacts across a broad field.

NI: National Insurance.

Niche: A small, defensible business segment.

NK: Publishers' report on a book which is "not known" by that publisher.

Notional rent: A figurative rent which is not actually charged (usually where freehold is owned), but which reflects the likely level of commercial rent if the property were to be leased.

NTO: Non-traditional outlet: in other words, somewhere that sells books, but is not a dedicated bookshop.

NVQ: National Vocational Qualification, a government-sponsored award for vocational training schemes.

NYP: Publishers' report on a book which is "not yet published". Variants may include an indication of the likely publication date (NYP/Oct).

OCR: Optical character recognition, or machine-readable characters that can also be read with the human eye.

Off pitch: *Property:* A retail property is not on a prime pitch.

OFT: Office of Fair Trading. www.oft.gov.uk

On stop: A supplier may put you on " stop" if you have failed to settle your account within an agreed time-frame. When your account is on stop no orders will be supplied until the account is settled.

ONIX: Online Information Exchange. www.editeur.org/onix.html

OP: Publishers' report on a book which is "out of print". Sometimes given as "O/P".

Opening stock: The value of stock at the beginning of the financial year – *cf.* closing stock.

OS: Publishers' report on a book which is "out of stock". Sometimes given as "O/S".

Overheads: *Accountancy*: The working costs of the business. Often separated into fixed and variable overheads. Variable overheads increase as volume of business increases; fixed overheads remain constant.

PA: The Publishers Association of The United Kingdom. www.publishers.org.uk

PAYE: Pay As You Earn: the system of taxation.

PC: *Computing*: Personal computer (an IBM-compatible machine).
Censorship: "Politically correct" in attitude and presentation.

Peppercorn rent: *Legal:* A rent where consideration is necessary for the contract, but does not have to be adequate. The idea being that a tenant might pay a single peppercorn to a landlord in consideration for a lease. Although such a rent is purely notional, the contract would not stand without it.

PERT: Programme Evaluation and Review Technique. A very early forerunner of JIT.

Pitch: *Property:* The location of a retail property within the town. Generally a pitch will be "prime", "secondary" or "tertiary", but often used to generalise for prime.

PLU: Price Look Up, the facility to obtain the price of an item from its product code – in the case of books, the ISBN.

POS: Point of sale. Usually refers to display materials such as posters, show-cards and other pieces of promotional material used to help mount strong displays for a publisher's lead titles.

Premium: *Property*: A sum of money that a prospective tenant must pay to encourage a landlord, or an existing tenant, in order to gain access to the lease of a valuable retail property.

Price elasticity: A measure of the elasticity of demand to changes in price, i.e. to what extent changes in price will affect volume sales.

Price leadership: A price strategy of using the lowest prices in the market so as to achieve a reputation as the cheapest outlet for your products.

Price matching: A price strategy of matching the main competitor prices in an attempt to demonstrate to shared customers that your prices are equally competitive.

Price point: A particular price which is accepted by customers and by those within an industry. An effective price point usually has an element of psychological pricing in it, so £9.99 is perceived as "significantly" cheaper than £10.00, even though everyone "knows'" it is not.

Price promise: A device designed to reassure customers about the value offered. Basically a guarantee that if a customer finds a product cheaper, having met certain specified criteria or limitations, then the retailer will refund the difference.

Prime: *Property:* The best pitch in a town. Properties on prime sites can command the highest rentals.

Privity of contract: A fundamental principle of contract law requires that you can only claim benefit under a contract if you are a party to that contract.

Pro forma: An invoice which is submitted for payment prior to goods being sent, usually because the bookshop does not have a credit account with the supplier. Once payment has been received by the supplier the goods are despatched.

Processor: *Computing:* The part of the electronics which processes data at a very fast rate. A Pentium processor is about the fastest processor in PC technology.

Profit & loss account: *Accountancy:* After the balance sheet, the second most important financial statement, explaining how the retained profit, as appears on the balance sheet, got there. It also shows how and why it changed over the period. Sometimes also referred to as the P&L.

PubEasy: www.pubeasy.com

Publication date: Date on which a title is officially published. Sometimes there may be an embargo on the retail sale of key titles.

Publishing News: Weekly book trade journal. www.publishingnews.co.uk

Purchases: *Accountancy:* The total value, at cost price, of purchases made during the trading period.

R&D: Research and development.

RAM: *Computing:* Random access memory, allowing for swift processing of data.

RAN: Returns Authorisation Number.

Rate of stock turn: (RST). The number of times the totality of stock is turned over each year. This allows the bookseller to assess the effectiveness of stock buying, since it gives an indication of how much capital is tied up in stock. The higher the RST, the more efficient the buying. Always calculated at retail value for both sales and stock.
Rate of stock turn = Sales ∏ Stock

Rent review: A defined date when a landlord reserves the right to review the rental on a lease. Usually done at five-year intervals. The rental will be set in line with other rent settlements within the immediate vicinity and will often be on an upwards only basis.

Rep: Publishers' representative, who seeks to persuade the bookshop to order the company's books. A freelance rep will usually represent a broad variety of publishers' lists.

Report: A response from a publisher or distributor indicating the reason why a book has not been delivered in response to an order *(cf. OP, OS, etc.)*.

Reserves from P&L Account: *Accountancy*: These are profits retained by the business after the payment of dividends to shareholders and after provision has been made for all other current liabilities. Businesses will use these profit reserves to finance expansion at some later date.

Returns: Books which are potentially returnable to the supplier for credit.

Reverse premium: *Property:* A premium paid by a landlord to induce a new tenant into taking a lease on a property. Sometimes also used by an existing tenant to encourage a new tenant to take assignment of the lease.

RFID: Radio Frequency Identification. A technology used in smart chips for security and logistical control purposes.

Risk capital: Shareholder's equity investments.

Romalpa clause: *Legal:* A clause quite often used in publishers' terms of trade whereby the ownership of goods supplied only passes to the retailer when the outstanding amount has been paid in full. The objective is to ensure that, should the retailer have to call in administrators or go bankrupt, the publisher can reclaim the stock rather than wait for settlement of the outstanding debt. Sometimes known as a Retention of Title clause.

Royalty: Money paid in return for exercising a right under a licence. An author receives a royalty from a publisher in exchange for the copyright licence to publish the work. Usually calculated as a percentage of earnings.

RP: Publishers' report on a title that is reprinting. Sometimes reported as "R/P". Variants include "RP/08" for reprint due in August, or "RPND" for reprinting with no date.

RST: Rate of stock turn *(q.v.)*. Sales divided by stock, both at retail value.

Sale or return: Goods ordered on sale or return are paid for in the usual manner and within the usual credit period, but the book shop has the right to seek (and expect) authorisation to return unsold copies for credit, usually after an agreed period.

Sales: The value of sales transactions over a specified period. When looking at a company's annual accounts the sales will be the sum of all transactions over a twelve-month period.

SAN: Standard address number, a unique reference denoting the bookshop's delivery address. www.sanagency.co.uk

SAV: Stock at value. A term used when buying or selling a bookshop as a going concern.

Secondary pitch: *Property*: A retail property that is not on a prime pitch, but is still in a potentially reasonable pitch.

See safe: Stock which is ordered from a publisher on the basis that unsold copies can be returned for credit after a pre-deter mined period.

Segment: A part of the market identified by one or more firms as a target

Shareholders' Interest: *Accountancy:* All of the issued share value (ordinary and preference shares), all reserves, retained profits and any other reserves.

Shareware: *Computing:* Software that is intended for widespread use, but which is still protected by a fee requirement. The fee is usually much lower than that required for proprietary software.

Shrinkage: A generic term to describe any activity which results in the active erosion of gross profit. The main cause is theft, but till errors, or paying for goods which never arrived and were not noticed missing on delivery can be further causes of shrinkage.

SKU: Stock Keeping Unit.

Small order surcharge: A surcharge that some publishers use to penalise book sellers who place orders under a certain volume.

SME: Small and medium-sized enterprises.

Software: *Computing*: Software denotes the programmes that are used to run computers, as opposed to hardware *(q.v.)*

SOR: Sale or return.

Scottish Book Trust: Scottish equivalent of Book Trust. www.scottishbook trust.com

SPA: Scottish Publishers Association. www.scottishbooks.org

SPWA: Spoken Word Publishers Association. www.swpa.co.uk

Split delivery: A split delivery occurs when all the boxes expected in a delivery fail to arrive in the same consignment. For instance, the first four boxes may arrive on a Thursday with the remaining three the following Monday. This is usually due to some difficulty at the distribution centre that the publisher uses. If a continual problem, it is worth discussing with the publisher concerned.

Spreadsheet: A computer-based worksheet developed for manipulation of figures. Utilising a cellular structure, it allows calculations to be based on the contents of various cell locations. Examples would include Microsoft Excel and Lotus 1-2-3.

Statement: A monthly summary of all invoices and credit notes for goods that a supplier has sent or received from a retailer. Payment is usually made within a set number of days of the statement date.

Stock control: The process of stock management whereby the bookshop tries to make sure that each individual title is stocked at the right level to ensure that no sales are lost, yet at the same time further ensure that no more capital than necessary is tied up in stock. Usually computerised.

Sub/sub order: Subscription order, for a new title that has not yet been published. Most often called a "sub".

SWOT analysis: An overview of a company's prospects in terms of the company's strengths, weaknesses, opportunities and threats.

Target market: The particular group or groups of people on which a firm has decided to focus its attentions. This focus may be exclusive – i.e. it will actively try to discourage non-target groups – or inclusive, encouraging the selected group(s) but welcoming non-target customers too.

TeleOrdering: Trade-wide electronic order transmission and collation system.

Test purchase: A purchase made by an unknown person to see how well a sale is handled, and/or whether the correct till procedures were used. A technique used by security companies to identify whether goods are being rung up properly, and also to identify possible dishonest handling of cash.

TOS: Publishers' report on a book temporarily out of stock.

TQM: Total quality management.

Transaction: Anything a company does that affects its financial position and its balance sheet.

TSO: Trading standards officer.

Unfair dismissal: When a dismissal is deemed unfair it usually means that the correct disciplinary procedures were not followed. If a member of staff has been employed for two years and is then unfairly dismissed he/she may ask an industrial tribunal to award compensation.

Upwards only rental: *Property:* A clause in a lease which allows for rentals only to be increased (and never reduced) at the rent review.

UK online for business: www.ukonlineforbusiness.gov.uk

URL: *Computing*: Uniform Resource Locator. The unique address for a web page on the World Wide Web.

VAT: Value Added Tax.

VDU: *Computing:* Visual Display Unit. "Monitor" is the term used more frequently at present.

VPN: *Computing*: Virtual Private Network. A secured private net work connection built on top of publicly-accessible infra structure, such as the Internet or the public telephone network.

Web site: A series of informational and possibly transactional pages at a given location on the World Wide Web. The site is specified by an address such as www.booksellers.org.uk

Welsh Books Council: www.wbc.org.uk

Wholesaler: Go-betweens who generally offer a broad range of services in the distribution of goods to retail outlets. Most book wholesalers stock wide ranges of books, but do not usually extend their stock much beyond books.

Windows: *Computing:* Operating system developed by Microsoft.

Word processor: A computer programme designed to handle words in digitised form. Used for correspondence, reports, adverts, and also for making use of such specialist functions as mail-merge and label production. Examples would include Microsoft Word, AmiPro, etc.

Working capital: Funding required for day-to-day operations to cover the gap between the payment for inputs (e.g. stock, wages, etc.) and the time when customers pay for goods. Technically, working capital plus fixed assets equal capital employed.

World Book Day: www.worldbookday.com

Write down: *Accountancy:* Percentage by which the retail value of stock is written down to give a realistic estimate of its cost.

Written down value: *Accountancy:* The value of assets in the books of a company. This is usually the historical cost less the cumulative amount of depreciation written-off at the balance sheet date.

WWW: World Wide Web.

Zone "A" rental: *Property:* The rent, in terms of £ per square foot, for the front 20 ft (30 ft in Scotland) of retail premises. The more desirable the property, the higher the Zone "A" rent.

Zoning: *Property:* A term to allow rental costs to be defined through premises. The first 20 ft of premises (30 ft in Scotland) is deemed to be Zone "A". The second 20-ft zone (or 30 ft) costs half the Zone "A" rate; the third 20-ft zone costs one quarter of Zone "A"; the fourth 20-ft zone costs one eighth of Zone "A". Upstairs and downstairs tends to cost one eighth of Zone "A" if used for sales, or one tenth of Zone "A" if used for storage.

Appendix 5

Bibliography

The following selection of books (some of which have already been mentioned in the text) may be useful as further reading around either the core subject of bookselling, or some of its more detailed aspects mentioned in the text.

Books and the Consumer Summary Report, Book Marketing Ltd, 2001

BA Directory of UK & Irish Book Publishers (including distributors, sales agents & wholesalers), Booksellers Association, annual

Book Retailing in Britain, Bookseller Publications, 2001

Book Sales Yearbook, Bookseller Publications, 2001

Cassell & the Publishers Association Directory of Publishing: United Kingdom, Commonwealth and Overseas annual*; Continental Europe* 1992 Cassell

Dibb, Simkin, Pride & Ferrell *Marketing* Houghton Mifflin, 1997

Deborah Elliott (ed) *Bookselling* (Teach Yourself Series) Hodder & Stoughton, 1990

John Hitchin *Planning the Opening and Running of a Bookshop* European Commission, 1997

Ros Jay *Low Cost Marketing* (Institute of Management Series) Pitman, 1994

Garry Jones *Running a Shop* (NatWest Business Handbooks) Pearson, 2nd edn 1995

Thomas Joy *The Bookselling Business* Pitman, 1974

Nicholas Negroponte *Being Digital* Knopf, 1995

Hilarie Owen *Creating Top Flight Teams* Kogan Page, 1996

Publishers in the United Kingdom and their Addresses Whitaker, annual

Leonard Shatkin *The Mathematics of Bookselling* Sun River Press, Butterick Company, 1997

Paco Underhill *Why We Buy* Orion Business Books, 1999

Arthur Young Management Consultants *Book Retailing in the 1990s*; Booksellers Association, 1987

Index

A

B

D

E

N

O

P

Q

R

S

T

U

V

W

Z